Misty Mornings and Moonless Nights

OTHER BOOKS BY THE AUTHOR

The Fisherman's Almanac by Dan Morris and Norman Strung
The Hunter's Almanac
Family Fun Around the Water by Dan Morris and Norman Strung
Camping in Comfort by Norman and Sil Strung
Spinfishing by Norman Strung and Milt Rosko
Deer Hunting

Misty Mornings and Moonless Nights

A WATERFOWLER'S GUIDE

by Norman Strung

Line drawings by C. W. "Wally" Hansen

Macmillan Publishing Co., Inc.

NEW YORK

Collier Macmillan Publishers

LONDON

Macmillan Publishing Co., Inc.
866 Third Avenue, New York, N.Y. 10022
Collier-Macmillan Canada Ltd.

Library of Congress Cataloging in Publication Data

Strung, Norman.
  Misty mornings and moonless nights.

  Bibliography: p.
  1. Waterfowl shooting.   I. Title.
Sk331.S78   799.2'44   74-8226
ISBN 0-02-615100-6

First Printing 1974

Printed in the United States of America

Contents

PART FIVE
TABLE FARE   233

Introduction

The fondest memories of my youth are of those times spent in the company of rough baymen on Long Island's South Shore. They were special men who scratched and snared their living from the waters of Great South Bay, unique as the converted catboats they used in their trade and salty as the bay itself.

Like specialists anywhere, they had a vocabulary all their own. It wasn't a different language, just an assortment of odd words that better described important things that ignorant laymen like myself lumped into one category. For example, I always thought a clam was a clam, but under their tutelage I learned that a clam could be a seed, a skimmer, a neck, a cherry, a chowder, or a steamer.

The word "hunter" received similar attention. There were those who were deer hunters, and those who were bird hunters. A "bird shooter" referred to someone who was primarily interested in upland game, and a duck hunter obviously shot ducks.

All these labels were spun off their tongues with glib ease, almost to the point of disdain, but a special verbal ceremony occurred when they called someone a "gunner."

A gunner was a waterfowler, but one of a distinct breed. He was the kind of person who would forsake all other duties to be out on a marsh when it was spitting snow and sleet. He would confidently challenge surly seas in a tiny boat and laugh back at wild whitecaps and stinging icy spray.

Gunners could look at a flight of ducks, merely fly-specks on the horizon, and say, with unerring accuracy, "black duck," or "broadbill," or "whistler." Their hands were hard and horny, well acquainted with the suspicious warmth of frostbite. Yet, with a few deft strokes of a penknife and paintbrush, they could breathe life into a stoic block of wood.

Today there aren't many men like that left. Their strange squat little clamboats with racked tongs and four-cylinder Ford engines have been replaced by company-owned behemoths that chew clams from the bottom with clanking conveyor belts. Two- and three-bird limits have destroyed the will to carve, maintain, and rig decoy spreads numbering in the hundreds. The baymen have grown old;

they've left the sea, and their odd pronunciation of words—boobie for buddy, loit for light—is now seldom heard on the tarry wharfs of Bay Shore, West Sayville, and Sag Harbor.

As in any natural process, however, a new breed of gunner has emerged to take their place, and you can always find a few of them on Sedam Point. For years, it was known far and wide as one of the best duck-shooting spots on the South Shore; then it gradually slipped between the jaws of progress.

A canal was dredged to the west, and small houses grew along its bulkheading. A yacht club found a home on the east shore of the point; then a marina was built even closer, complete with a yellow plastic scallop shell that turns and turns and turns, flaring ducks with its reflection on sunny days.

Today Sedam Point is a mere triangle of sand, barely big enough for two blinds, but the hopeful hunters still come. They're no longer baymen, but schoolteachers, students, insurance brokers, and laborers. They come when they can—before work, after school, on their days off—and set their rigs off the point to stare seaward and watch for black duck, broadbill, and an occasional mallard. They don't know the total intimacy that comes with life rooted in an estuary, but still they all share that quality I found so distinctive many years ago: a deep and abiding respect for, and fascination with, waterfowl. They know the delight of three wobbling teal appearing out of nowhere on a misty morning. They are awed by the sounds of a flock of geese passing overhead on a moonless night. They sense the mystery and romance of waterfowl as they follow the sun and fly with the wind to some unknown destiny.

Misty Mornings and Moonless Nights is a book written for this new breed of waterfowler. It's primarily a how-to book that records all aspects of duck and goose hunting, from the art of carving a decoy to the craft of setting out a rig to the science of how waterfowl react to the weather, including choosing the right gun and dressing warmly in a damp, cold blind. Sound advice on how to be more successful and comfortable afield. But it's also a book about history and hunters—why different duckboat designs came about, antique decoys, and some of the tricks used by old market shooters, illegal now, but a vital thread in the fabric of waterfowling today.

It isn't just a hunting guide, or a novel, or a textbook; yet it's all these things, unified by a spirit that will endure even when the last grain of sand on Sedam Point is cemented and lawned over. It's written for a very special kind of sportsman.

A Waterfowler's Guide is the only subtitle I find appropriate.

PART ONE

Waterfowl

1 | The Ways of Waterfowl and Whys of Management

Rolvaag's *Giants in the Earth* contains a memorable passage about shooting ducks in a North Dakota marsh in the late 1800s—it makes me weep for kingdoms lost every time I read it.

The late Tom Sicard would spin blind-side yarns about the millions of southbound mallards that would pass over his father's Montana homestead in the fall, then triple the injury by pointing across Meadow Lake, saying, "—yep—right up there on that marshy little bench. That's where dad's place was." (He always timed those stories to coincide with utterly dismal duck days.)

Even today, when the shooting slacks off around eight at Sedam Point, Joe Steigerwald focuses his eyes on someplace my generation will never see and weaves stories of gunning from a sink box when a case of shells ran out before noon and he had to go home disgruntled with a mere seventy-five birds to soothe his black-and-blue shoulder.

They're stories of a time when nature was allowed to take care of her own: the halcyon days of frontier innocence when men and horses tilled the soil, and a rich bounty of waterfowl swept across

3

the nation. But those days and the ducks are gone, relegated to the pages of history books and the memories of old men.

It wasn't the hunter that blotted out the flights—it was the changes that man molded into the land with his infernal machines: draining marshes, clearing brush, building along the banks of rivers and streams, and creating huge impoundments that flooded rich lowlands. To mourn or malign the practices after the fact is pointless; it was done.

As a purely natural system with its intricate rhythms was gradually replaced by man's "improvements," it became evident that severe gaps were being created in the life cycles of all wildlife, especially waterfowl. The biggest problem facing ducks and geese was the destruction of vital habitat, which in turn increased vulnerability to hunting pressure and predation and forced changes in long-established patterns of life. By the 1940s it was plain that, if waterfowl were to survive, man had to intervene on nature's behalf. He had to begin filling those gaps he created, functioning in part as waterfowl's protector and provider.

The first step involved understanding some of the life processes of the creatures he hoped to maintain.

THE LIFE CYCLE OF WATERFOWL

Migrations might seem romantic to some, but there's a good argument for waterfowl movements being good hard sense. I regularly follow the ducks north to Montana in the spring, and south to Mexico and Florida in the fall, and find it's a mighty agreeable way to spend a year. But personal value judgments aside, let's take a look at motivations, movements, and why and how they occur. Migrations find birds moving north in the spring and south in the fall. There's often a great deal of mystery connected with these movements, but closely analyzed, they amount to a perfectly logical response to ground rules and limits laid down by nature.

No matter their range and scope, waterfowl migrations are largely triggered by light. As daylight increases in southern latitudes, birds get restless and begin to move north. When days in the north shorten, waterfowl respond by moving south.

Depending on how far south they've wintered, waterfowl begin to indicate the spring urge to move north as early as February. I've seen huge flocks of pintail queuing up for migration as early as February 15 in Altata, Sinaloa, a tiny town on the west coast of Mexico, seven hundred miles south of the United States border.

Birds wintering in more northerly climes move later. Quite a few mallards spend the entire winter in the warm springs near my Montana home, and they'll often remain in the area until April.

When birds do decide to move, their migrations are not nonstop affairs, but something of a northward drift: a leisurely trip up-country. Movements are further slowed when birds become tired and must stop along the way to rest and feed. Storms make navigation difficult and churn up unfavorable headwinds.

The duration of daylight plays another part in regulating migrations. As waterfowl work their way into more northerly latitudes, the days get shorter again, creating a braking effect.

The sum of all these difficulties and detours is one of the many facets of nature's marvelous clockwork. Although their origins, routes, and destinations are widely divergent, the bulk of migrating waterfowl arrive at their chosen breeding grounds coincidental with the melting of ice from the lakes and the departure of frost from the earth.

Migrations don't occur en masse. If you ever spend some time watching a marsh that constitutes either summering or wintering grounds, note arrivals or departures. There is a flow of birds that begins with the first few hardy adventurers and increases in intensity as more and more waterfowl get the message carried by the winds.

Migrations, if plotted on a chart, would reveal a classic bell-shaped curve, beginning with a level line of light activity, then rising to a rounded dome during the height of movement, and falling back to zero as the last birds leave.

The place and time where that peak or bell occurs—the month and the specific locale on the continent—are functions of latitude. For example, during a northerly migration around Big Bend, Texas, the curve would start to rise in late February, peak out in mid-March, and fall to nothing by mid-April. In Bismarck, North Dakota, the curve would start in March, peak in April, and flatten out in May. The top of the bell—the bulk of activity—follows the majority of birds moving north. The same holds true during the southerly migrations in the fall. In the far north, near the Arctic Circle, peak activity usually occurs around mid-September. Mid-November is when migrating birds are heaviest through the northern tier of states, and the South doesn't get heavy populations of waterfowl until mid-December and early January.

With these stages of activity there's also a degree of segregation by species. Certain species migrate before others, and there seems to be a broad correlation with size—the smallest birds moving south first.

There is a certain logic to this, not based solely on strength. The smaller a body, the greater its ratio of exposure to the air, and consequently, the greater its heat loss.

Like the high school chemistry sugar-cube experiment that proves small cubes dissolve faster than big cubes, or the cook's knowledge

6

that finely diced potatoes will cook faster than the whole vegetable, smaller birds will expend more energy keeping warm in a cold climate than larger birds.

So the smallest species are the first to migrate—doves and the tiny teals. These birds migrate so early that many northern states have special teal seasons in September; resident gunners can get a crack at flights that will long have been gone from their area by regular openings.

The next birds to get restless are the mid-sized ducks: gadwalls, shovelers, redheads, ringneck ducks, and wood ducks. These are the species that will usually make up the bulk of an early season bag.

The largest ducks are the last to leave their summer homes and the last to arrive in the South: greater scaup, whistler, mallard, and black duck. The very last flights of these birds often occur in December and January, and it's these biggest and hardiest examples of the species that hunters call "northerns," "Canadas," or "redlegs," and prize as table fare above all other waterfowl.

Geese, too, exhibit a migratory schedule based on size. Early in the season, along primary flyways, it's the small cackler or lesser snow goose that makes up the bulk of the action. Toward mid-season the greater snow geese predominate, and the last birds to move through will be the big Canada geese.

It's also interesting to note that these larger birds—Canadas, mallards, and black duck—normally winter at more northerly latitudes than the smaller birds, also tending to support the body-size/heat-ratio theory.

Migratory Routes   Like the cause of migrations, how waterfowl select their routes has undergone investigation. What was once mystically referred to as "instinct" seems to be a case of education and memory.

It's hypothesized that migratory patterns evolved by a process of natural selection. No one knows which came first, the chicken or the egg, but major flyways tend to follow fertile farm belts. They also act as passes to channel weather systems, funneling southerly winds in the spring and northerly winds in the fall. Birds that chose to fly these routes survived the journey and taught others; those who took a path that afforded little food and adverse winds perished along the way. Major routes were thus established.

Evidence of "teaching" or leadership is often observable during

7

migrations. The classic wedge of Canada geese functions as an air-foil, with the lead goose breaking the air for those behind him. Leaders are frequently changed during long flights, with the stron-gest geese moving toward the front of the formation where the work is the hardest. The very old, the very young, and the weak fly toward the rear of the formation where little effort is required to remain aloft.

You'll also notice an element of leadership if you carefully watch any flock of waterfowl lost in a storm or just heading out for morning feed. They'll often break ranks, mill around, then regroup with obvious intent and heading.

I've seen this a lot while gunning broadbill. Upon seeing my de-coys, the flock will rise off their close-to-the-water flight path, ball up, then either continue on their way or head for my rig. It appears that indecision on the part of individual flock members results in temporary group confusion. Then a leader or leaders will take over to give positive direction, and they re-form. I've seen exactly the same thing occur with herds of elk and packs of coyote.

Navigation Systems   The leadership notion also helps explain how waterfowl find their way. At least some of the birds remember landmarks. Exactly how much detail they commit to memory is any-body's guess, but major features of the landscape and sky are surely utilized along each route: rivers, prominent mountains, low passes, islands, cities, and man's traditional fixes, the stars, sun, and moon.

Dave Wolny, a Montana rancher, and I run a hunting and fishing guide service; and our big-game camp is on his ranch, high in a grassy swale that rests at the base of Wolny's Mountain. That great pile of rock and timber is surely a fix for waterfowl, for at least once a season, when the sky is smoky with the blowing snow of a storm that hasn't touched down yet, we hear ducks or geese.

It's usually early in the evening, and we're sitting down to a few hands of poker. Then someone motions for silence, and gradually the calls become more distinct.

The sound is a magnet. Every man, including the guy with the winning hand, throws down his cards and steps out the door.

They always come from the north, gradually taking shape and form in the misty sky, and they're never in a coherent formation. They gabble, they honk, they quack—their shifting numbers con-stantly changing the shape of the flock. Then one or two birds recog-nize the mountain looming up out of the mist. Suddenly the bickering stops. They circle our cabin two or three times and then queue up. By the time they disappear the geese are in wedges or the mallards in a line, and always on a southwesterly heading, a direct route to the Madison River.

It's an interesting thing to witness—interesting in that every man watches in silent awe, like a little boy entering a big church. But it's also interesting in that Dave's mountain is far far away from anything approximating a flyway.

Birds venturing over that cabin are thirty miles from the route they're looking for: the valley of the Madison, a major pass in our area. Yet one or more of their numbers know the geography well enough to recognize Wolny's Mountain. And they must, for the direction they eventually take is the shortest air route to intersect the river.

That waterfowl do indeed follow a prescribed pattern in their movements is also supported by banding studies. They show that ducks and geese return each year to nest close to their place of birth, and regularly winter in the same locale. Their movements north and south aren't aimless wanderings engendered by simple stimulus/response motivation, but an intellectual matter of choice, selection, and problem-solving, based on memory and past experience. Not a mystery, but nonetheless a marvel.

Breeding and Nesting   Upon reaching the destination determined by memory and desire, flocks break up, and pairing and mating take place. There are many strange antics associated with the mating ritual among waterfowl: pirouetting dances that whirl across the water, footraces between male and female that explode in a shower of spray, chases, deep dives, calling, fighting—truly a circus of wild activity and odd behavior that's guaranteed to be a delight if you're fortunate enough to witness it. Once mating is accomplished the female begins to build the nest, and in some species (primarily geese and swans) she is assisted by the male.

As the young waterfowl mature, they'll likely face several threats to their survival. Predators are one danger to their existence. Skunks and raccoons often raid nests and eat the eggs lying there. Fox, coyote, snapping turtles, and fish like big bass and northern pike delight in a duckling meal.

Even more important to survival is the weather; too little rain will dry out ponds and leave broods stranded and unprotected on mud flats. Too much rain floods them out. From an average clutch

9

Manitoba Department of Tourism

Breeding and nesting take place in the north around the time of summer solstice, when the days are warm and long and the sun hangs in the evening sky till midnight.

of seven to nine eggs, biologists estimate that only six young survive to adulthood.

Assuming the elements are kind and coyotes none too quick, duckling down is eventually replaced by flight feathers; and the young of the year approach a point where they begin to fly.

At about this same time adult birds go into molt. This is nature's way of replacing feathers that have been lost during the year's activities, but it renders adults nearly helpless since they can't fly for a two-to-three-week period. Some compensation occurs, however, in the form the new plumage takes. "Eclipse" plumage emerges drab and nondistinctive in both hens and drakes, affording some protection through camouflage.

Fall migrations are essentially a reverse of those made in the spring, with a few exceptions. Ducks tend to segregate themselves by age and sex at this time, with young birds-of-the-year moving south first, followed by adult hens and adult drakes. Swans and geese migrate as a family unit.

The most important factor present in the fall that wasn't there in the spring is the hunter. As waterfowl move down the flyways, they're culled to a point approximating the number needed to nest and reproduce successfully the following spring.

At the end of the fall migrations lie the wintering grounds, and habits that are in sharp contrast to the solitude and small family groups of summer. Ducks, geese, and swans become quite gregarious at this time, "flocking up" into huge bunches that appear to pave southern lakes and bays with bobbing backs. There the waterfowl bide their time until again stirred by lengthening days and the wakening warmth of spring.

WATERFOWL MANAGEMENT

All living things need food and shelter to survive. In order for a species to survive, it must also reproduce. Indeed, when there is sufficient food and proper habitat, it is a characteristic of nature's creatures to multiply and prosper—overproduce if you will.

There are, of course, limits to overproduction. The land, the habitat, the resource can grow just so much food and afford just so much room. If a farmer puts ten cattle in a pasture that has enough grass for five, the animals certainly will not thrive and some will eventually die. This is exactly what happens with wildlife.

Whether a deer, a duck, or a songbird is hunted or not, his numbers are infinite. No one shoots robins in this country; yet the ground doesn't seethe with them as they search for worms, nor do they blacken the sky. Nature eliminates surplus robins by disease, predation, and starvation, and keeps them in balance with their environment.

So-called "game species," of which waterfowl are part, would be similarly regulated by nature if left unmolested; but game has a special attraction for many Americans. Some of us enjoy watching waterfowl, some of us enjoy hunting them, and most of us enjoy both. There is a demand for these birds—a reason to ensure optimum numbers of ducks, geese, and swans within the limits of available habitat.

This is the purpose of waterfowl management: to ensure that "pasture" is as productive as it can be, that important waterfowl nesting, resting, and wintering areas have the right balance of food, water, and protection from harassment. Once these conditions are realized, maximum reproduction follows naturally, and it is then the job of management to make sure the surplus of birds is properly harvested by the hunter.

Nesting Habitat—The Key to Waterfowl Production   The success of the nesting effort is *the* critical factor influencing the numbers of waterfowl that will inhabit our flyways each year.

Fall hunting removes surplus waterfowl, and the birds that are left function as next year's breeding stock. If that stock can't replenish itself, can't increase its numbers through reproduction, any mortality losses the following fall will cut seriously into future waterfowl production.

To look at this another way: under normal conditions, 2,000 ducks would produce in the neighborhood of 6,000 young during a normal summer, making for a total of 8,000 birds to fly south in the fall. A bag of 6,000 birds could then be harvested from that flock, and a stable population would be maintained. If, however, nesting conditions were poor and only 2,000 birds reached adulthood, a normal harvest would virtually wipe out the entire population.

What, then, determines nesting success? The weather is one important factor. The greatest part of the breeding and nesting habitat on this continent is dependent upon the waters of winter runoff and spring rains for maintenance. If little snow falls during the winter and the spring rains are scant, many marshes, ponds, and potholes will be dry and afford no nesting opportunities.

Spring storms are another side of the weather coin. Occasionally they are of such severity and duration that they flood or freeze out nesting waterfowl. Flooding and drought are not so critical, however, in terms of long-range effect. Waterfowl can have several bad nesting years, but so long as a basic stock is maintained and protected, they'll bounce back strong as soon as the weather enters a more temperate cycle.

In the long run the real culprit that cuts into waterfowl numbers isn't the weather. It's habitat destruction.

Virtually all of the northern half of the United States and Canada serve as potential breeding grounds for our waterfowl. Nesting sites normally occur in little isolated marshes, along the banks of wooded streams, and in farm ponds.

Now, look at human living patterns. We place a premium on just those places waterfowl need to nest: stream banks, lake shores, salt marshes; they're being dredged, filled, and built upon. Cities characteristically spring up near water, and the mere pressure of human population is often enough to discourage nesting, even when suitable sites are available.

There are also several areas on this continent that can be pinpointed as "duck factories"—places that attract great concentrations of nesting waterfowl. As such they contribute especially significant numbers of ducks and geese to the overall population. Many of the ponds and marshes in our best duck factories are constantly under the threat posed by drainage projects.

The most fertile factory in this category is the pothole region of the northern plains. This area encompasses western Minnesota, the two Dakotas, eastern Montana, and huge chunks of southern Manitoba, Alberta and Saskatchewan. The pothole country isn't only rich in ducks—the land is some of the best in the world for raising grain, primarily wheat.

In order to place more land in production, farmers regularly drain potholes and plow them under, removing them as nesting sites forever.

The significance of such habitat destruction, especially in this geologic region, might not be immediately apparent. Wildlife is inexorably tied to "edge" areas. Whitetail deer do best when they have an environment that incorporates tall timber and the low, brushy growth that sprouts up around the perimeters of thick forests. Wild turkeys will thrive when between 10 and 30 percent of a forest is logged over. Ducks and geese are similarly encouraged by an "edge" situation, theirs being the shallow, shoreline margins of ponds. These places are perfect nesting sites in that they provide food and protection. There are insects and certain types of shallow-water plants to eat, and tall rushes and grasses to hide among. Logically, the more of this type of edge area available to waterfowl, the more nesting sites there will be, the more young will be produced.

With these pond-edges in mind, then, envision a lake that is a square mile in size. It would incorporate an approximate shoreline of four total miles. Now imagine two lakes crammed into that space. Their total shoreline would be around three miles each—two more miles of shoreline than one large lake. Now envision hundreds of tiny ponds crammed into that square mile, ponds that look like the pockmarked battlefield of a modern-day Armageddon when viewed from the air. The total shoreline, the total "edge" area, the total potential duck-breeding grounds are increased ten- to twentyfold.

Now multiply that edge area by the vastness that is the northern prairie—thousands upon thousands of square miles dotted with ponds. The product should give you some inkling of the importance of this region to waterfowl production—and the negative effect as more and more ponds disappear each year.

The tundra/Arctic Circle region of the Far North is another major breeding ground. This area is rather secure in terms of waterfowl production because it's marginal land by human standards and wants. The growing season up there is too short for farming, and the winter is too long to be attractive for settlement.

But the area is used almost exclusively by geese. Bread-and-butter ducks like mallard, canvasback, and pintail don't normally nest so far north, so they benefit little from its pristine nature.

The tundra area, too, is not without some inherent problems that result in population ups and downs. If a first nesting attempt is frustrated by severe weather, waterfowl will make a second, even a third, try at raising a brood in more southerly climes. But in the far north the nesting season is so short that there isn't time to raise a second brood before freeze-up. The first attempt must succeed, or the females simply absorb their own eggs.

This is precisely the situation currently facing our brant population on the East Coast. A late thaw and severe storms have disrupted brant breeding activity in the Maritimes for the third consecutive year, and the birds are currently far down in numbers.

There are, however, some bright prospects on the waterfowl

breeding horizon. Existing habitat and the chances that it won't be plowed under have been given a shot in the arm by a shift in the attitude of several government agencies. At one time the U.S. Department of Agriculture encouraged the draining of swamps, wetlands, and potholes, and even subsidized the operation. Now they advise farmers to retain all the water they possibly can, and not only for the benefit of wildlife.

Montana Fish and Game Department

This pothole pond in eastern Montana is a classic example of prime nesting habitat. Note the extensive "edge" areas created by the many islands of grass and pond weed.

A network of ditches rids the land of surface water in a hurry, and in the process a great deal of erosion occurs. Another negative result of marsh elimination is that such rapid draining raises the possibility of severe floods downstream. There's also the matter of groundwater; when water drains off quickly, the soil absorbs and retains less moisture than when water is allowed to stand, and the effects of any period of drought are intensified.

In the drainage of wetlands, the alteration of a natural scheme, man has discovered that perhaps nature's system was best to begin with. "A healthy environment for wildlife is a healthy environment for man" is far more than just another slogan.

No appraisal of waterfowl management, past accomplishments, and future prospects would be complete without pointing out the contributions made by a private organization of waterfowlers and naturalists known as Ducks Unlimited.

It was formed in the 1930s to solve a potentially disastrous problem. The pothole country of Canada was being despoiled. Ponds were being drained for farming, drought was on the land, and the once-great populations of waterfowl that nested there were dwindling below subsistence levels.

More troubling still, the funds collected from United States sportsmen through the sale of duck stamps and a federal excise tax on sporting goods could not be used to alleviate the emergency.

By law, these funds can only be used within the borders of the United States. Even though the majority of the ducklings dying on Canadian prairies would have been harvested by this country's sportsmen in the fall, our government could do nothing to help. In that milieu Ducks Unlimited was born.

Through private donations, Ducks Unlimited raised money to purchase valuable Canadian wetlands before they were cut deep by draglines. They built levees, dams, and headgates on many of these marshes, so water could be controlled.

With these man-made controls, water could then be held back and conserved during dry periods, and allowed to flow freely during any flooding situation that threatened established nests.

The result was a buffer effect. Even though waterfowl populations are still at the mercy of the weather, Ducks Unlimited's marshes were, at the very least, sufficient to maintain a suitable breeding population of waterfowl species each year. Although flights might be small and bag limits lean, these wetlands ensure enough broods will hatch out and survive to produce good crops of young once climatic conditions arise that are more conducive to breeding.

Ducks Unlimited is an active force in waterfowl management and conservation legislation today. It continues to purchase more marshland in Canada, to create more stable wetlands, and its most recent project involves the acquisition of vast waterfowl wintering grounds in Mexico. It goes without further note that every waterfowler owes it to himself and his sport to join. The price of membership in the organization is $10.00 a year, with larger donations gratefully accepted. Write to: Ducks Unlimited, P. O. Box 66300, Chicago, Illinois 60666.

"Habitat preservation" is pretty broad, both as a term and a practice, and it involves a lot more than putting the brakes on development. A listing of some individual techniques wildlife personnel are currently employing to increase breeding opportunities would include:

• Planting and maintenance of key waterfowl foods and cover. This increases the number of birds that can and will be attracted to nest in an area. Many ponds with barren shorelines can also be converted into breeding grounds through this method.

• Providing prefabricated nests also attracts birds. These nests are usually boxes on elevated posts for ducks, and open platforms for geese. The posts prevent nest-robbing by predators like skunk and raccoon.

• Building small islands in shallow ponds increases the edge effect, and they're especially attractive as nesting sites because they offer a safety zone of water between brood and shore.

• Further protection is achieved by closing important nesting areas to the public during the mating and incubation period so the parent birds aren't disturbed or inadvertently frightened away.

Reestablishment of past traditions is a particularly absorbing aspect of waterfowl management.

While the need and desire to migrate are universal among waterfowl, they don't all migrate to the same place, or travel the same routes. Waterfowl migrations are a little like the daily movement of workers from Long Island to New York City. Some of the commuters originate in Queens, some in Nassau, and some in Suffolk. When they arrive in the city, some go uptown, some downtown, and some to Brooklyn.

Within the framework of home-to-work movement, each individual has his own starting point, way to travel, and his own desti-

17

Planting and maintenance of waterfowl foods and cover vegetation can turn an unproductive stockpond into a mini-duck factory.

nation. This same sort of situation takes place when waterfowl migrate.

They all move from the south to the north in the spring and north to south in the fall, but each flock or family group flies its own route from and to different places. The selection of these routes, and the places these birds regularly choose as nesting and wintering sites, are called waterfowl "traditions."

Traditions are learned during a duck's growing-up period, just as a child learns that stoves burn, and how to recite his ABCs. Because traditions are learned and not instinct, biologists have discovered that if a duckling is removed from the nest site to grow, and is allowed to become familiar with a new place, the chances are good he'll return to that new home the following spring.

Montana Fish and Game Department

The ability of waterfowl to learn and accept new traditions might well result in much greater numbers of waterfowl than now fill the North American skies, for there are many breeding and nesting opportunities neglected by our waterfowl. It's theorized that the middle regions of the United States were once major breeding grounds. Because these areas were the first to be settled, resident birds were heavily pressured. Not just in the fall, but during the nesting period as well. Young, tender ducklings and easy-to-catch molting adults were just too much of a table temptation for a struggling settler to ignore. Waterfowl were harvested to a point where those with southerly nesting traditions were extinguished.

Because young birds placed in new surroundings often adopt these environments as "home," it's felt that this type of introduction

19

Montana Fish and Game Department

Reestablishment of extinguished traditions, coupled with nesting opportunities, could mean a vast new source of waterfowl. Here, a Canada goose glowers at the photographer from her man-made nest.

might well reestablish nesting ducks and geese in habitat that's currently ignored, but otherwise perfectly suitable for waterfowl reproduction.

Farm ponds are another type of frontier. Before the dust-bowl days of the 1930s, few farmers made any effort to trap and store surface water. Learning their lessons from those dry years, virtually every farm west of the Mississippi now has at least one small pothole within its borders. If these places were made attractive to waterfowl through habitat management, with nesting traditions established there, a new and potentially fertile source of ducks and geese could be created.

The Refuge System   Waterfowl historically favor specific places for food and rest stops during their migrations. Many of these spots achieve a degree of fame as hunting meccas. Because they attract both hunters and hordes of ducks and geese, it is conceivable that the birds using them could be discouraged from returning there in the future—to their detriment. Consequently, it's a necessary move to turn at least some of these spots into refuges.

Sportsmen's dollars, collected through the sale of duck stamps and an excise tax on sporting goods, go toward the federal purchase of these key areas. In addition, states develop their own refuges, and some private duck clubs contribute to the effort by keeping portions of their lands off-limits to hunting, or under close regulation.

The effect is a system of sanctuaries that spans all four flyways—patches of marshland, river bottom, and tilled fields that are available as safe havens to birds on the move. They function as places to temporarily escape hunting pressure in the fall, or to wait out possible adverse weather in the spring. Many of these refuges also double as breeding and nesting grounds.

Some of these places are huge, like the 17,000-acre Horicon Marsh in Wisconsin, the 50,000-acre Bear Refuge in Utah, and the 40,000-acre Malheur Refuge in Oregon. And some are small. I know of a beautiful little sanctuary near Sag Harbor, on Long Island, that can't be much more than 500 acres; and another small chunk of land is reserved for migrating mallards near my home in Montana's Gallatin Valley.

These refuges, no matter what their size, not only benefit waterfowl, but also the waterfowler.

Forsyth, Montana, in my experience one of the best places in the country to hunt Canada geese, wasn't always that way. Old-timers tell me of "the good old days" when a visitation by a flock of these big birds amounted to hot news that was talked about in the community for a week afterward.

Then the nearby Yellowstone River was made a refuge. Waterfowl could not be hunted below the spring high-water mark. Geese and ducks gradually began to use the river on their southbound travels, resting on the water during the day, feeding in the rich corn and wheat fields along the river morning and evening. Soon area residents had a hunting opportunity that never existed before— thanks to a refuge.

Realize, too, that the word refuge doesn't necessarily mean "no hunting." Many of the larger refuges permit controlled hunting.

Short-Stopping: A Modern Management Problem   It's a little ironic that two management techniques, teaching new traditions and the refuge system, have combined to produce a monumental headache for sportsmen and biologists alike.

"Short-stopping" is a frequent and legitimate gripe among southern waterfowlers. At one time ducks and geese migrated to the Gulf Coast through the Central and Mississippi flyways, and down the Atlantic flyway to Georgia and Florida. Now many ducks and the great bulk of geese spend their winters in South Dakota, southern Illinois, Tennessee, and North Carolina.

The reasons why amount to newly acquired traditions. Federal preserves were established at certain points along the flyways to provide a place where migrating birds could temporarily escape hunting pressure and feed in relative peace. The system worked— too well in fact, for many birds have learned that they don't have to fly beyond these places. This not only robs the southern gunner of his share of the harvest; it's a potentially destructive tradition.

It is conceivable that extremely severe weather could decimate these short-stopped birds—essentially catch them in a vice of ice and starvation from which there's no midwinter escape. Since the birds that survive hunting season are the source of next year's crop, this would be a serious tragedy indeed.

Disease is another possibility. When the old traditions were observed by waterfowl, they dispersed over a rather wide area upon reaching their wintering grounds. Short-stopped birds, however, bunch up in staggering numbers in close proximity—perfect conditions for the spread of sickness and an epidemic. In fact, a very large kill of short-stopped waterfowl occurred in South Dakota last winter as a result of disease.

Because traditions are learned, however, waterfowl can eventually "unlearn" the short-stopping tradition if they're encouraged to do so. This could be achieved by elimination of winter feeding, and programmed harassment at the time birds would normally head farther south.

THE HUNTER'S ROLE AS WATERFOWL MANAGER

A symbiotic relationship exists between waterfowl and the waterfowler. The birds provide sport, relaxation, and that indefinable something that comes over anyone who's ever watched a flight of canvasback against a gray sky.

The hunter, in turn, provides for the well-being and very existence of the birds.

The hunter cares for waterfowl in a way that goes far beyond harvesting the surplus. It's a seldom-recognized fact that the sportsman has long taken the lead in conservation, preservation, and protection. He has provided not just words, but hard cash as well, for waterfowl research, wetland acquisition, the purchase of refuges, and law enforcement. As a political lobby, sportsmen have also initiated and helped vote in significant legislation to protect wildlife environment as well as endangered species. It's more than ironic that those who see hunting as a threat to wildlife would do it immeasurable good if they'd regularly purchase hunting licenses and duck stamps, and join a gun club.

The Whys of Waterfowling Laws   • "Man, you tell me we're not being taken! We pay five bucks for a duck stamp, have a bunch of bureaucrats tell us all we can have is one black duck a day because there's so few of them, and then you see something like this."

My young companion embraced the expanse of Long Island's Moriches Bay with a sweep of his arm. The gesture took in a panorama that began at Pattersquash Island and scribed a wide circle all the way to the Coast Guard Station opposite Moriches Inlet—a distance of some five miles. Everywhere his hand passed there was a black duck.

The bay was thick with them—beelike swarms of birds trading back and forth—velvet strings of resting flocks—thousands and

23

thousands of black duck, and of that uncountable number we were only allowed one per day per hunter.

It's sometimes difficult to grasp the need for restrictive laws in terms of waterfowl, because scenes like that on Moriches Bay are common, and so are low limits. To understand the reasoning and the right behind their existence, look first at the hunting situation as it exists with upland game.

Imagine a hundred-acre farm that's well supplied with wildlife. As the hunting season progresses and game is bagged, their numbers dwindle. Where there were two rabbits to the acre, there is now one. The two clutches of pheasant, numbering perhaps twenty birds, are now reduced to eight. Through hunting harvest, game numbers are reduced and animals are comparatively scarce. Hunters have to work twice as hard, walk twice as long, before a bird or bunny busts from cover.

The normal reaction to this situation usually is for hunters to move on—to find greener pastures with greater concentrations of game. So, even though the season is still open, the remaining resident wildlife goes unhunted. In upland hunting there is a self-limiting factor in terms of harvest.

This is not the case with waterfowl. Because of their gregarious nature, their travels, and their traditions, it's quite possible for a poor hatching year to result in low populations. Yet the concentration of those scant populations might appear great indeed in scattered areas. Realize, too, that in such concentrations, birds are extremely vulnerable. It is conceivable that under the right circumstances whole breeding stocks for next year could be wiped out by concentrated gunning pressure in the right place at the right time.

To prevent this from happening, some complex laws have evolved regarding waterfowling. At times they appear unfair—as when you see ten thousand birds but are only allowed to bag one—but their purpose is preservation, not frustration. The flyway system is one example.

• FLYWAYS. In their semiannual migrations from south to north and back, waterfowl follow one of four roughly prescribed routes called "flyways."

In diagram form, flyways look like hourglasses, funneling widely scattered birds into a narrow neck as they migrate, then distributing them over an equally broad range when they reach their destination.

Although there's minor mixing of different flyway residents on wintering and breeding grounds, this natural division of North

American waterfowl into units permits a degree of management and control.

For example, waterfowl along both the Mississippi and Central flyways nest heavily in the Canadian duck factory. If that region has a poor nesting year, bag limits along these two flyways can be reduced to prevent an overharvest. On the other hand, only a few birds on the Atlantic and Pacific flyways nest in that plains region; so nesting success in mid-Canada has little effect on the numbers of birds that will be trading down the East and West coasts. Bag limits for these flyways must be set in relation to their individual breeding record, compiled on their separate nesting grounds.

There's also the matter of exposure. The Mississippi and Atlantic flyways include large population centers like Chicago and New York. Concentrations of people also mean concentrations of hunters, so a three-bird limit on the Mississippi flyway would result in a far greater total harvest than the same limit on the Central flyway.

Flyways afford a better system for management than nationwide regulations that might result in too heavy a take along one flyway and an underharvest on another. That is the basis for the four separate sets of rules and regulations regarding waterfowling issued by the government each year.

• THE POINT SYSTEM. A valuable new addition to migratory game laws is the point system. This system is based on the knowledge that in any year there will be certain species of waterfowl that achieve maximum populations and others that fall below optimum levels in each flyway.

When a bird is deemed down in numbers—let's say mallards had a bad nesting year in the Central flyway—a premium is placed on their possession. Drakes might be worth thirty points, and hens, because they're the ones that represent next year's numbers, might be worth ninety. With a limit of 100 total points, plus one duck in possession, this means that the guy who shoots two hen mallards is done for the day. If he holds out for drakes, he can shoot a total of four.

Should a particular species be undergunned, like the teal and shoveler commonly are, they can have a low number assigned to them, thereby encouraging hunters to harvest them. Recent regulations have assigned ten points to a whole slew of species in the Central flyway: whistler, teal, gadwall, drake pintail, shoveler, and scaup, to name a few; so under this system it's quite possible

ATLANTIC FLYWAY

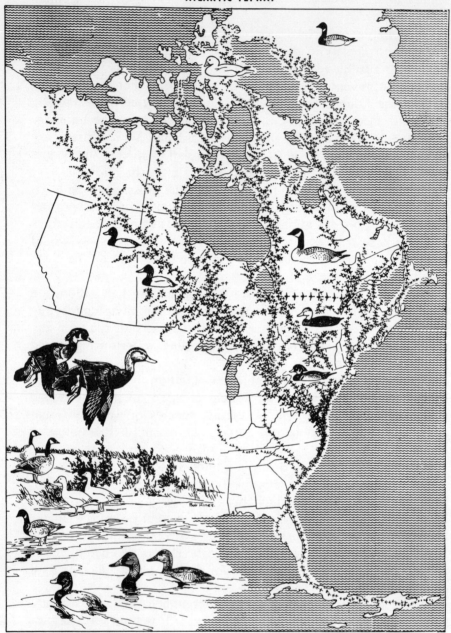

UNITED STATES DEPARTMENT OF THE INTERIOR • FISH AND WILDLIFE SERVICE

U.S. Fish and Wildlife Service

"Flyways" are the four main migration routes traveled by waterfowl in North America. Their existence permits regulation and management by units, rather than nationwide laws and policies that could result in too heavy a kill in one flyway and too light a harvest in another.

MISSISSIPPI FLYWAY

UNITED STATES DEPARTMENT OF THE INTERIOR • FISH AND WILDLIFE SERVICE

Waterfowl

CENTRAL FLYWAY

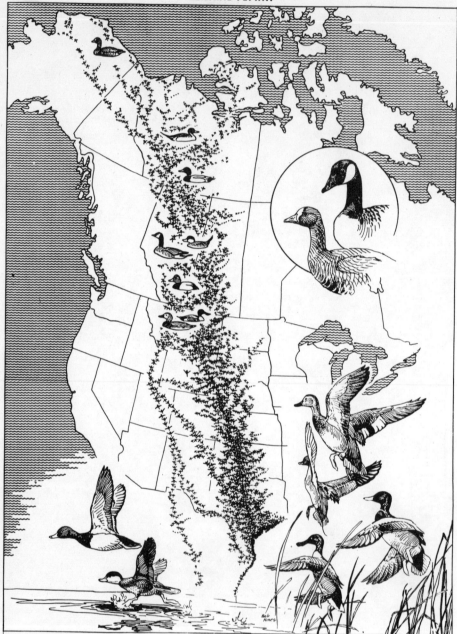

UNITED STATES DEPARTMENT OF THE INTERIOR · FISH AND WILDLIFE SERVICE

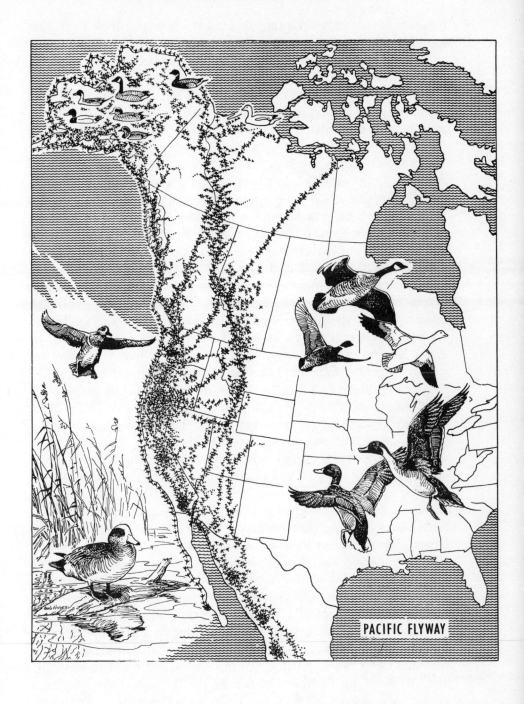

PACIFIC FLYWAY

to shoot eleven birds in a day. No matter how you look at it, that amounts to real gunning action!

There is one problem inherent in the point system: you must be able to identify ducks. You'll get the most mileage out of your day if you can do it on the wing—admittedly difficult given poor light conditions and the eclipse plumage of early season. You absolutely must be able to identify birds in the hand, or run the risk of breaking the law.

• EVIDENCE OF SPECIES. It is the law that you can't destroy all evidence of a bird's sex and species by completely dressing and plucking it, until you reach your home refrigerator or freezer. This has to do, in part, with those who would hedge on the point system; but, more important, by leaving the legally required wingtip (from the last joint) intact, examining biologists can determine age, sex, and species of the dead bird.

This is important to waterfowl management because of what are called "age-distribution characteristics." To understand their significance, consider a family of ten ducks born one spring. In the fall perhaps five of the group would be killed. Of the five that survived, let's assume they have a total of twenty young the following spring. The next fall, then, that total "family" would number five 1½ year-old birds and twenty birds-of-the-year. A proportion of them would be removed by hunting—perhaps two of the older birds and twelve of the younger birds. They would again breed and produce more offspring the next spring, so that the family winging south the third fall would be composed of three 2½-year-old birds, eight 1½-year-old birds, and perhaps forty birds-of-the-year.

Note the pyramidlike structure of age groups, with the oldest birds always having the smallest numbers, and the youngest the largest. This amounts to a normal age-distribution pattern.

By comparing the age-group profiles of harvested birds with previously established normal distribution, it is then possible to determine if populations of ducks are growing, stable, or on the decline. For example, if it were found that birds-of-the-year mallards made up a smaller portion of the hunter's kill than was normal, it would be a sign that the total numbers of mallards, and next year's breeding stock, were down. This, in turn, would point toward the need to build up numbers in the future through a readjustment in the point system, a lower bag limit, a shorter season, or the removal of the bird from "game" classification entirely. These are the kinds of measures taken to bring back the redhead and canvas-back and, most recently, the Atlantic brant.

• Banding is a cooperative program between the United States, Canada, and Mexico that involves the live capture of waterfowl, then permanently identifying them by means of a strong steel band around their leg. The band bears a code number, and it will be worn by the bird for the rest of its life. The band is harmless in terms of life processes—it doesn't interfere with flight, feeding, or swim-ming, and is absolutely painless.

Upon recapture by biologists, or harvest by hunters, the code number then reveals things like age and migratory patterns. In terms of the numbers of bands returned by hunters, they also pro-vide some indication of the size of the annual harvest.

Hunters, of course, must take the time to inform the Fish and Wildlife Service of their kill; a postcard with the number, your name and address, and where the bird was shot will do. You'll then receive information from the service about where and when the bird was banded.

Aside from helping with waterfowl management, the history of the bird could prove downright fascinating. Ducks banded in the United States have been downed in Siberia and South America, and birds shot in California have been banded in Quebec. If there is any doubt about the applicability of any particular law, you should consult a local Fish and Wildlife official for clarification.

Waterfowling laws are designed to protect the birds from over-harvest and preserve the best of the sport for future generations. Although the following is by no means a complete list (you should get a new synopsis each year from your local post office), it does provide a list of the basic do's and don't's of waterfowling.

• When hunting migratory birds (including doves), you will need both a state hunting license and a federal duck stamp. Duck stamps are available at any post office. The stamp must be signed with your name in ink, across its face.

• It is illegal to use a net, trap, crossbow, rifle, or pistol to hunt waterfowl. Shotguns may not be larger than ten gauge, nor may they be capable of holding more than three shells.

• Live birds may not be used as decoys or as callers. Electronic calling devices are likewise illegal.

• Baiting is illegal. This means you can't scatter grain or other forms of waterfowl feed with the intent of luring birds. It is, however, legal to hunt over feed that has occurred naturally, as the un-harvested corn or grain that escapes a picker or combine.

• You must shoot within legal hours. Those hours differ by region and circumstance, the most liberal ranging from one-half hour before sunrise to sunset. Check with local regulations.

• "Sink boxes," floating craft with less than three inches free-board, used to conceal a gunner, are illegal.

• Livestock may not be used as a blind.

• Disturbing or rallying resting waterfowl is illegal.

• Shooting waterfowl from any motorized conveyance—boat, car, etc.—is illegal.

INCIDENTAL MORTALITY

Harvest by hunters and natural predation are not the only causes of waterfowl deaths. There are other causes, all of them wasteful, since they satisfy neither the schemes of nature nor the wants of man. It's interesting to note that all of them, directly or indirectly, are the result of our collective use (or misuse) of the environment.

Perhaps most insidious is death from oil slicks. These slicks occur on inland settling ponds and the high seas, the result of the refining process, accidental spills, tankers blowing their ballast, and ships cleaning their bilges.

On the water, oil slicks have an attraction for waterfowl, espe-cially during rough weather, since they calm choppy seas. The birds land in the mess, assuming it's a safe haven, and as soon as they touch the stuff oil begins to soak into their feathers. If they remain in the spill for any length of time, the seeping oil robs their feathers of loft, and without the buoyancy of trapped air, the birds sink and drown.

Even if they should leave the spill immediately, the oil they have come in contact with gradually works its way into their feathers, and their down loses its insulating qualities. They then die of out-right freezing.

Should they survive that possibility, feathers and their function are so altered that unusual energy is required to fly and to go about a day's normal activities. Birds quickly become emaciated, with breastbones that protrude like knifeblades. If they're finally killed by a hunter, who indeed performs an act of mercy, they're unfit for the table—the smell and taste of oil permeates their flesh.

In the same breath, hunters aren't exactly lily-white either. Lead poisoning from expended shotgun pellets is at least as big a killer as oil spills.

This situation is particularly acute in areas where there is concentrated hunting pressure. The spent shot end up on pond and river bottoms, and before the shot can sink into the mud, feeding waterfowl ingest the pellets, thinking them to be either small seeds or pebbles that they'd normally use as grit for their crop.

Unless the shot are expelled, they lodge in the crop where they indeed function like grit, grinding food preliminary to digestion. When that food is hard and flinty, like corn or, to a lesser extent, wheat or rice, the lead is eroded and transformed into a substance that is readily absorbed into the blood stream. It doesn't take much to kill a duck in this manner; one or two fully digested pellets of #6 shot are enough. Lead levels build up in the system; the bird declines in vigor and quality and eventually dies.

The solution to this problem lies in finding a substitute for lead, but the telling is a lot easier than the doing.

Because of lead's density (the relationship existing between lots of weight and little bulk), lead shot carry farther and penetrate more deeply than any other practical substitute. Soft iron shot, the alternative most often suggested, perform about as well as lead up to ranges of thirty-five yards, but beyond that point lead's superior qualities count heavily in terms of the energy packed in each pellet and resulting clean kills.

Translated into field application, this means more wounded and crippled birds that will elude capture, but not death, if lead substitutes are used.

Truly, the use or non-use of lead shot, and its consequences, are a sportsman's dilemma.

"Natural" mortality, as opposed to human causes of waterfowl deaths, does occur; and of natural causes two stand out in terms of sheer devastation: fowl cholera and botulism.

Both these diseases are capable of wiping out huge numbers of birds. Fowl cholera, the least understood of the two, is an infection that appears to originate in domestic fowl. It strikes fast, with the disease running its course among a flock of waterfowl in a matter of days, often reducing the numbers of exposed birds by 90 percent. Aside from removal and burning of infected carcasses, there are no known cures or preventative measures that may be taken against the spread of this disease.

Botulism, also known as "western duck sickness," is equally deadly, but more is understood about the disease. Botulism is actually a form of poisoning, the poison being the product of toxic bacteria.

The bacteria are thought to grow in the carcasses of aquatic insects exposed to the air as water levels in lakes with gently sloping shores recede, due to dry spells or drawdowns. When the lake is again reflooded, waterfowl feed in these previously exposed areas and ingest the deadly bacteria.

Antiserum can be used to revive sick ducks, but the prospects of finding and injecting sick birds in time to save them make this a marginal practice. Careful control of water levels on marshes subject to avian botulism is a more practical method of prevention and control, and the one most often employed.

Realize that these diseases, while "natural," are encouraged when man meddles too much with natural order. The effects of fowl cholera are greatly multiplied when it develops among flocks concentrated by the attraction of refuges and feeding programs. Avian botulism is most common around man-made reservoirs.

There is a message contained therein: that we can't go too far in "managing" nature and her creatures; that, ultimately, our responsibility is to preserve and protect at least a portion of the wild world and its schemes that evolved over eons of time—not create man-made substitutes for it.

And in that maxim lies a good measure of what, to me, is essential to the sport of waterfowling.

2 | Waterfowl Identification

Being able to identify birds on the wing and in hand is a skill every waterfowler should learn. The reasons are both pragmatic and aesthetic. Certain species of duck and goose are seasonally placed off-limits to shooting, and you must be able to identify them as such as they come into your decoys or pass overhead. There's also the matter of the point system on certain flyways. When you know the bird you're aiming at before you pull the trigger, you can enjoy true bonus shooting with a limit up to eleven ducks.

There is, too, a deeper sense of understanding, accomplishment, and downright pleasure that accompanies the ability to look at a knot of birds on the horizon and say with conviction, "Mallards," or "Brant." It develops into the kind of intimacy with nature that leads you to rig out in the spring to watch the antics of courtship and mating, and that finds you building wood duck boxes in your spare time.

Waterfowl identification is one of the many components of gunning that make the sport infinitely more than shooting at a bird.

Habitat: The First Clue   The terrain and types of water favored by individual species of waterfowl provide the first step in identification. Ducks can be divided into two categories: divers and puddlers.

Diving ducks are creatures of big water: large lakes, bays, and the ocean. They characteristically dive completely under the water to feed. Some examples of more common diving ducks would include canvasback, redhead, scaup, whistler, merganser, and bufflehead.

Puddle ducks favor shallow water. While they can and will dive when pursued, or under unusual circumstances, they prefer to feed by "dabbling"—stretching their long necks underwater while their tails reach skyward in a "bottoms up" attitude. Because of their feeding preferences, puddler species are usually found around small ponds, creeks, and the shallow marshes and bays of our big lakes and coastal waters. Examples of common puddler species include mallard, black duck, pintail, gadwall, and the teals.

The clues provided by the habitat where you shoot or see a duck are just rules of thumb, however. I've occasionally shot lesser scaup over small creeks in Montana, and watched black duck raft up on a calm Atlantic Ocean. For real oddball behavior, though, nothing beats the scene I witnessed last year. Ornithologists and seasoned gunners alike accuse me of having pipe dreams, but I saw what I saw.

I was in the lakeside home of a friend on Long Island, and it was near the end of the gunning season. The marshes on Long Island are becoming scarce, and consequently ducks adaptable to civilization seldom go there, knowing they'll hold hunters. Instead, the birds become thick on the little house-rimmed ponds of suburbia where people feed them bread.

This pond was just that kind, with no hunting allowed along its shores. In addition to mallards, the pond also had a few pairs of baldpate and about a dozen whistlers (goldeneye).

Whistlers are divers; so it was a bit unusual to see them on a four-acre close-in pond. But what really bugged my eyes out were those crazy mallards; they'd learned to dive, I'd assume, by watching the whistlers.

Just like a diving duck, they'd snake under the surface, using their wings to swim. They'd stay under for 30 seconds, then bob back up to the top. The fellow who owned the house claimed the pond was between eight and twelve feet deep.

Ducks at a Distance   Although habitat alone can be a questionable yardstick of identification, when you couple it with the behavior and appearance of ducks at a distance you come closer to positive identification of the type and species of bird it might be.

Puddle ducks characteristically fly and rest in small groups seldom larger than a dozen birds. Divers like a lot more company, traveling with twelve or more companions and sometimes rafting and flying in numbers that reach into the thousands.

Behavior on the water is another indicator; when you see birds diving under the surface, it's pretty safe to assume you're looking at divers. Puddlers are similarly identified by a bunch of tails bobbing about.

In the air, divers tend to fly low on the water, and individual members of the flock change position very slowly, creating a visual effect that's a little like watching an amoeba. They also appear to have a steadier, slightly faster wingbeat than puddlers, though this tendency will be revealed only after you've looked at a lot of ducks.

Puddlers fly high, as do geese, and puddlers are forever changing their position relative to the flock; so that, aloft, the configuration of birds appears to have no real definition. The same can be true of geese when they're semipermanent residents of an area and flying to or from feed. When covering great distances, however, geese assume a very definite pattern—the classic V for Canadas and wavy lines for snows and blues.

When approaching a rig of decoys or a raft of real birds, puddlers will come in high, set their wings, and slowly drift down.

When alarmed in flight, puddlers have the ability to transfer their forward motion into near-vertical rise, and "fly up a stovepipe." Many gunners miss their target because of this part of a puddler's behavior; they fail to anticipate that rise and shoot beneath the bird.

Divers approach a rig low on the water and travel at high speeds until the moment they decide to sit in. If they flare, they do so by peeling off—usually away from the blind and with the wind. Because their flight is less erratic than that of a puddler, they're a bit easier to hit—or so people tell me.

Waterfowl Up Close   A duck's profile on the water is another way to tell the difference between puddlers and divers. A puddler rides highest in the rear, with his tail plainly out of water. The tail on a diver slopes down very nearly to meet the water, and the thick-

Even though they're not in the classic V-formation, the large size and slow wingbeats of these birds should make it a cinch to identify them as Canada geese.

est part of his body will appear to be around mid-back.

Takeoff is another giveaway. A puddle duck leaps into the air in a spangle of spray as if his feet were attached to a springboard. He rises near vertically for six to ten feet, then levels off into flight like a pheasant.

Divers, on the other hand, run across the water as they flap their wings to gain airspeed.

The landing characteristics exhibited by each type are likewise divergent; divers skid into a landing, a little like an airplane, and puddlers plop down like a helicopter.

INDIVIDUAL SPECIES IDENTIFICATION

It's rather easy to get the hang of quick differentiation between puddler and diver types, but when you get into individual species identification things get a bit tougher.

It helps immensely to have some idea of the birds common to your area, and the time of year that they're around. For example, blue-wing teal are always early migrants, often passing through our northern states long before the regular season begins. If you were hunting in Minnesota in November and saw a puddle duck the size of a tiny teal, you would know immediately that it couldn't be a blue-wing.

Cinnamon teal seldom stray east of the Rockies, and they, too, are early migrants; so chances are slim that the bird could be a cinnamon.

That leaves only one other teal common to North America: the green-wing. Without referring to any markings or distinctive color, by knowing relative size, how a puddle duck behaves, and what birds might be around, you've correctly identified the species.

Knowing something about general markings helps too. If you see two or three high-flying birds with rather slow wingbeats, flying in an erratic pattern, you're looking at one of the larger puddle ducks. If you note a light-colored underwing that seems to flash in the sun, that can mean one of two birds: a black duck or a mallard. If you were hunting in the West, it could only be a mallard. There are no blacks west of the Mississippi. If you were on Maryland's Eastern Shore, you'd probably be looking at a black, because they are in significant majority there. But you can make even more positive identification by observing the tone of the body of the bird. Black duck are of a rich burnt umber color and show up quite dark. Mallards, both hens and drakes, appear much lighter overall—not much darker, in fact, than the flash of their underwings.

At this point it might be worth noting that I'm purposely not mentioning specific color markings, like the green head of a drake mallard or the reddish-brown head of a canvasback. I think the biggest mistake hunters make when trying to identify a bird on the wing is to look for these specific shades and markings. First, at fifty yards, many of these details will be ill-defined. Under the constantly changing light conditions encountered during a hunter's day, the green head of a mallard can look black, and every hen of every species appears to be the same allover shade. There's also the complicating matter of eclipse plumage.

Virtually every picture painted or published of a duck portrays the creature in his gaudy mating colors, and it's usually a drake at that. But in the beginning of the gunning season, birds are wearing their drab, mottled, tough-to-define eclipse plumage.

It takes an exceptional eye to differentiate between a hen redhead and a hen broadbill in the hand at this time, much less on the wing and flying by at forty-five yards; it's even tough to identify the hen and drake of the same species!

However, if you'll concentrate on things like flying form, outlines, environment, and what ducks should be around at what time of the year, you'll be amazed at the accuracy your predictions will show.

The start of the season is the toughest, and I'll be the first to admit occasional mistakes. After all, it's been nine months since correct identification counted so heavily. So don't feel too badly when you show a warden a hen gadwall and he points out that it's a bird-of-the-year mallard.

But if you'll commit to memory the following lists and charts, relative to the species predominant in your flyway, you'll find those mistakes surprisingly few. And by the end of the season, with the grace of full plumage and experience, you'll be delighted to discover that you can indeed tell a whistler from a canvasback from a bufflehead at a hundred yards; and you will find the subtle difference between a greater and lesser scaup to be comparable to night and day once they're in hand.

Excellent pocket guides are available at no charge from the Bureau of Sportfisheries and Wildlife, Department of the Interior, Washington, D.C.

Their Hunters Duck Identification Guide, reproduced on pp. 42-43, is a simple and near-foolproof way to identify birds in the hand by a process of elimination. Other good guides include "Ducks At A Distance" and "Know Your Ducks."

U.S. Fish and Wildlife Service

DUCKS

Baldpate or Widgeon

LATIN NAME: Mareca americana.
REGIONAL NAMES: Widgeon, baldface, wheat duck, poacher.
SIZE: 20 inches, 2½ pounds.
IDENTIFYING CHARACTERISTICS: Males: forehead and back of head white, giving a bald appearance. Prominent stripe of glossy green on the side of the head. Brownish gray above, rust and white below. A green wing patch, bordered by black, and a small narrow bill are common to both sexes. Hens: yellow-brown above, brown and white below. On the water, baldpate appear to have an exceptionally short neck and are often found in the company of geese and swans. On the water, and in the air, the reedy whistle of the drake is hard to miss and sure identification. It sounds just like the whistle that's found in kids' and pets' rubber toys.

If you don't hear the whistle, the baldpates' white forewing will be obvious as they fly, and it is common to both sexes. Baldpate move about in small groups—rarely more than six—and, when alarmed, flare into the wind. This finds them momentarily drifting back before flying off, affording a good opportunity for a second shot with camera or gun. Baldpate are puddle ducks.
DISTRIBUTION: Common across the nation.
HABITAT: Small woods ponds early in the season. Larger waters, including the sea, with the coming of cold weather. Baldpate favor aquatic plants and, like the gadwall, frequently steal the food other ducks have brought up from the bottom. They have the common nickname of "poacher."
HABITS: Baldpate are shy, wary ducks, easily flared and hard to fool.

Bufflehead

LATIN NAME: Bucephala albeola.
REGIONAL NAMES: Butterball, butter duck, buffalo-head, hell-diver.
SIZE: 14 inches, 1 pound.
IDENTIFYING CHARACTERISTICS: Male: prominent white patch on side of crested iridescent purple-black head. Upper body black with white striping, lower half white. Females: slight crest on head, overall color grayish brown. Bufflehead are diving ducks and noticeably on the small side. They always fly in small groups. Drakes are easy to pick out because they show so much white that appears to flash on and off as they fly.

Bufflehead are easy to differentiate from teal in the air by a rather straight, low flight, and a slate-gray overall appearance. Teal appear buff-brown.
DISTRIBUTION: Ranges from border to border and coast to coast.
HABITAT: The bufflehead can be found in both fresh and salt water during gunning season, but shows a marked preference for big expanses of water—

41

Waterfowl

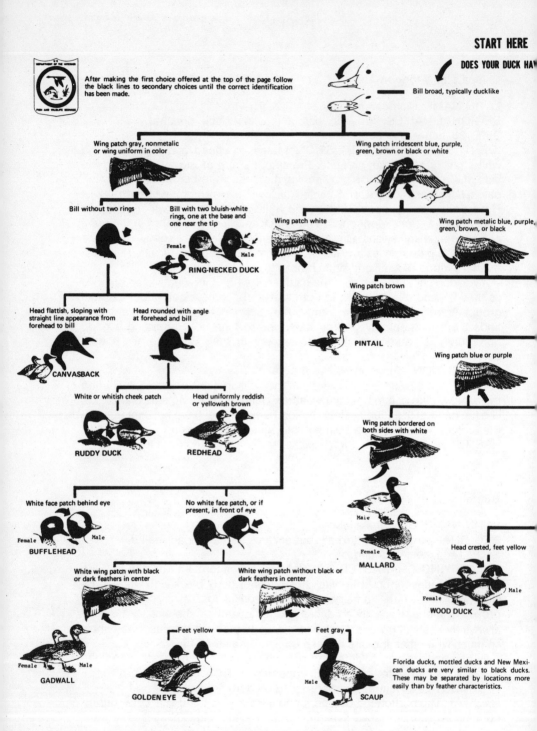

After making the first choice offered at the top of the page follow the black lines to secondary choices until the correct identification has been made.

START HERE

DOES YOUR DUCK HA▪

Bill broad, typically ducklike

Wing patch gray, nonmetalic or wing uniform in color

Wing patch irridescent blue, purple, green, brown or black or white

Bill without two rings

Bill with two bluish-white rings, one at the base and one near the tip

Female   Male   RING-NECKED DUCK

Wing patch white

Wing patch metalic blue, purple, green, brown, or black

Head flattish, sloping with straight line appearance from forehead to bill

Head rounded with angle at forehead and bill

Wing patch brown

PINTAIL

CANVASBACK

Wing patch blue or purple

White or whitish cheek patch

Head uniformly reddish or yellowish brown

Wing patch bordered on both sides with white

RUDDY DUCK

REDHEAD

Male

White face patch behind eye

No white face patch, or if present, in front of eye

Female

MALLARD

Female   Male

BUFFLEHEAD

Head crested, feet yellow

White wing patch with black or dark feathers in center

White wing patch without black or dark feathers in center

Female   Male

WOOD DUCK

Feet yellow

Feet gray

Female   Male

GADWALL

Male

Male

GOLDENEYE

SCAUP

Florida ducks, mottled ducks and New Mexican ducks are very similar to black ducks. These may be separated by locations more easily than by feather characteristics.

42

Guide For Hunters Duck Identification

This pictorial aid is designed to assist in recognizing ducks in the hand after they have been bagged.

The shape of the bill, wing markings, color of feet or head crest are some of the typical characteristics used to identify ducks in the hand. This is quite different from identification of ducks in flight or sitting on water. When flying or on water other identifying features are used such as silhouettes, mannerisms of flight, wing beat, speed of flight or color patterns on body and wings. Every effort should be made to learn to recognize ducks before they are shot. By doing this the hunter is able to take much greater advantage of his sport.

Although occasionally seen inland, sea ducks are not included in this key. They are most frequently found in open salt water areas.

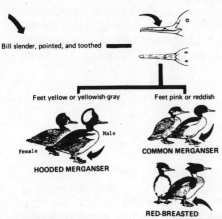

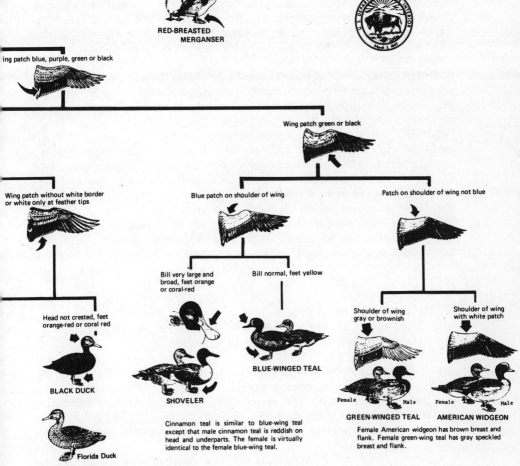

Cinnamon teal is similar to blue-wing teal except that male cinnamon teal is reddish on head and underparts. The female is virtually identical to the female blue-wing teal.

Female American widgeon has brown breast and flank. Female green-wing teal has gray speckled breast and flank.

large lakes, bays, and sounds. They're fond of following shore lines and consequently are frequent visitors to decoys.

HABITS: Bufflehead are relatively easy to decoy. Their call is a diminutive "quack." Once they stool in, they'll likely dive rather than fly if they sense danger. When they do take off, however, they jump into the air like a puddle duck. The bufflehead and hooded merganser are the only diving ducks that do this.

Canvasback

LATIN NAME: Aytha valisineria.
REGIONAL NAMES: Can, white-back, shelldrake (an insulting misnomer).
SIZE: 24 inches, 3 pounds.
IDENTIFYING CHARACTERISTICS: Males: head and neck reddish brown. Wide black neck collar. Bill, slate gray. Back, mottled black and white, giving an overall bright gray color. Bill on both sexes close to a straight line from top of head to tip of bill. This is the easiest way (together with size) to differentiate them from the look-alike redhead. Females: head and neck yellowish brown, body grayish brown. Cans regularly fly in Vs or wavy lines; so you've got a good hint of their presence from afar. Drakes peep and growl when they call, and hens quack much like a mallard. When tolling to decoys, the drab hens usually come in first and closest to the blind, explaining, in part, why many of them are mistakenly shot.
DISTRIBUTION: Border to border, coast to coast.
HABITAT: A big-water duck, favoring large bodies of fresh water and the sea. Canvasback, though diving ducks, choose their diet largely as a vegetarian. Their favorite food is wild celery, explaining their unbeatable taste.
HABITS: Cans like to travel in big bunches. They're hardy ducks and don't leave favored spots until they're literally frozen out; so look for them late in the season. Because of their fine meat and their ready response to decoys, they've been hunted incessantly. In the past fifteen years limits on cans have been very low, so it's especially important to be able to identify this species.

Coot

LATIN NAME: Fulica americana.
REGIONAL NAMES: Mud hen, marsh hen, mud coot, crow duck. The true coot is not to be confused with the scoter, but often is.
SIZE: 16 inches, 1¼ pounds in weight.
IDENTIFYING CHARACTERISTICS: Overall slate gray color. Grayish white bill prominent. A frequent diver and one of the most ungainly wild fowl you'll ever see. They take off by running across the water like a mouse-frightened matron with her skirts held high. The landing procedure is just as short on grace, roughly resembling a flying boxcar coming to roost without landing gears.

A coot's profile on the water finds his tail appearing to be submerged. In addition, their heads nod in chickenlike time to their paddling legs as they glide along. Airborne, a coot has a markedly straight profile from head to tail and carries his feet stretched behind his body. Coot fly very low on the water.

DISTRIBUTION: Border to border, coast to coast.

HABITAT: Shallows in both sea and lakes, where they dive to the bottom and wrench free aquatic vegetation.

HABITS: Coot seldom fly into a stool, but they'll often swim in, usually with plenty of company.

Duck, Black

LATIN NAME: Anas rubripes.

REGIONAL NAMES: Black mallard, dusky mallard, red-legged duck.

SIZE: 22 inches, 3 pounds.

IDENTIFYING CHARACTERISTICS: Color, dark brown; legs, rich orange; beak, dull yellow to olive. No white borders on blue wing patch—the quickest way to tell the difference between a black and a hen mallard, which both male and female blacks resemble. Their whitish gray underwing appears to flash on and off in flight and can be seen from a mile or more away.

DISTRIBUTION: Blacks are Eastern ducks, found in both salt and fresh waters east of the Mississippi.

HABITAT: Blacks are shy birds by nature and seek out wild, untouched sections of beach and woodland for food and shelter. Their favorite foods are wild rice, grains, aquatic plants (both salt and fresh), grasses, acorns, and berries.

HABITS: The black is a puddle duck with a deserved reputation as one of the toughest of all waterfowl to fool. They prefer to feed early and late, often before and after legal gunning hours. Around salt water they do show some deference to tides, feeding on the high tide. Blacks are decided loners, usually traveling singly or in pairs. When coming into a rig, blacks normally make one pass with the wind on the outside of the stool, then swing into the wind to land. If anything seems out of place or wrong, the birds are quick to flare. There's an old saying about black duck and those who hunt them that I've found quite true: "Anyone taking them regularly and in large numbers is probably cheating."

Duck, Ring-Necked

LATIN NAME: Aythya collaris.

REGIONAL NAMES: Ring-necked scaup, marsh bluebill, bastard broadbill.

IDENTIFYING CHARACTERISTICS: Except for two bluish white rings that encircle the bill, one at the base and one at the tip, and a poorly defined chestnut ring around its lower neck, the ring-necked duck resembles the scaup in size, appearance, and habits. They're frequently found together. (See Scaup.)

Duck, Ruddy

LATIN NAME: Oxyura jamaicensis rubida.

REGIONAL NAMES: Fool duck, mud-dipper, tough head, steelhead, bull-neck.

SIZE: 16 inches, 1½ pounds.

IDENTIFYING CHARACTERISTICS: A ready diver who'll go under water before he'll fly. Both sexes carry their longish tail in an erect position when swimming. Males have a dull white cheek patch; otherwise they're similar to females. Upper half of body brownish gray, lower parts dull gray-white.

DISTRIBUTION: Nationwide distribution, but not one of our more common birds.

HABITAT: Both fresh and salt water, but prefers fresh. Favorite foods include aquatic plants, grasses, occasionally shellfish and crustaceans.

HABITS: Usually swims into decoys in lieu of flying.

Duck, Wood

LATIN NAME: Aix sponsa.

REGIONAL NAMES: Woodie, summer duck, bridal duck, wood widgeon, tree duck.

SIZE: 20 inches, 1½ pounds.

IDENTIFYING CHARACTERISTICS: Males: prominent crest of iridescent purple. Narrow white line over the eye. Iridescent green-blue coloring above, chestnut and mottled white below. A drake woodie is a strikingly beautiful bird. Females: brown above, light brown and white below. Both sexes have small bills and long soft tail feathers.

DISTRIBUTION: Common nationwide.

HABITAT: Fresh-water marshes and swamps where they can find plenty of seeds, aquatic plants, and nuts.

HABITS: Woodies have a fast, arrow-straight flight, and in the air they carry their heads with the bill pointed down, as if they're watching the ground below them. They often twist their heads from side to side during flight. These birds are commonly early migrants, so expect them to be around during the first few weeks of the season.

Gadwall

LATIN NAME: Anas strepera.

REGIONAL NAMES: Gray duck, poacher, specklebelly, creek duck.

SIZE: 20 inches, 2½ pounds.

IDENTIFYING CHARACTERISTICS: Gadwalls are puddle ducks, frequently found in the company of diving species. They're fond of snatching food away from other ducks as it's brought up from the bottom; hence the nickname "poacher." Both sexes are similar in markings: a dull brown above and gray below. The easiest way to identify them is through a close inspection of their wing patch. It's pure white, and no other puddler has it. Gadwall fly in fast compact flocks and follow a rather straight path.

DISTRIBUTION: Border to border, west of a line drawn from Illinois to North Carolina.

HABITAT: Creeks, streams, rivers, marshes, and ponds; occasionally salt-water estuaries. Gadwall eat aquatic plants and grain.

HABITS: Gadwall are ready decoyers. Drakes issue a shrill whistle, hens quack. They will come to a mallard call.

Goldeneye, American

LATIN NAME: Bucephala clangula.
REGIONAL NAMES: Whistler, garrot, goldeye.
SIZE: 18 inches, 3 pounds.
IDENTIFYING CHARACTERISTICS: When goldeneyes fly, their wings make a warbling whistle; hence their nickname "whistler." Males: head, indescent purple with a prominent white patch. The body of the male is basically black, but with plenty of dazzling white showing. Both sexes have bright golden eyes and crested heads. Females: head and back brown, underparts grayish.
DISTRIBUTION: Border to border, ranging as far south as central California and northern Florida.
HABITAT: Prefer large lakes and rivers until cold weather begins to freeze the countryside. They then move on to salt water. Goldeneyes eat crustaceans and vegetation with equal gusto.
HABITS: These birds move around in small groups, but raft up in big flocks. They're wary birds and hard to decoy. Goldeneye are divers and especially like to fly along the leading edge of shoals or ice. Should this bring them close to shore, they make for fine pass shooting. Goldeneye are not responsive to a call.

Mallard

LATIN NAME: Anas platyrhynchos.
REGIONAL NAMES: Greenhead, stock duck, northern, wild duck.
SIZE: 22 to 24 inches, to 3 pounds.
IDENTIFYING CHARACTERISTICS: Males: bright green head, white neck ring. Blue to deep purple wing patch, white border. Females: buff to mottled dark brown appearance, yellow to orange bill, blue or purple wing patch bordered with white. Their light gray wing is quite prominent during flight.
DISTRIBUTION: From coast to coast and border to border. Concentrations of mallards are found in America's midsection.
HABITAT: Mallards are puddle ducks and prefer fresh-water ponds and rivers that are near a source of food. A mallard's favorite meal includes grains of all kinds, alfalfa, duckweed, wild rice, and celery.
HABITS: The mallard is equally at home on water and land and is the duck found feeding most frequently in grainfields. They prefer to rest and sleep around the safety of water, however, and will return to ponds and lakes after their morning and evening inland feeding periods. Mallards are quite responsive to calling.

Merganser

LATIN NAME: Mergus merganser.

REGIONAL NAMES: Shelldrake, fish duck, sawbill, American merganser.
SIZE: 25 inches, 4 pounds.
IDENTIFYING CHARACTERISTICS: There are three species of merganser, the American, the red-breasted, and the hooded merganser. All three types are readily identified by a sharp, toothy, pointed bill and crested head, a very straight profile in the air, and an unusually low profile in the water. The hooded merganser, the smallest of the three birds, is rather rare and should not be shot. Mergansers don't make the best table fare and are usually shot by mistake or purely for target practice.
DISTRIBUTION: Common nationwide.
HABITAT: Fresh-water lakes, ponds, and rivers until frozen out. Then they move to salt water. They eat an exclusively fish diet.
HABITS: Mergansers usually fly right on the deck and in single file. Their occasional call is a low croaking quack.

Old Squaw

LATIN NAME: Clangula hyemalis.
REGIONAL NAMES: Long-tailed duck, old wife, cowheen, cockawee, cow duck.
SIZE: 17 inches (plus 6 inches of tail on the male), 2 pounds.
IDENTIFYING CHARACTERISTICS: Males: long, slender, swallowlike tail; prominent white on head and body. Both sexes have a short neck and small, slender bill. Females: gray-brown above, white-shaded below. Old squaw are diving sea ducks, only occasionally found on large inland lakes. They have a distinctive call that falls somewhere between the moo of a cow and the grunt of a goose.
DISTRIBUTION: A northerner, seldom found south of northern California, the Great Lakes, and, on the eastern seaboard, North Carolina.
HABITAT: Open water where they feed on shellfish.
HABITS: Their incessant chattering has led to their name of "old squaw." Generally these ducks are reluctant to come to stool, preferring great stretches of open water far from land for their resting place. A brisk offshore breeze will sometimes have them flying close to shore, when they may be pass-shot from points.

Pintail

LATIN NAME: Anas acuta.
REGIONAL NAMES: Sprig, sharptail, spiketail, pheasant duck, sea widgeon, gray duck.
SIZE: 25 inches, 3½ pounds.
IDENTIFYING CHARACTERISTICS: Long slender neck, sharp-pointed tail (5 to 9 inches long on male). Males: gray above, dull white below; prominent stripe on side of head. Females: yellowish brown neck, dusky brown body. Both sexes have a greenish wing patch. In flight, pintails have a slender, almost fragile appearance. Very fast flyers.
DISTRIBUTION: Token populations on East Coast with concentrations of birds in the West.

HABITAT: Shallow ponds and marshes. Pintails feast on grasses, aquatic plants, and grain.

HABITS: Pintails are puddle ducks, ready decoyers that will come to mallard or black-duck stool. They are responsive to mallard calls. Because of their fondness for shallows, they'll frequently land at the head of the stool, providing for close-in shooting. When coming into a rig, pintails first execute some classy aerial maneuvers, hovering overhead while they make sure all is well. They're masters of flight and, in a strong wind, can and will drift backward. Pintails will feed in a dry grainfield, though not with the wild abandon of mallards. The real drawing card for pintails is a flooded rice field.

Redhead

LATIN NAME: Aythya americana.

REGIONAL NAMES: Poachard, raft duck, red-headed broadbill, gray-back, fiddler duck.

SIZE: 20 inches, 2½ pounds.

IDENTIFYING CHARACTERISTICS: Males: head, reddish brown, melting into a wide black collar; back silvery gray. Both sexes have a short blue bill with a prominent inverted arch between bill tip and the top of their head; this is the easiest way, together with size, to differentiate them from the canvasback. Females: pale brown neck, dark to dusky back.

DISTRIBUTION: Common throughout the nation.

HABITAT: Redheads prefer big water—lakes, large rivers, and the sea. They feed with equal gusto on aquatic plants and crustaceans.

HABITS: Redheads are ready decoyers, so ready, in fact, that a Michigan friend of mine who's hunted them extensively calls them "dumb ducks." They like plenty of company and raft up on bluebird days (days with clear blue skies and no wind), but stormy weather gets them moving in groups of six to twelve. When flying about, they "knot up" like a swarm of bees. Their approach to a stool of decoys is one of the most classic and beautiful in waterfowling.

Scaup

LATIN NAME: Aythya family.

REGIONAL NAMES: Bluebill, broadbill, greenhead (not to be confused with the mallard), mussel duck.

SIZE: Greater scaup, 20 inches, 3 pounds; lesser scaup, 17 inches, 2½ pounds.

IDENTIFYING CHARACTERISTICS: Males: green-black head, neck, and foreparts. Rest of the body mottled black and white, giving an overall grayish appearance. Females: dusky brown above, yellowish brown below.

DISTRIBUTION: Scaup are found nationwide but are seldom seen far away from very large lakes or the sea.

HABITAT: Big-water ducks that are fond of both fresh and salt water. They feed with equal gusto on vegetation and animal life and love to rest in great rafts.

HABITS: Scaup are hardy ducks and one of the last breeds to migrate in the fall. They're never around in large numbers until bays and estuaries start to show skim ice and hard north winds begin to blow. Unlike most other species, this breed of birds has been on a numerical upswing for the past decade, and as a result, special seasons and bonus limits on broadbill are common.

They're a ready decoyer, coming to stool with such conviction that a friend of mine once quipped, "I'd rather hunt broadbill than any other duck in the world! Mallards or blacks fidget and fiddle around stool, but a broadbill—he bares his breast and just takes what's coming!"

Scaup aren't impressed by a conventional duck call, but often drop their feet when encouraged by a high-pitched mouth-produced "b-r-r-rt, b-r-r-rt, b-r-r-rt."

This sound is made by speaking those letters in a falsetto tone and letting your tongue flap against the roof of your mouth, much the way kids imitate the rattle of a machine gun.

Scoter, American

LATIN NAME: Oidemia americana.
REGIONAL NAMES: Coot (misnomer), sea coot, black coot.
SIZE: 21 inches, to 4 pounds.
IDENTIFYING CHARACTERISTICS: Male: entirely black, bill black with a yellow knot at base. Female: sooty brown, color brightening toward abdomen.
DISTRIBUTION: Primarily a sea dweller, but found on the Great Lakes. This scoter seldom strays farther south than central California in the West, North Carolina in the East.
HABITAT: Large bodies of water, preferably salt. Scoters are deep divers. Fishermen have pulled them up in nets from seventy-five-foot depths. Their primary food is mussels.
HABITS: Scoters of every variety are easy to decoy and will come to any block vaguely resembling a duck. Once they land, they're prone to dive in lieu of flying. When they do fly, they're fast.

Scoter, Surf

LATIN NAME: Oidemia perspicillata.
REGIONAL NAMES: Sea coot, surf duck, surf coot, horsehead.
SIZE: 21 inches, to 4 pounds.
IDENTIFYING CHARACTERISTICS: Both sexes similar to other scoters, except the head on the males includes two triangular white patches. The one on the forehead points forward; the one on the nape of the neck downward. Surf scoters have no white speculum.
DISTRIBUTION: A marked preference for the sea, though occasionally found inland. Winters south as far as lower California in the West, North Carolina in the East.

Scoter, White-Winged

LATIN NAME: Melanitta deglandi.
REGIONAL NAMES: Sea coot, bull coot, brant coot, sea brant, velvet duck.
SIZE: 24 inches long, to 4½ pounds.
IDENTIFYING CHARACTERISTICS: Male: all black save for a white wing patch. Sides of bill reddish, shading to orange on top. Females: prominent white wing patch, sooty brown above, pale gray below.
DISTRIBUTION: Primarily a sea duck, but occasionally found inland, always around big water. Southern limits of the white-winged scoter's range are northern Florida in the East, southern California in the West.

Shoveler

LATIN NAME: Spatula clypeata.
REGIONAL NAMES: Spoonbill, spoonbill teal, broady, swaddle-bill.
SIZE: 18 inches, 2 pounds.
IDENTIFYING CHARACTERISTICS: A prominent, broad bill that's wider at the tip than at its juncture with the head. Male: green head, white forebreast. Wing patch on both sexes rich green. A light blue forewing is prominent on both sexes. Females: ocher to dusky brown; prominent flecking.
DISTRIBUTION: Occasionally found in the East, but common from mid-central states west. Winters south as far as Texas and Mexico.
HABITAT: Shallow fresh-water sloughs and ponds. A shoveler's bill is designed to sieve small plants and insects from water and mud, and these make up the bulk of the diet.
HABITS: Shovelers are early migrants; so look for them at the first of the season. They're relatively easy to decoy and respond to a mallard call.

Teal, Blue-Winged

LATIN NAME: Anas discors.
REGIONAL NAMES: Blue-wing, summer teal.
SIZE: 16 inches, to 1¼ pounds.
IDENTIFYING CHARACTERISTICS: Large, dull-blue wing patch above a green speculum on both sexes. Flight fast and erratic. Males: dark and light brown above, yellowish gray with black spots below. Females: dark brown above, dull white below with brown spots.
DISTRIBUTION: Border to border, from New York state west. Greatest concentrations in the Midwest.
HABITAT: Puddles, small marshy ponds, and tiny sloughs. Blue-wings feed on grains, insects, worms, and snails.
HABITS: Blue-wings are the earliest migrants of the teals, leaving nesting grounds in the north with the first dusting of frost.

Teal, Cinnamon

LATIN NAME: Anas cyanoptera.
REGIONAL NAMES: South American teal, red-breasted teal.
SIZE: 17 inches, to 1½ pounds.
IDENTIFYING CHARACTERISTICS: Overall rich cinnamon color on male; bright green wing patch framed with white. Females: dark brown and brownish white variations above, mottled dull white below.
DISTRIBUTION: Cinnamon teal breed along our northern border, usually beginning their migrations well before gunning season. For that reason they're largely limited to the Southwest as a shootable bird.

Teal, Green-Winged

LATIN NAME: Anas carolinensis.
REGIONAL NAMES: Green-wing, mud teal, winter teal.
SIZE: 14 inches, to 1 pound.
IDENTIFYING CHARACTERISTICS: Prominent green wing patch on both sexes. Fast erratic flight. Males: gray and rust above, white and rust below. Females: flecked brown above, dull white below.
DISTRIBUTION: Common across North America. Densest populations from the Mississippi west.
HABITAT: Sloughs, streams, and small fresh-water ponds. Occasionally found in salt water when cold weather freezes them out. Teal eat grains, wild rice, insects, worms, and snails.
HABITS: All teals drive shotgunners mad. Pour a cup of coffee, break out a sandwich, or step out of the blind on a nature call, and it's the teal's cue to come rocketing out of nowhere, sizzle across your stool, and disappear before you can lay hands on a gun.

GEESE

Brant, American

LATIN NAME: Branta bernicla glaucogastra.
REGIONAL NAMES: Atlantic brant, common brant, eastern brant, clatter goose, croaker.
SIZE: 24 inches, to 4 pounds.
IDENTIFYING CHARACTERISTICS: Head, neck, and breast black; five or six prominent white slashes on throat. Neck slender, short beak. Body coloration above, brownish gray; below, ash and white.
DISTRIBUTION: Brant are late fall and winter visitors to the East Coast, migrating as far south as North Carolina. They can occasionally be found in the interior, but seldom stray west of the Rockies.
HABITAT: Brant prefer salt water: bays, estuaries, and the ocean. They particularly favor offshore islands where they can dine on their favorite meal, eelgrass.
HABITS: Brant visit shallows of two to three feet in depth to feed. This feed-

ing usually takes place morning and evening. They're hard to decoy when bluebird weather has them rafted up in flocks of thousands, but quite simple to fool when nasty weather breaks them into smaller groups. Because they stick close to open water they're seldom jumped or pass-shot.

Brant, Black

LATIN NAME: Branta nigricans.
REGIONAL NAMES: Pacific brant, burnt goose. Many names applicable to the American brant are also used for the black brant.
SIZE: 24 inches, to 5 pounds.
IDENTIFYING CHARACTERISTICS: The black brant closely resembles the American brant. Primary differences of the black brant include the black coloring that extends over the head, breast, and most of its underparts.
DISTRIBUTION: The West Coast from Alaska south to central California. Occasionally found inland, but primarily a salt-water dweller, it's seldom found east of the Continental Divide.
HABITAT: Shoals and offshore bars in bays, sounds, inlets, and the ocean.
HABITS: Identical to the American brant. (See Brant, American.)

Goose, Blue

LATIN NAME: Chen caerulescens.
REGIONAL NAMES: Blue brant, blue snow goose, brant (misnomer).
SIZE: 28 inches, to 5 pounds.
IDENTIFYING CHARACTERISTICS: Sexes similar. Head and neck white, body gray.
DISTRIBUTION: East of Texas, north to Nebraska and southern Illinois.
HABITAT: Large bodies of water or protected preserves near a source of food. Grains such as wheat, corn, oats, and barley are favored goose foods.
HABITS: Blue geese are wary birds, fond of flying high and thoroughly scouting an area. They will drop in on snow-goose stool. All geese come more readily to decoys in a field than decoys in water.

Goose, Canada

LATIN NAME: Branta canadensis.
REGIONAL NAMES: Canada, honker, wild goose, big gray goose, reef goose.
SIZE: 40 inches, 10 pounds and up.
IDENTIFYING CHARACTERISTICS: Head and neck black, prominent white patch extending from one side of the head under the throat and up to the other side. Body, brownish gray on top; dull white underneath. Neck, long and slender. Canadas fly in V formations. Once you've heard their plaintive "gahonk" call you'll never forget it. With the cry of the loon and the howl of a coyote, it's one of the most nostalgic sounds in the wilderness.

DISTRIBUTION: Common nationwide with concentrations in America's midsection.

HABITAT: Large bodies of water or preserves near sources of food. Grains, particularly corn, are a Canada's favorite meal.

HABITS: Like all geese, Canadas feed in the morning and evening, and rest, preferably on a large river or lake, during midday and at night. When they alight, either to feed or rest, they always post a sentry—one lone goose—whose sole job is to watch for danger. As a result, they're extremely hard to jump-shoot.

Goose, Ross's

LATIN NAME: Chen rossii.

REGIONAL NAMES: Little wavy, China goose, galoot.

SIZE: At 3 pounds, Ross's goose is the smallest species of goose in North America.

IDENTIFYING CHARACTERISTICS: Very similar in plumage and habit to the snow goose, but smaller. All white except for black wing tips and bill. The easiest way to tell the two apart is by their bills. A snow goose's bill is smooth. A Ross's has warty protuberances near where the bill joins the head.

DISTRIBUTION: Breeds in the Great Slave Lake region in Canada, then migrates southward to the shores of the Pacific. Few states east of a line drawn from Montana to New Mexico have huntable populations of this bird. (For further information see Snow Goose.)

Goose, Snow

LATIN NAME: Chen hyperboreus hyperboreus.

REGIONAL NAMES: Wavy, white brant, white goose, Mexican goose.

SIZE: 25 inches, to 4 pounds.

IDENTIFYING CHARACTERISTICS: Entirely white with the exception of their wing tips. This bit of black is easily spotted during flight or at rest and makes for quick differentiation between snow geese and swans. Bill, short and reddish in color. Sexes similar.

DISTRIBUTION: Found from border to border, west of the Mississippi.

HABITAT: Large bodies of water or preserves near abundant grainfields.

HABITS: Like the blue goose, snow geese do a lot of scouting before they drop in. They usually travel in wavy lines and do plenty of high-pitched chattering. Their call sounds a little like a series of falsetto "whos." Although they're wary birds, their willingness to come to stool increases proportionately to the number of birds out.

Goose, White-Fronted

LATIN NAME: Anser albifrons.

REGIONAL NAMES: Laughing goose, cackling goose, speckle-belly, speckled brant.

SIZE: 30 inches, to 6 pounds.

IDENTIFYING CHARACTERISTICS: Forehead white. Overall grayish brown cast with prominent dark patch on lower breast. Bill, pink with a white tip. Sexes similar.

DISTRIBUTION: Border to border west of the Mississippi.

HABITAT: Large bodies of water or preserves near abundant grainfields. Speckle-bellies like to eat grasses, grains, nuts, and snails.

HABITS: This goose flies in the characteristic V formation of the Canadas, but can quickly be differentiated by its incessant cackling that sounds a bit like laughter. They will come to other breeds of goose stool.

3 | Waterfowl and the Weather

A thousand geese flew by last night
  I saw them in the cold, blue light
of dying winter's last full moon

They swung twice around our town
  rattled the darkness with their sound
then left on the wings of a hard, south wind.

Today old men who come to the square
  will tell everyone the geese were here
(a pagan prayer to muddy spring)

Since time began, men have measured the progress of seasons and predicted the weather by waterfowl movements. Early sightings of northbound birds have always been considered a sign that spring-like weather will also come early, and the passing of the last great flights of mallards on their way south counts as the start of winter in the northern border states.

Although fluctuating daylight is the major force that spurs waterfowl to migrate, weather plays its day-to-day part and is particularly important to the hunter.

Ducks and geese virtually always move southward during periods of north winds. The birds know that they'll have a tail wind to speed their flight and help them conserve energy.

Just how important that tail wind is to waterfowl can be quickly demonstrated by comparing ground to air speed. A duck that averages forty-five miles an hour air speed, flying into a thirty-mile-an-hour wind, is actually only covering fifteen miles an hour on the ground. Conversely, if that wind is blowing in the same direction that he's headed, he'll be covering seventy-five miles each hour. With help like that, migrations that consume thousands of miles become more comprehensible.

The beginning of the migratory period occurs at a time when the weather patterns could be termed as warring. In the fall, the prevailing southerlies of summer are colliding with, and gradually being overcome by, the northerlies of winter. In the spring, the reverse situation takes place.

It's a little oversimplified, but when such a "collision" occurs, the result is usually a low-pressure system and a storm.

To see how a storm influences waterfowl movements, let's take a look at a typical fall situation. At the approach of the low, barometric pressure begins to drop and winds blow strong from the south. These amount to unfavorable head winds, so waterfowl sit tight.

As the low passes, winds back around through the easterly quadrant and finally end up in the north. Skies clear, winds become favorable to southerly movements, and waterfowl take to the wing.

It is this post-storm combination of north winds and pleasant weather that amounts to a poor time for waterfowling. Birds will be sky-high and moving south, but even though you might not get much gunning, it's still a delight to be in the marshes on these bluebird days.

One of my favorite spots for this variety of "hunting" is a blind I maintain in Montana's Madison Valley. The Madison is a major migratory route for swans, snow geese, Canada geese, and mallards, and during clear weather from mid-October on, I can depend on a daily splendor of wave after wave of birds heading south. I just lie back and let it happen, usually cradling a fishing rod on my knee.

At no time is the sound of their call beyond my ears, and on the better days, birds will always be in sight—long wedges of Canadas or wavy lines of snow geese that appear on the horizon before the flock that preceded them is directly overhead. On the best days I've picked out three and four separate flocks at once, whistling, honking, yelping, and filling the clear western air with their sound.

The movements continue throughout the night if there's a full moon, and I regularly go to bed, in the little lakeside shack I rent, with their symphony to put me to sleep.

The plaintive calls, the cold blue light, the taste of fall in the air—it's a delicious moment in life.

Although pleasant weather finds waterfowl covering great distances, their flight south is never nonstop. They get tired and hungry, and must rest and feed along the way; so, even during bluebird weather, spotty action can occur around traditional stopovers. Flocks filter in to these places, usually refuges, and build into huge populations as they enjoy the warm weather of Indian summer.

This is the time when locals say the birds are "in." Waterfowl will remain in these stopovers until driven out by hunting pressure, a dwindling food supply, or the frosting of winter as colder temperatures and other storms creep farther southward.

While new arrivals make for good hunting, a few days' experience teaches them well where blinds, refuge lines, and hunters are likely to be. So even though there are ample waterfowl around, hunting in bluebird weather will be tough.

This picture changes, however, with the approach of a storm. I mentioned earlier that migrations are flows of birds rather than mass movements. Because this flow conforms to a general north/south pattern, and weather in the hemisphere moves from west to east, any storm occurring during periods of migration will interfere with birds in the air. The snow, rain, fog, and winds that accompany these weather systems make for impossible flying conditions; so the birds must come down.

I've heard that waterfowl have a barometerlike organ in their heads that puts pressure on their optic nerves when atmospheric readings are low. More logical perhaps is the presence of ice crystals, moisture, and head winds in the upper atmosphere. Whatever the reasons, waterfowl have a sixth sense about the weather. They know when it's going to storm, and for two or three hours before it happens they search for a place to sit it out.

This desire to get out of bad weather, no matter what the consequences, has had some strange results—many of them funny and a few of them sad.

Airports are occasionally tied up by waterfowl on the runway, lured there by lights gleaming in the night. I can remember one snowy evening in Missoula, Montana, when thousands of lost geese circled the lights of the town until 3 A.M., keeping residents awake. They eventually settled down in one of the city parks until morning. Wes Sommers, a good friend of mine from Washington state, once related a story about Canada geese raining down on a roadway, and creating a real traffic hazard in the process. The roadway was covered with frozen rain, and when night closed in, the headlights of cars reflecting off the ice made it look like open water to the birds.

Although the results of waterfowl coming in out of the weather aren't always that spectacular, hunters can plan on great activity just before a heavy blow. Birds perfer to sit out a storm in big water; so that's the place to hunt.

When they arrive at this sort of resting spot, waterfowl raft up. The combined effect of hundreds of breasts and paddling feet is to break up heavy waves and wind and provide a degree of protection and comfort for individual birds.

The spot they choose to raft up in will be some sort of a lee — the downwind side of a point, shore, shoal, or bar that will serve both as windbreak and breakwater. These semiprotected spots amount to choice locations for a blind and decoys.

Waterfowl will be active right up to the time the storm breaks, with arriving migrants and residents searching for a safe haven.

Once the storm hits and heavy rains or snows begin, birds will settle down and sit tight, and the smart hunter does likewise. There will be little activity; so you might as well enjoy the comforts of a roof over your head and a warm fire.

There is, however, one notable exception to waterfowl waiting out a storm in one spot: windshifts.

Low-pressure systems produce a cyclonic or counterclockwise flow of air that commonly begins as a gentle breeze from a southerly quadrant, then increases in velocity as the wind backs around to easterly. When it reaches due east, the full fury of the storm wind is on the land, and the lee the waterfowl choose to weather out the winds usually offers good protection from this direction.

However, as the storm moves east it's followed by a high-pressure system with an anticyclonic or clockwise flow of air whose initial and strongest thrust begins in the north. By the time the winds from the low back around to the north and skies begin to clear, they're joined by the winds from the high; and the combination often results in velocities nearly as severe as those encountered during the full

U.S. Dept. of Commerce, National Oceanic and Atmospheric Administration

In this typical fall weather pattern, waterfowl moving South would bump into inclement weather over much of the U.S. Note the correlation between areas of high pressure and clear skies, and areas of low pressure with clouds. A barometer is an unlikely but valuable tool for the waterfowler.

fury of the storm. The significant thing about these winds is that they're now blowing from a different quarter than the waterfowl initially anticipated, and it's quite possible they might have to find a new lee.

It's under these conditions that I've encountered some of my most memorable gunning. Whole rafts of birds, numbering well into the hundreds, tired of fighting the wind and waves without the protection of a lee, leave their choppy resting place in twos and threes to find a better-protected spot. When you can locate the lee they want, you'll also discover one of the few opportunities to lure today's birds with the laughable deceptions of yesteryear: paper bags, blobs of mud, and third-rate decoys. Even educated blacks will readily come to stool under these conditions, with gunners outside the blind and decoys rolling over like pinwheels.

Another blessing of weather-system gunning can occur when birds raft up on tidewaters. The easterly winds of a low often push extremely high tides inland. Birds that chose the protection of a mid-bay bar at the beginning of the storm lose that lee as the waters rise, and are forced to move. It's a prime time to use a coffin blind or grassboat right on flooded marsh meadows, for that is where the birds are likely to head.

Unfortunately, not all waterfowling areas afford the opportunity for this type of mid-storm gunning. Either there's no big water around and birds wait out the weather on land, or the place they pick to rest offers good protection from all quarters. After the storm subsides, however, you can expect waterfowl activity to reach another peak.

The wind will now be northerly and birds will be tired and hungry, having expended quite a bit of energy as they waited out the weather. As soon as it clears, they'll leave their big rafts in small groups, intent on finding a meal. If you'll rig out in a place you know to hold food, or build a blind along some pass birds use to reach feed, you'll always get good gunning right after a hard blow.

Hunting storms is one of the most dependably productive tactics at the waterfowler's disposal, but storms don't happen every day. The bulk of waterfowling opportunities usually come in relatively pleasant weather conditions.

When the sun shines strong and the sky is blue, it's important to capitalize on waterfowl feeding habits. These usually include peak activity in the early morning and late evening, and a resting period during midday. Easily the best place to set out decoys, or jump or pass shoot, is around an area that could conceivably serve as both a feeding and resting place—the shallow shore of a large lake, for example.

Plan to be in place before legal gunning hours begin, for in nice weather birds will begin to fly with first light. That first hour of light will provide the most action as birds mill about looking for a meal. Shots will then taper off until two or three hours into the day. It's at this time that most marsh rats get discouraged and start to pick up stool or gather their belongings—and then do a lot of cussing as ducks suddenly begin to appear again. If you've got the time and patience, plan to remain in your blind for four to five hours, no matter how dismal the hunting might appear around 9 A.M. Ducks and geese returning from feed and looking for a safe spot to spend the day will produce a period of renewed activity later in the morning.

Aside from those first few days of the season when birds behave the way they should, I've never had good evening gunning in blue-bird weather. The sunset closing of gunning hours is in force nation-wide, and waterfowl seem to have learned this. Except for the odd early bird, so rare as not to rate mention, ducks and geese wait until the sun dips below the horizon before taking off for their evening meal.

A few other words deserve to be said about gunning in nice weather. When birds stay in one area for a week or more, they get to know the lay of the land and those spots hunters favor well. This makes them most difficult to fool. To be successful on such edu-cated birds, you've got to use the finest decoys, build the best camouflaged blind, and be capable of skillful calling.

The more these birds are hunted, the wiser they get. After three weeks' worth of season without storms or fresh migrants, I just don't bother to hunt waterfowl very seriously, using instead those Indian summer hours to catch fall trout, shoot grouse, or watch Saturday afternoon football.

There's one other weather condition that affects waterfowl and waterfowling: temperatures cold enough to produce ice.

In the far north it's the finality of ice that ultimately drives the last great flights south. They are simply and literally frozen out of lakes, ponds, and sloughs; for even geese—more grazers than water-feeders—need the presence of some open water to survive.

Farther south, however, the presence of ice can have a positive effect on hunting. One result of ice is a concentration of waterfowl. Virtually every area I've ever gunned that is subject to icing has some places that never freeze over—either warm-water sloughs, springs, or river or tidal currents that keep water open. When the weather is cold enough to lock in lakes, ponds, and slow-moving streams, waterfowl are forced to concentrate in whatever open water there might be. Under just these circumstances I've enjoyed some top gunning—jump-shooting mallards from warm-spring creeks in the West, and shooting broadbill over open potholes in the frozen Great South Bay.

Realize, however, that ice is a boon only if it's a temporary thing. If you're far enough north to experience winters that lock in tight and stay tight until spring, you'll have good gunning for the first few days that permanent ice is in, but once birds realize that the ice is there to stay, they'll move south. Waterfowl will tolerate crowding by ice as a temporary expedient, but not as a permanent condition.

Author

The arrival of ice can signal the best hunting of the season.

On the other hand, if the region where you gun is subject to sporadic icing, you've got a good thing going for you. Waterfowl will remain in the area so long as there's a food supply; hopefully, you can count on ice's concentrating effect to occur regularly.

Another big plus from ice in these climes is when you've got large expanses of water. When a solid sheet of ice thaws, it breaks up into flows and moves with tides and winds. A flock of waterfowl is then hard pressed to find a spot where it can raft up all day. They locate open water, ice moves in on them, and they're forced to move out. This happens again and again, resulting in fragmented, easy-to-lure flocks, and birds that are tired from the constant rallying.

If you can find a lee that's open and protected from the moving ice—say a long finger of land, or jetty with a southern exposure during a northerly wind—you'll draw birds with only a handful of stool. Thanks to a diver's habit of following the leading edge of moving ice, you can also enjoy land-based pass shooting at diving ducks when this situation arises.

Several years ago I was gunning a point in the Great South Bay with Joe Arata and Dick Freidah. It was a warm day in the 50s that followed several days of cold temperatures and north winds. The winds had blown and jammed ice up against the south side of the bay; so the north shore where we gunned amounted to a long lead to open water that stretched perhaps a mile out from the beach.

We all knew the warm weather was a harbinger of a strong south wind. A light breeze from that direction was already blowing. So we kept a sharp eye out for any signs of moving ice; it has the power of a hundred bulldozers, and will easily sweep up a rig and crush it— as well as any hunters who happen to be in its path.

Joe spotted the first signs of movement, and the three of us hustled out to the water to pull in the forty-odd blocks we'd set. We were intent on wrapping stool, not birdwatching, so we didn't immediately realize that the crunching, grinding ice was disturbing every bird on the bay. The potholes where they rested were closing in, the lead where we gunned was narrowing, and every broadbill and whistler within five miles was aloft. True to instinct, they started winging along the edge of the ice sheet that was moving in on us. Dick was the first to realize the possibilities, and as soon as we had the stool safely back from shore he motioned us into the blind.

Every minute hundreds of birds were trading by our point, following the ice that now lay 150 yards offshore. The ice came closer and the birds came closer, their wingbeats so loud that we had to yell to be heard. At 60 yards, we opened up, our pounding guns barely drowning out the whistle and rush of wings. And the birds came and came and continued to come, strung out down the beach as far as we could see.

I don't know how long the barrage lasted—five minutes perhaps. But when the ice finally crunched into shore we had our fifteen-bird limit, and a wild story to tell that friends doubted then and have since.

Although that combination of good fortune and situation has never occurred since, I've learned that in smaller ways weather plays an important part every day I'm afield.

As Joe Steigerwald once told me on a stormy day when the broadbill were flying down our gun barrels:

"You can talk all you want about top-notch decoys, duckboats, and special ways to rig out, but 90 percent of duck hunting is knowing when and where to go."

Correctly interpreting the weather and its effect on waterfowl will give you just that information.

PART TWO

Blinds, Boats, and Pits

4 | **Shore Blinds**

The finest blind I've ever seen was on a small fresh-water marsh pond, close to Chesapeake Bay on Maryland's Eastern Shore. It was owned by a very wealthy man who held controlling interest in a large oil company.

Aside from its size and a grassing job that looked like it had been done by Frank Lloyd Wright, there was nothing odd about the structure from the outside. It looked like a hundred other blinds I've seen. But inside and underneath, its design and appointments were nothing short of exquisite.

The seats were padded and fitted with backrests. There was a kind of shallow cistern, lined with indoor/outdoor carpeting to function as a comfortable place for a wet retriever. The dog was also provided with his own spring-loaded door.

The blind was heated with a thermostatically controlled propane unit, and it had a double-burner hotplate for morning coffee or a bowl of soup. It even had its own telephone.

There were padded racks for guns and shelves for shells, and the shooting vent, set well back from the roof and pond-side wall, was a hinged, wooden-framed piece of plexiglass that sprang up and out of the way at the touch of a button.

The entire structure, roughly fifteen feet wide and seven feet deep, was built on a platform supported by pontoons. When a good nor'easter blew high tides onto the flats, the blind floated up with the water, anchored in place by driven steel bars that slid through sockets set on the corners of the blind.

There was a place that once held loudspeakers too—and an electronic caller until that practice was made illegal about fifteen years ago. As housewives have their dream houses, this place was certainly a waterfowler's dream blind.

I hunted that blind once. The comfort it provided made the experience a never-to-be-forgotten pleasure, but it was also a moment of revelation. For all its opulence, and a price tag that must have numbered in the thousands of dollars, it hid its occupants and fooled waterfowl no better and no worse than the simple affairs to which most of us gunners with more limited incomes are relegated. As a matter of fact, we had very poor shooting that day; waterfowling is a great leveler.

BLIND BASICS

You don't have to go to great lengths or a lot of expense to have a blind that will effectively mask your presence from waterfowl.

Choosing the location is the first order of business, and blinds should be built as close to potential landing areas, among decoys or as near to flight paths, as is practical. This is primarily a matter of available natural cover. If thick cattails grow right up to the water's edge, the blind can be put there. There are limits to the type of cover where a blind will work, however. Especially in heavily hunted areas, waterfowl learn to recognize thick thatches of brush where a man can easily be concealed, and avoid flying near those places. In general, medium-to-sparse cover, three to four feet high, will afford the opportunity for you to hide, and waterfowl will approach it freely.

Cover means the material you use to mask a blind. Rather than building materials, cover is camouflage. Cover can be grass, hay, brush, rush, paint, burlap—or a hundred other materials—but what it must do is approximate the shade and texture of your surroundings.

It would be foolish to build a blind of yellow straw for pass shooting over a stream lined with evergreens, or paint a blind in the bright greens of spring when you're hunting on a marsh tinted with the browns and golds of fall. But on a less obvious level these kinds of mistakes are commonplace.

For example, let's say you are building a blind along a lakeshore that has washed-up vegetation at the water's edge and ten feet of sandy beach, then a stand of four-foot-high cattail.

The correct cover under these conditions would imitate the visual stratification of the lakeshore with collected water weeds at the blind's base; sand or a suggestion of sand, like burlap, above that; then cattail, thick and dense close to the ground, but thinning to sparse wispy heads as the blind reached full height.

Although matching a background in this manner sounds both simple and logical, I've seen hunters throw together a blind of brush and driftwood, draped with dark seaweed, to "match" just the conditions previously described. You could spot that blind a mile away—literally—and I'm sure waterfowl could too.

When gathering materials for cover, nothing beats getting them from the immediate blind area. But don't cut grass or rush too close to the actual blind site. Leave enough natural cover nearby so your blind doesn't stand out like a ship on a calm sea. Which brings us to another observation about camouflage.

Avoid building or using a blind that stands higher than the surrounding natural cover.

A grassy meadow is an attractive spot for waterfowl to fly over because the lack of cover gives them confidence that nothing could be hiding there.

But if the place you choose to build your blind has no more cover than two-foot-high marsh hay, and the walls of your blind are four feet high, the structure will appear distinctively unnatural.

While its obvious presence might not flare birds away, it will make them wary and quick to pick out any other signs of danger—to the hunter's disadvantage.

In this case, then, that rule about matching cover would also involve getting down to its level, either digging a shallow pit or keeping the walls low and lying down at the approach of waterfowl.

Another possibility in this situation is creating your own cover. "Frosty" Dick Freidah, pride of the Moriches marshes and a long-time gunning buddy, yearly builds his blind on a long point that grows no cover but salt hay. To better mask his blind, he hauls in a few cut evergreens, and "plants" them by tying them to stakes driven into the mud. The effect is quite good; it looks like a small grove of natural growth. He does this several weeks in advance of the season to give the birds a chance to get used to this new feature of the terrain.

Eliminating outlines is another component of effective camouflage. Ever since man learned to walk on two legs, he's been hell-bent on forcing nature to conform to his ideas of order. Grecian temples were magnificent studies in geometry; Augustinian gardens were carefully balanced so a tree viewed on the right side of a hedge had a perfect mate on the left; and today the legions of suburban ticky-tacky are laid out in checkerboard squares.

While such order might satisfy some primal human insecurity common to all of us, it doesn't have a place when you're building a duck blind.

Nature certainly has patterns, but they're patterns on a grand scale. When you view an individual bush, a field of grass, or a stand of cattail, there are no fine lines of definition. Branches ebb into the sky, blades of grass grow high and lush and sparse and low like waves on a lake, and bulrushes don't stop at a street corner. They gradually thin out as you get farther back from the water's edge.

No matter how well camouflaged a blind might be, it will still be plain to see if you fail to eliminate suggestions of straight lines. A perfect example occurred when I put up my newest blind at Ennis five years ago. I was very careful to cover the wood completely with native material that perfectly matched the background, and I did the job very neatly. I bent the blades of cattails around corners to cover any wood there, and stapled rushes to the roof. When I was done, the blind seemed to blend in well when viewed from gun range.

But when I returned to my car that night and drove to the top of a high bluff overlooking the lake, there stood my blind. It was easy to pick out at a distance in excess of a mile.

The giveaways were the square, boxy sides, the angle of the roof, and the roofline itself. They simply didn't fit in with the helter-skelter pattern of nature.

I returned the day before the season opened and wove, stapled, and nailed some rushes so they stuck up beyond the roof, the walls, and the sides. It didn't take much work, just an odd piece here and there. But when I looked again from the bluff that evening, the blind no longer was there. Sure, there was a dark spot close to the water's edge that had to be my blind, but there was nothing about it to reveal that it was a man-made structure. Its outline had successfully been broken by the addition of a few strands of rush, arranged in a most sloppy, unneat, untidy, and unhumanlike way.

BLIND DESIGNS

No matter the nature or construction of a blind, good camouflage is what makes it work. But behind that screen of deception lie many possible variations of design, each suited to different hunting tastes and habits.

Author

A blind made of shoreside flotsam will effectively fool ducks. The trick is to use native material for camouflage and break up severe outlines. Note the effect of the cut brush.

Makeshift blinds are probably the most common type of hunting blinds used. They're constructed on the spot with whatever native materials are available: driftwood, tree stumps, brush, grass, and rushes. Makeshift blinds, if built with all the rules about correct camouflage in mind, can be as effective as any other. But you're never assured the materials needed for construction will be available at the site, and a really first-rate job takes time and patience. Both commodities are usually in short supply when the dawn breaks red, wings start whistling overhead, and the hands on your watch indicate five minutes till gunning hours.

Portable blinds are a wiser way to go. They can be set up quickly, and if, indeed, you do find the time and material, native vegetation and bracing can be added before shooting starts to create a really first-rate job of camouflage.

I've found the most practical portable blinds to be light and easy to carry; not a dense impregnable fortress, just something to break up another telltale outline—yours.

The simplest of these blinds is nothing more than sewn-together scraps of cloth. The structure is supported by five stakes pushed into the soil, and the cloth when laid flat measures twenty-four feet in length and four feet in height. When the stakes are in place, the blind is enclosed on all sides except for an entryway. The enclosure measures four by ten feet—ample room for two gunners and a retriever.

Erected in front of some tall cover like bulrushes or willow, with a few sprigs of grass or twigs laid up against the walls to break up solid colors and lines, such a blind does an acceptable job of hiding hunters.

When constructing this blind, always choose cloth material that matches the background where you'll be hunting. Army-surplus camouflage cloth is best for green backgrounds, burlap works well around sand or dead grasses, and when there's ice and snow you can use a few old bedsheets. Another useful material is a ¼-inch-mesh minnow seine, twenty-five feet long. You don't have to sew anything together with these nets, and their color is quite close to the fall browns common in and around salt and fresh-water marshes in the north.

I like to use 2 x 2s for supports. This dimension of wood is stout enough to be pounded into hard earth without splitting, but it's not overly heavy. Buy them five feet long, sharpen one end, and

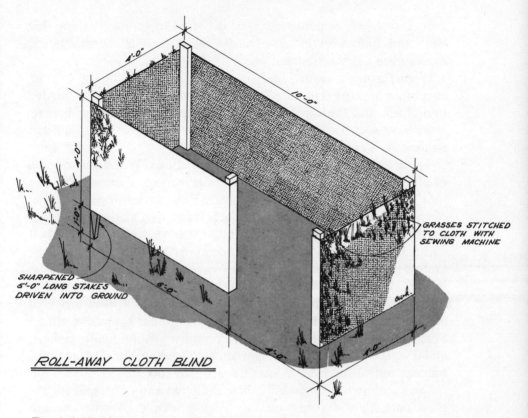

ROLL-AWAY CLOTH BLIND

GRASSES STITCHED
TO CLOTH WITH
SEWING MACHINE

SHARPENED
5'-0" LONG STAKES
DRIVEN INTO GROUND

The cloth blind is the most practical design for a portable blind.

staple or tack them to the cloth. For transport, roll up the blind like a rug.

I've found simple cloth blinds sufficient for hunting diving ducks. Divers approach a rig over water and seldom swing over shore; so sophisticated overhead camouflage isn't too necessary.

Puddlers are a different matter, though. They're always skeptical, and their approach usually carries them over land and overhead. When you hunt these birds a lot, I'd recommend extra attention be paid to your portable blind.

Set up a sewing machine out of doors and wide-stitch some grasses native to your favorite marsh to the cloth. You don't have to cover the cloth totally with grass; just create a suggestion of nature's disorder to hide man's neatness.

Overhead cover is a big edge too. No matter how still you remain, a duck swinging directly overhead is bound to spot something that will spook him: a bright box of shells, the shine of a Thermos bottle, or the glint off your barrel.

When using a cloth blind, overhead cover is difficult to incorporate into the structure. You can't engineer the rigidity needed into cloth, and the top will blow and flap in the slightest breeze. But I have seen a workable alternative that made use of a jon boat, painted in a camouflage pattern.

These are squarish craft with pram-type bows. When constructed of aluminum, a ten-footer weighs under seventy-five pounds, and they're available in camouflage colors. You can car-top a jon boat of these dimensions with ease, launch it at water's edge, fill it with all your gear, and walk it to your blind site. Once there, support it with four poles driven into the sand or marsh on each quarter of the craft. Turned upside down, it will provide overhead cover, and it can be quickly dismounted to pick up cripples that have fallen out of wader or retriever range. All in all, jon boats are a most practical adjunct to any duck hunting trip, and not all that expensive either. Sears, for example, sells just such a boat for around ninety dollars, and if you're a fresh-water fisherman, you'll get plenty of pleasurable mileage out of the boat in that department too.

I've seen other "roll-away" blinds designed and used, and for the most part, they're based on the same principle of erection and deception outlined here. Common construction materials include woven-wire sheep fence, chicken wire, and lath-type snow fence. These blinds are more sturdy than cloth, but they're bulkier and more work to handle, carry, and set up. The only place I can think of where I'd call them preferable is in hunting situations that involve strong buffeting winds.

Roll-aways aren't the only portable blind at the waterfowler's disposal. A sampling of other types I've seen or used—and some observations on their practicality—would include:

• Collapsible frame blinds. One design I've seen is a clamshell-like aluminum and canvas structure that can be packed on your back. But it must have been homemade, and I can't envision its intricacies of construction and erection as either practical or able to withstand hard use.

Then, too, these blinds are one-man propositions, and much of my waterfowling pleasure is derived from hunting with a buddy. There's also the matter of sheer volume of equipment: guns, shells, decoys, hot coffee, *and* a large blind for any and every gunner amount to quite a bit of gear to lug around in the mud.

• SCREEN BLIND. A more acceptable arrangement, if only because of its simplicity, is a lightly framed three-sided blind made from thin wood and window screening. The screening is grassed, and the walls of the blind bolt together. The blind is light and sturdy, but bulky; it must be car-topped or carried in a pickup.

• Three New York gunners I occasionally run into on Long Island's South Shore have put together a fully enclosed three-man blind of plywood, screening, and grass. They carry it in the back of a pickup truck, and when they find a promising point or cove, they just plop it in place. It's light enough to be carried by two men, comfortable, and affords excellent camouflage, but it requires that truck for transport and is too heavy and bulky to carry much beyond a point that's attainable by vehicle.

• Boat blinds are walls of grass or cattail, wire, and wood framing that bolt or snap on to the gunwales of a boat. The boat then becomes the blind and you hunt from it.

The idea sounds good, but this arrangement doesn't pan out that well in practice. When the blind wall isn't being used, like going to and from the hunting site, it's carried inside the boat. It's extremely bulky, and the wispy ends of cattail, rush, or other natural camouflage are easily broken. This creates an unnatural-looking wall between you and the birds and a lot of garbage in the bottom of your boat.

The cover it takes to hide a fourteen-foot boat isn't that easy to put together or maintain. It's been my experience that when you want to bring a blind with you, the word "portability" counts heavily. And no other blind is so portable and compact, yet functional, as one made from cloth and stakes.

Permanent Blinds   My views are equally narrow about permanent blinds. The best blind is going to be a boxlike, roofed structure with a shooting vent. These blinds, when correctly grassed, completely hide a hunter and provide protection from the weather and wind.

They're most practical and economical when built of ⅜-inch exterior plywood, with floor dimensions of four feet by eight feet. This size blind will accommodate three hunters and a dog. Because plywood comes in four-by-eight-foot sheets, building along these lines means less cutting and less scrap left over when you're done.

I also recommend using 2 x 2s for most of the supports, rather

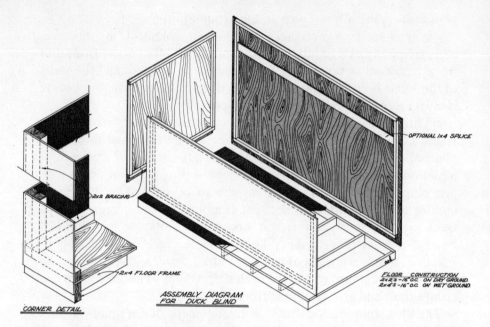

OPTIONAL 1x4 SPLICE

2x2 BRACING

2x4 FLOOR FRAME

FLOOR CONSTRUCTION
2x2'S -16" O.C. ON DRY GROUND.
2x4'S -16" O.C. ON WET GROUND.

ASSEMBLY DIAGRAM
FOR DUCK BLIND

CORNER DETAIL

The enclosed duck blind affords protection from the elements and from detection by birds swinging overhead.

than more conventional 2 x 4s; 2 x 2s are of more than sufficient strength for such a small structure, they're cheaper than 2 x 4s, and with half the weight, they make moving either the finished blind or basic materials a lot easier.

Construction is much easier if you prefabricate the blind in your garage or home workshop, then move it in pieces to the hunting site. The availability of power, warmth, a place to work out of the weather, and lighting at night make easy work of what could be backbreaking labor in the marsh.

The simplest version of this blind requires five sheets of plywood, and 128 feet of 2 x 2s. A quick look at construction steps should help you understand the plans.

• The floor is braced underneath on each edge, and on sixteen-inch centers. This is the one place where you might consider using 2 x 4s. If the ground where you'll be hunting is mucky or boggy, that extra two inches of height will help keep the floor up off the marsh, dry and less likely to rot.

Shore Blinds

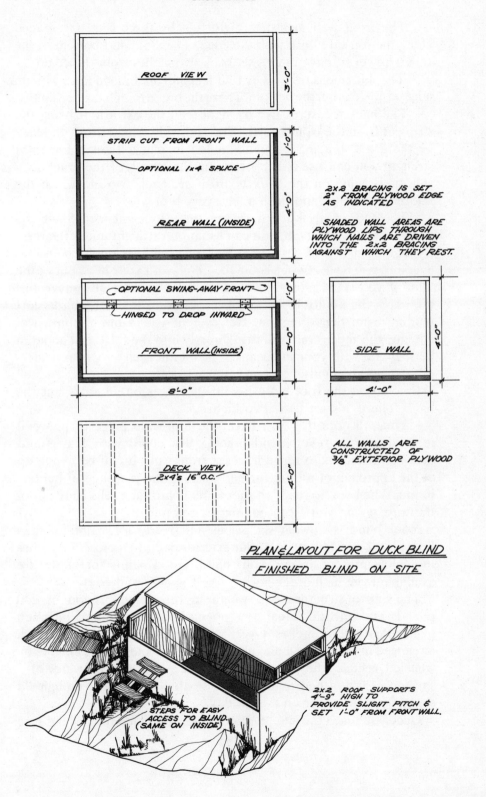

ROOF VIEW

3'-0"

STRIP CUT FROM FRONT WALL

OPTIONAL 1x4 SPLICE

REAR WALL (INSIDE)

1'-0"

4'-0"

2x2 BRACING IS SET
2" FROM PLYWOOD EDGE
AS INDICATED

SHADED WALL AREAS ARE
PLYWOOD LIPS THROUGH
WHICH NAILS ARE DRIVEN
INTO THE 2x2 BRACING
AGAINST WHICH THEY REST.

OPTIONAL SWING-AWAY FRONT

HINGED TO DROP INWARD

FRONT WALL (INSIDE)

1'-0"

3'-0"

8'-0"

SIDE WALL

4'-0"

4'-0"

DECK VIEW
2x4's 16" O.C.

4'-0"

ALL WALLS ARE
CONSTRUCTED OF
3/8" EXTERIOR PLYWOOD

PLAN & LAYOUT FOR DUCK BLIND

FINISHED BLIND ON SITE

STEPS FOR EASY
ACCESS TO BLIND.
(SAME ON INSIDE)

2x2 ROOF SUPPORTS
4'-9" HIGH TO
PROVIDE SLIGHT PITCH &
SET 1'-0" FROM FRONT WALL.

• The front wall measures eight feet by three feet. It's braced along the top side flush with the edge. The sides and bottom of the sheet, however, have braces set back two inches from the edge.

• The sides measure four by four feet and are braced flush with the edge on all sides but the bottom. There the brace is set back two inches.

• The back measures five by eight feet, the extra foot being the strip cut from the front board. The strip will be held firmly in place by the 2 x 2 bracing once it's nailed in place, though for extra strength you can use a 1 x 4 running the length of the crack as a splicer. Bracing on the back board is set back two inches on the bottom and sides, and flush at the very top.

• The roof of my blind measures three by eight feet. Since the blind is only five feet tall, you can't stand up straight under the roof. By making that roof only three feet long, with its pitch taken into account, you have enough room to stretch with your head out of the blind if you stand close to the front wall. Another advantage this affords is the ability to look in back of you should the birds start tending from that direction. However, if you're hunting in a wet climate, this means rain will drip directly into the blind just about in perfect line with your kneecaps. You'll either have to wear waders or incorporate a gutter system into the roof.

Bracing on the roof is flush with the edges on all sides but the back. There, it's set back two inches.

• You will note that you have one foot-wide piece of plywood left. I'd heartily recommend bracing this board with 1 x 2s and making provisions to hinge it to the front wall. It can be swung up at the approach of a bird, further masking the presence of hunters inside. When you're ready to shoot, the board then falls back out of the way, giving you more gunning room.

Your blind is now in six pieces and ready for painting, then transport. Use a top grade of flat exterior paint that closely matches the colors present around your blind. Good paints for blinds are available from mail-order houses like Cabela's and Herter's.

The entire structure will weigh in the neighborhood of 200 pounds, and with individual components laid flat, shouldn't be much higher than twelve inches. Over land, the blind can be car-topped, or carried in the bed of a pickup. If your blind site isn't attainable by wheeled vehicle, the pieces can be laid across the gunwales of a small boat, or lashed together and floated into place, though I'd suggest you do either on a calm day.

Once you reach the site, the floor goes into place first. Make sure it's on a perfectly level surface and that the joists all touch ground.

Erection of the structure takes only a few minutes. Put the front of the blind in place and you'll note the bottom edge of the wall overlaps the bracing on the floor of the blind by two inches. This affords nail holds from two directions—through the plywood from the front and through the inside bracing, straight down. When tacking walls in place, don't use a lot of nails. I used only six on the front wall of mine (three through the plywood and three through the inside bracing) and followed a similarly miserly pattern throughout the structure. It's still standing today, five years later, and in a spot that's often buffeted by seventy-mile-an-hour winds.

Another wise move is to use double-headed nails when you're putting the finished product together. These nails have two heads, so when they're driven home you still have one head sticking out. With these nails you can take your blind down as easily as it went up, without damaging wood. In places where the structure might be subject to vandalism, you can break your blind down and take it home after the season ends.

All that's left is installation of two 2 x 2 roof braces, and a seat. When bracing the roof, remember to incorporate a little pitch. An inch per foot is plenty. Seats are easiest to install when they're a simple bench. I don't bother with a door; instead I just hammer a few blocks of wood close to the front corner of the blind. They function as steps, and I go up and over the front of the blind.

The final chore is careful and total grassing.

This basic design is also eminently practical for two other types of blinds: the floating and the stake blinds.

• Stake blinds, also called "boobie blinds," are built out over the water on stilts. They're most advantageous when flight paths carry birds far from shore, or when the shore is heavily populated. But be sure gunning over water is legal.

Stake blinds do have several drawbacks, however. When you use them in salt water in cold climates, the grip of ice on their legs, coupled with the rise and fall of the tide, works them loose from the bottom in a matter of days. In a river subject to icing, current-carried floes can snap their legs like twigs. You also have to locate them in a spot that doesn't constitute a hazard to navigation.

When building a stake blind, the procedure and materials are identical to a shore blind, with the exception of the blind floor. In this case, I'd flatly recommend using 2 x 4s for bracing, and heavier flooring material—either ¾-inch exterior plywood or tongue-and-grooved 1 x 6s. A stake blind also requires some sort of a door—either a trap underneath where you hide your boat or a conventional door in the back or side of the blind.

• A floating blind makes a bit more sense to me than a stake blind, especially when you build one along the lines of a multipurpose craft. A good friend of mine living in Minnesota has a house on one of its ten thousand lakes. It's a recreation home: a place to fish and swim in the summer, and hunt ducks and deer in the fall. Larry built a ten-by-eight-foot raft, and floated it on two pontoons. He also put an outboard bracket on the back.

In the summer the raft functions as a diving platform, sunbathing spot, and boat dock, and, with an outboard and a few lounge chairs, is a great way to spend an afternoon slowly trolling around for walleye and northerns while you sip cold beer.

In the fall he erects his blind on the raft, camouflages it and any exposed decking, and is in a position to hunt every bay and potential flyway on that lake. And his ingenuity goes even beyond that.

When he welded the pontoons for the bottom, he made them big enough so the underside of the raft would have enough clearance to accommodate a ten-foot jon boat, making the job of hiding his pickup boat a cinch.

Two other types of permanent blinds deserve mention, but not detail because their use is restricted to narrow areas.

• Tree blinds are occasionally used in the swamps of the South. Tree blinds usually aren't elaborate affairs—just eight-to-ten-foot-high platforms next to a trunk of a tree. Hunters hide behind camouflage-pattern clothing. While I've hunted from them only for woodies, I don't doubt they'd be quite effective for any other species of duck that frequents a thickly forested swamp area.

• Curtain blinds are deadly indeed. They are cement or steel boxes that rest on a bay bottom. The boxes have flexible canvas sides, or "curtains," that are rolled up and down as the tide rises and falls. The hunter is then concealed below the surface of the water as in the old "sink-box" design, one of the basic tools of the market-gunning trade.

Waterfowl have always come freely to this type of blind, never even vaguely suspecting the presence of a hunter. While these blinds are effective, they're expensive to construct and maintain, and a pump must be carried aboard the tending boat. They fill with water when not in use.

Because of the effort and expense involved with curtain blinds, they're usually employed only by professional waterfowling guides.

There's also the matter of the spirit of the law. Technically they're not sink boxes because they're anchored to the bottom, but in function and effect they're identical to that device, outlawed because it worked too well. I've never been too impressed by the brilliance of those who find loopholes in the law, especially when the law's intent is clear. Sink box, curtain blind, call them what you will—I find them a little offensive to my sense of sportsmanship.

Blind Comfort   All a blind has to do to "work" is conceal a hunter, but holding to that sole essential makes for Spartan conditions.

• Seats are a virtual necessity. Without them you'll be sitting on cold, wet ground, and in a position where it's difficult to get up quickly to shoot.

Seats needn't be elaborate. If you're building a blind on the spot, or toting along a portable blind, and you know there's driftwood in the area, a flat board propped on two mounds of earth or tree stumps will be enough. If you have doubts about the availability of dimensioned lumber, bring along a folding camp stool. My old standby for makeshift blinds is a wooden milkbox. I've got two of them, and I guard them jealously since they're practically antiques.

Another eminently practical way to bring a seat is to buy one of those ammo-gear boxes that make into a comfortable seat. They're available through both Herter's, Mitchell, South Dakota, and L.L. Bean, Freeport, Maine.

When you're hunting in cold weather, I'm also a fan of that padded seat known commercially as a "hot seat." It's soft and comfortable, filled with a styrofoam substance that gets wonderfully warm when you sit on it.

a move I heartily endorse if you'll be out all day in near-freezing or colder weather.

In an open blind you can make a charcoal heater of a large coffee can. Poke holes in the bottom and lower sides of the can for air, wad some paper in the bottom, and throw a handful of charcoal on top. The coals will catch quickly.

Once they do, if you bury the can deeply enough to cover the air holes, you'll slow down combustion and the coals will last most of the day.

A word of warning, however: only use a charcoal heater in an uncovered blind. Glowing charcoal produces a great volume of deadly carbon monoxide. So much, in fact, that you'll get a splitting headache from the stuff if you use it in any sort of covered blind.

If you're gunning out of a covered blind, invest in a modern catalytic heater. They're safe and relatively cheap to run; if you buy one with a grate arrangement on top, you'll be able to heat coffee and foil-wrapped sandwiches. The combination amounts to a gourmet's repast when sprinkled liberally with a few duck feathers, the smell of gunsmoke, and a snowflake or two.

5 | Duckboats

A duckboat is a form of blind, a dry way to conceal a hunter intent on drifting down upon or sculling up to waterfowl, or luring a flock to his decoy spread. I'm rather sensitive about the term, too. I've heard some odd craft labeled "duckboats": jon boats, semi-vee outboards, even canoes. These aren't duckboats any more than I'm Henry VIII. While they could be altered into "boat blinds," that doesn't make them duckboats.

To me, a duckboat is a low flat-bottomed craft with a lot of decking fore and aft and along the gunwales. It has a small cockpit capable of holding one or two gunners who hide from view by lying flat on their backs. They're then concealed from ready detection by the covering decking.

Duckboats aren't just blinds, however. They're a wonderfully easy way to transport equipment. The energy it takes to pole or pilot a duckboat full of decoys is far less than would be spent if you had to slog your gear across the marsh afoot.

A duckboat also means a blind with mobility; miles of marsh, shoreline, and open water are within easy reach. And you aren't

A top-notch duckboat rates as the best tool at the modern gunner's disposal.

anchored to just one spot. If the birds change their flight pattern in the middle of the day or the wind swings around and spits sheets of sleet in your teeth, you can quickly pick up and move to a more promising location.

Another advantage offered by a duckboat in heavily hunted areas is that, because you bring your blind with you, you don't have to worry about the first-come-first-served rush for a spot at four in the morning. You can launch at a more gentlemanly hour and be rigged in time to greet the first purple glow of dawn with a hopeful prayer and full load of fours.

Duckboats are more, too, that might not be immediately perceptible to the novice's eye; they embody a fascinating study in waterfowling history and marine engineering that's worth recounting.

DUCKBOAT DESIGNS

What once was just a tiny boat used to reach a point or marsh where ducks were profuse gradually evolved into several vehicles of uncommon deception during the days of market shooting: highly specialized craft that could be rowed, sailed, poled, pulled, skidded across a marsh, and even piloted over a sheet of ice at sixty miles per hour.

Once the destination was reached, the boat was either slipped into a cut in the marsh or anchored in open water to function as an efficient blind. Sometimes the boat also did duty as shelter.

The most famous of these exceptional craft were named after the regions where they were developed.

• The Louisiana (also known as Arkansas) double-ender was a craft that looked much like a kayak: narrow of beam, low in profile, and decked over fore and aft with a small cockpit for the gunner. Like the durable pirogue, this was a boat suited to swamp travel. It could be rowed or poled backward or forward with ease. It sliced through the water silently and it threaded the needle channels between cypress knees and live oak like a curling snake.

I once owned a Louisiana double-ender, long gone to rot. It was a marvelous craft for jumping ducks on small rivers, and for gunning the margins of quiet ponds. But it proved to be a death trap in heavy weather or an angry chop: extremely unstable and as seaworthy as a bathtub.

I once made the mistake of laying out for broadbill in that boat and took on so much water that, in the span of a few minutes, I was in danger of swamping. The water was making ice then, too, which salt water doesn't do until it drops to 27 degrees. Exposure to that kind of temperature can kill a man in a matter of minutes.

But I was young then—seventeen if memory serves me right—and the boat was never designed for such youthful folly. I didn't realize it when I launched that dark morning, but I discovered a great deal about open-water boats before I got back to shore. That's another thing about waterfowling: you learn an awful lot, even on bad days.

• The Maine sharpy makes a nice study in contrasts. It isn't really a duckboat according to my personal definition, but it is a boat used to hunt sea ducks: old squaw, scoter, and eider on the open rough water of Maine harbors and the Atlantic itself. If you've never hunted them, sea ducks aren't too bright. They'll gladly decoy to plywood cutouts and, once shot at, will swing around for a second run through the gauntlet if you'll wave a gunnysack at them.

Maine Yankees being practical people first and foremost were quick to realize that a cleverly camouflaged boat made no difference to a sea duck; so they built their duckboats with a wild ocean in mind. The Maine sharpy includes in her lines a broad but graceful beam for stability, an extremely high profile with exaggerated sheer fore and aft, a bit of curved decking over the bow to cast the breaking sea back to its own, and a narrow transom that comes neighborly close to making the boat a double-ender.

This design fully discouraged the roughest waves from slopping in, and the narrow stern sliced a following sea like a knife, eliminating at least part of the danger of broaching. If you're a westerner and have no idea of what a Maine sharpy might look like, take a look at a McKenzie River boat. Whatever wild man decided he could navigate those burly western rivers surely had a sharpy in mind when he built his amazing craft.

In keeping with those two divergent designs and the very different conditions they were expected to encounter, some very interesting blends occurred halfway between Maine and the South.

• Perhaps the most famous of all duckboats was the Barnegat Bay sneak box. This craft had decking all around that sloped down to meet the bottom at the chine. So constructed, the boat had virtually no profile on the water, but resembled a muskrat lodge or floating clog of weed. The rounded sloping deck performed still another function—in heavy weather any wave breaking over bow or stern rolled back on itself, stymied by the pitch of the deck and the high coaming around the narrow cockpit.

The twelve-foot-long, four-foot-wide sneak box looked something like a melon or pumpkin seed when viewed from above, and its bottom was a bit like the dish of a spoon. Its modified-V bow rode shallow enough to allow the boat to be pushed or poled across tidal flats; yet it was deep enough to slice through an oncoming sea and to quiet a slapping ripple as the craft slipped up on a flock of ducks.

Although the boat was essentially round-bottomed, its broad beam made for a degree of stability for shooting—a matter of no small consequence, since the craft functioned as a blind as well as transportation. Most sneak boxes were also fitted with a leg-of-mutton sail, rudder, and daggerboard so they could be sailed to the gunning grounds. These places often lay many miles from home ports and gunners would stay out for several days, sleeping in, as

SNEAK BOX

The Barnegat Bay sneak box was the best-designed duckboat ever built. The advent of outboard power rendered it outdated, but not ineffective. Many of the best modern-day designs trace their lineage to the sneak box.

well as hunting from, their sneak boxes. Their sails also functioned as either a tent or blanket.

It is said that form follows function in enduring art, and viewing an old sneak box is indeed an artistic experience. Her lines speak softly of the sounds and smells of lonely marshes. There is something in every gentle curve and strake of wood that says it's for a purpose: to hold camouflaging grass, to ward off an angry sea, to drift silently.

Rotting in a marsh or in a museum, with the lightest dusting of imagination a sneak box conjures up the rushing wings of a thousand canvasback, the smell of black powder, and the pounding of guns. You can almost feel the touch of the cold-cracked hands that piloted her through decades of gray dawns. A sneak box is the symbol of waterfowling in a bygone era.

As the days of market gunning began to wane and duck shooting took on the cloak of gentlemanly sport, the phenomenal versatility of a sneak box was no longer necessary. Duckboats didn't have to function as shelter, and larger, more comfortable sailing craft could be used to tow the duckboats close to the marshes. In this milieu the Halleck skiff was born.

• The Halleck skiff was originally used as a pole boat to carry supplies across the shallow tidal flats of the Great South Bay. There were several lighthouses along Fire Island barrier beach, and this was the most practical way to provision them.

The Halleck skiff boasted low sharpy sides, seldom more than six inches high; so it maintained a low profile. This also meant that both bottom and decking could be built without the severe pitch common to sneak boxes, producing a less seaworthy boat in a heavy blow, but one that was infinitely more stable to gun from and that could be more easily camouflaged.

Like the sneak box, the Halleck skiff had a small, fully coamed cockpit, but it also had a flat afterdeck with railings or boxy sides built up around it. This was where the hunter carried his decoys—in far easier reach than tucked under the gunwales and foredeck, as was the case with the sneak box.

I once owned a modified Halleck skiff, not constructed along precise historic lines, but close enough to qualify as that type of craft. It was an extremely practical boat for setting out stool, and it seemed to disappear when it was slid into place along a marsh bank.

You can see a few originals around today, still in use. I recently dropped by a boat basin in Bellport, New York, and was delighted to find several of these skiffs tied up next to their tenders. Most of them belonged to members of the Pattersquash Duck Club, a rather tweedy, but delightful, group of old-time gentlemen black-duck gunners, whose club lands are legend in the area. I had a chat with one of the members and was a bit saddened to learn he was retiring his Halleck.

"The club voted to permit the use of outboards on our skiffs," he said, "and I'll be damned if I'll put a bracket on my boat. It's a little like forcing your best girl into prostitution, you know."

His plans were to donate the beautifully preserved and cared-for craft to a museum. While I applaud the gentleman's taste, his refusal to compromise ideals, and his desire to share his beautiful little boat with future generations, I think it's a damn shame that working waterfowlers won't have the pleasure of bumping into that little piece of history during a normal day on the bay.

Like the demise of the railroad steam engine, another passion of mine, that's progress for you.

• Coffin blinds were a kind of boat. They were built in the shape of a long box, big enough for a man to lie down in, with a pram-type bow.

Coffin blinds were usually carried on the deck of a boat, then towed by hand into place on a flooded marsh. They were extremely effective—and still are—when birds are forced to seek shelter inland due to high tides and winds.

Coffin blinds, the double-ender, the sneak box, and the Halleck skiff were essentially marsh and swamp craft, designed to be slid into a cut or slough and covered with grass. As such, they were used primarily in the pursuit of puddle ducks. The craft used to hunt diving species that prefer open water are yet another genre.

• The sink box, illegal since the 1930s, is the classic of the kind. Sink boxes were literally waterproof boxes of sufficient dimensions to hide one or two hunters. They were towed into position, or carried on the deck of a tending boat and put overboard.

Large canvas or wood "wings" extended from the top of the box, appearing a little like the open flaps on a cardboard box, but much longer.

The wings stabilized the craft, and they also kept out the chop. They angled gently downward from the lip of the box that floated inches above the water's surface. Like sloped decking on a boat, or the gentle rise of a sandy beach, the wings functioned to subdue oncoming waves, breaking their force before they sloughed over into the interior. Even with these wings, however, sink boxes could not withstand a hard blow; they were calm-weather craft, and wet even then.

Sink boxes also utilized cast-iron or lead decoys. These heavy decoys were placed on the wings to weight the craft down; on a dead-calm day the water level could be safely brought to within an inch of the top of the box. On rougher days fewer iron stool would be used, allowing the craft greater freeboard and the gunner some insurance against a dunking.

The net effect of a sink box was a pit blind smack in the middle of a bay or lake—a deadly deception that never failed to draw birds, and because it was so effective, the sink box was banned.

• Scooters are surely the most unusual, and exciting, of the open-water boats. They're large by duckboat standards, often exceeding sixteen feet, and they're broad in beam with a decided pumpkin-seed shape. Scooters have low sharpy sides, a bottom with only the gentlest curve to it, plenty of decking, and a large, roomy cockpit.

They also have a graceful bowsprit and four steel-sheathed rails that run nearly the length of the craft. Many of these boats also have either daggerboards, centerboards, or leeboards, and a rudder.

Scooters can be sailed in open weather and are low enough in profile and shallow enough in draft to be slid up against a marsh bank and grassed. Their broad flat bottoms make them excellent lay-out boats for open-water shooting because of the stability the bottom provides. But where these boats really stand alone is when winter locks in tight and bays freeze up.

When salt water freezes, tidal currents always maintain open leads no matter how cold the weather is. These potholes might occur along a deep channel, where tides sweep up and over a bar, or at the mouth of an inlet. Wherever they might be, they draw water-fowl like cracked corn.

With its steel rails and broad beam, a scooter will slide across the thinnest ice without breaking through, in much the same manner as a pair of skis will support a man on thinly crusted snow. Power is supplied by a man in the cockpit, pushing with a long-handled ice hook, essentially a sharpened boat hook. This combination, then, provides both access to potholes and a blind when the hunter gets there.

"Pole-power" is the means of locomotion when the ice is soft. When it's hard enough for a man to walk on, these craft can be

Author

The Great South Bay scooter incorporates the unique combination of duckboat/sail-
boat/iceboat.

sailed like an iceboat; and Lordy, do they go!

The rigging on these craft is a modified Marconi, with a smallish triangular mainsail; so the effect is a near-equal influence of wind on both sails. This is the way they're steered on ice—not with a rudder, but with a sail.

The system works simply. Since there are forces close to equal being exerted on both sails by the wind, if you slack up on the jib the pressure on the mainsail forces the boat into the wind. Slack up on the mainsail and cinch the jib down tight, and the boat turns with the wind.

I've had the good fortune to sail an ice scooter several times. We weren't after ducks, just fun on a cold winter's day, but it's an experience to remember.

As the first puff of wind catches your sail, the scooter hikes up a bit and begins to move. Salt ice is seldom millpond smooth, and as the boat picks up speed the ice begins to rumble and crunch under the hull. All the decking acts like the sound box on a guitar, and when you're up around forty to fifty miles an hour, the din approaches a cross between an express train and being inside a snare drum during a rock concert.

Then a puff of wind hikes you up higher. The boat is now resting on the outside rail and is at a crazy angle. To counterbalance, you lean far to the windward side, out over the whizzing ice. A thin stay is your only handle—the only thing between you, a hard fall, and a skin-tearing slide.

And then you see it looming up—an open lead of cold, bitterly cold water. I defy anyone to maintain a regular heartbeat as that little craft makes its approach to cross a lead. You simply think it's all over.

Suddenly the rumble is no more, just the silent hiss of the little scooter skimming across the water and wild cold spray jangling in the sunlight. When you hit a lead at high speeds the little boats plane—like a man on water skis. They lose speed fast, but leads usually aren't too wide—fifty yards is about average—and their momentum is often enough to carry you clear to the other side. There the scooter pops back up on the ice like a pleased penguin.

If the lead is too wide to be fully crossed on plane, the boat is sailed to the other side, then pulled up on the ice again with a hook.

There are still a few grizzled old baymen who sail their scooters in search of ducks, but for the most part, men who own them are interested in scootering, not hunting. It was surely an indescribably exciting way to fill a bag with birds.

• Puntys are of more modern design and are frequently in current use. They evolved chiefly after the banning of the sink box, as an alternative method to gunning open water.

They borrow their lines from the scooter, but like the Halleck skiff, their design is more specialized and the boat less versatile. The punty is solely a boat built to handle open water and heavy seas. It is towed into place by a tender and anchored. Puntys ride flat, keep dry, and are usually large enough to accommodate two gunners lying side by side. It can get awfully cold in a bouncing, spray-laced punty around December, and that kind of misery not only loves company, it demands it.

Puntys are painted off-white or battleship gray for camouflage, depending on weather conditions. When ice is prevalent, white is used to make the craft appear to be a floating floe. Battleship gray, roughly the color of water, is preferred during warm weather.

• Scull boats are the final category of historic duckboats. These were long, low, and slender craft that were propelled by an oar through the stern or by paddles strapped to the hunter's hands as he lay prone in the cockpit. They looked a bit like a modern rowing scull, but were deep enough to hide a man lying on his stomach.

These were the deadliest boats at the market gunner's disposal; with them, the hunter could silently slip up on huge rafts of waterfowl and kill hundreds of birds at a time.

Such large bags were made with the help of things like bow searchlights for night hunting, punt guns, and batteries.

Punt guns were huge cannons of O gauge or more that carried shot measured in pounds. They were mounted on the bow of a scull boat, their recoil being cushioned with ropes. Batteries were guns incorporating up to a dozen barrels that were likewise mounted in the bow of a sculler. They were triggered singly if the flock rose in progression, or all at once if it got up in a knot.

While contemporary sportsmen are justifiably appalled at this kind of slaughter, in context the sculler with his punt gun can't be entirely faulted.

He worked his trade at a time when there were millions of waterfowl and ample habitat for them to maintain their numbers. Then, too, his technique was hardly without danger, and of no guarantee. Scullers often maneuvered for a full day—even into the night—to get close enough to a flock of skittish waterfowl for a shot.

Ice floes, murderous tides, and sudden storms that raised moun-

Author

This beautifully preserved relic of a bygone era has graceful lines for ease in rowing and a low profile on the water.

Its modern-day counterpart, designed to be towed into place by a powered tender, is flat and squat to dampen rocky seas.

tainous waves were all part of the job. When they got close enough for a shot, there was more excitement involved than the sight of a thousand birds on thunderous rise; the homemade punt carried battery guns that often exploded, blinding or maiming the gunner. If they held together, but weren't correctly cushioned, the cannon-like punt guns could tear the bottom out of a scull with their recoil. Death by explosion, exposure, or drowning was always a possibility.

CONTEMPORARY DUCKBOATS

Buying a Used Duckboat   Although locating an original design amounts to a historic find, there are many recently built duckboats that incorporate features of one design here, another there, with a few of the original builder's ideas about what a duckboat should be and do thrown in for good measure. These boats are forever being traded or sold, and buying them used is one way to get a boat of your own. There are a few things you should consider, however, before buying a second-hand duckboat. The most important are:

• DRY ROT. Fresh water, especially rainwater, causes dry rot, and duckboats usually reside in open back yards during the off-season. Check for dry rot wherever water might collect. Push a knife blade into the wood. If it meets resistance, the wood is sound. If it finds an easy entry look for another boat. Tapping the wood is another test. Solid wood should produce a nice resounding knock. Rotted wood, because it's soft, will respond to a tap with a thunking sound: a muted thud.

• LEAKING. Before you buy, try the boat in the water. I've seen sound, dry-appearing boats that took on water like they had no bottom at all. If a boat you're planning to buy does leak, check from where the water is coming. You might be able to make it bone-dry by merely fiberglassing the seams—a simple job, but if it has to be done you should get a reduced price.

• WEIGHT. It's a reliable rule of thumb that heavy boats are best in open water. They bob less, hold a truer course, and are less affected by wind than feather-light craft. If your purchase is going to function primarily as a punty, weight is of no concern since you'll be towing the craft with a tender.

However, a heavy boat needs a boat trailer, and a trailer usually requires a constructed ramp for launching. A heavy boat will also draw more water, and it will take plenty of muscle power to draw it up to or push it around a marsh.

Generally, you're best off to choose a light craft for a marsh boat, a heavy craft for a punty.

• Sheathing amounts to a strip of hard covering, tacked, glued, or otherwise affixed around the waterline of your craft. Sheathing is a must if you plan to use a wooden boat around ice, as even the thinnest skim ice will cut, tear, and dig into wood like a knife.

Boats should be sheathed at least from a point beginning at the bow to slightly aft of the boat's broadest dimension. Once you've forced a path through the ice, your narrower stern quarters won't come in contact with the stuff. In addition, sheathing should be at least six inches wide—three inches above the waterline and three below.

Fiberglass sheathing is acceptable, but ice will eventually chew through it; so you'll have to replace it seasonally. Lead or copper sheathing is the best. Tin works, but it's hard to make it conform to the contours of your hull.

• CAPACITY. I favor open-water puntys that will hold two. Hunting from a grass boat is more fun if you can do it with two, but most of these boats are designed for one. If you think you're buying a two-man marsh boat, try it out with two people lying down with all their paraphernalia: clothes, guns, the works. Remember safe load capacity. The boat might be big enough to hide two gunners, but can it safely carry your decoys and an outboard as well if they are in your plans? Cast a critical eye at camouflage too—are the hunters indeed well hidden?

• DECKING. I can't think of any craft worthy of the designation "duckboat" that doesn't have plenty of decking. Decking helps blend in a boat with its background; it hides a good portion of the hunter's anatomy from view and it keeps waves from sloughing aboard in heavy weather. If you're buying an open-water boat that will be used in rough weather, remember that the longer the decking and the more precipitous its slope, the better it will tame the carry of a breaking wave. With this in mind, also remember that high seas dictate high coaming around the cockpit.

• PROFILE. The lower your boat's profile from the waterline to its highest point, the more effectively it will mask your presence, but there are limits. You need room to slide your feet and legs under the decking, and a paper-thin profile is an invitation to trouble when the water is rough.

• Keels and skegs are a big help when towing, rowing, or poling a boat, since they help you maintain a straight course. But they do make your boat draw more water, and it will lie on its side when drawn up on a marsh unless you do some propping under the stern.

• HULLS. The best boats should have some slight sheer to the hull rather than being perfectly flat. It makes them tow or row more easily, quiets the slap of waves, and because of the depth it creates amidships, allows for a low profile.

• Outboard brackets on second-hand duckboats deserve some careful attention. Many of them amount to an amateur conversion job on an old, noble design. Check for proper bracing, and be very careful about overpowering these conversions; usually the original boat was built to be propelled by musclepower, not horsepower.

What happens when you do overpower a hull not designed for a motor can have some interesting results. I once went hunting with an acquaintance from North Carolina who had a rather unusual boat—a fourteen-foot marsh rig, big enough for two, with a canvas bottom stretched over some light straking. It was an old boat too, with a place where a mast could be stepped for sailing the boat. I'm sure it was built before the advent of the outboard.

Someone had converted it to outboard power, and we had an engine on that day in the neighborhood of fifteen horse. Between it, the gas, a hundred-odd decoys, and the dumbest retriever I've ever had the misfortune to encounter, the boat was a bit over-loaded; but we knew we'd never venture into water any deeper than four or five feet during our crossing from shore to a small islet.

As we hunted, a good blow worked the channel into a fair chop; and by the time we were ready to return, the waves wore whitecaps. Because the water was so shallow, the sea wasn't running heavy; but it looked wet and snotty, so I donned my chest waders to keep dry in my bow position.

It was wetter than either of us had planned, and the boat began to take on a lot of spray. Bob cast a weather eye on the water ac-cumulating in the bilge and made an executive decision to get to shore in a hurry before we went under. He goosed the outboard up to full throttle—and drove the bow right under a wave. Down went the boat, pearl diving like an errant surfboard, until it hit bottom. And as it went down, I stood up, the top of my waders keeping perfect pace with the rising water. When I stepped from the boat and onto the bottom, shore was reasonably close, with the water a good six inches from the top of my waders. Bob wasn't so lucky; he was wearing hip boots, but he enjoyed a belly laugh any way. His damn dumb dog didn't want to get wet, and was trying to scramble up on my shoulders!

Buying a New Boat   There's a very real sense of charm, place, and history involved in locating and using an old duckboat; but as the years roll on, more and more of these venerable craft go under, and they're becoming difficult to find.

Surprisingly, not too many manufacturers turn out commercial duckboats either. But of those that do, I've found some makes upon which I'd be willing to place my stamp of approval.

• The Ducker, made by Aluma-craft, 325 Julien St., St. Peter, Minnesota 56802, is a delightfully light aluminum car-topper that can easily be handled by one man. The boat is comfortably broad in beam, flat-bottomed, and a good rig for gunning marshes and protected waters. It also makes a superior drift, row, or pole boat on rivers and in swamps.

At the writing of this book, production of the Ducker has been suspended; but if a demand for the hull arose I'm sure the boat would be made again. It's one of the best commercial designs I've ever seen.

Worthy of particular note is the anchoring system utilized on this craft. There are two tubes sealed in the decking, one fore and one aft, that run completely through the hull. To anchor the boat on bottom, close-fitting wooden or aluminum shafts can be slid down through the tubes and driven into the marsh mud. The result is marvelous stability; you neither drift nor rock, yet the craft is free to rise and fall with a tide.

The boat comes in dead-marsh color, but oddly enough the manufacturer doesn't make provisions for the boat to be grassed. It doesn't require much work for you to do this—just a few washered bolts drilled through the decking and nutted to grass boards.

• Tide-Craft, P. O. Box 796, Minden, Louisiana, produces what appears to be a well-designed duckboat made of fiberglass. I haven't had a chance to test the boat personally, nor have I seen it beyond a catalog description and pictures.

• Herter's, Mitchell, South Dakota, makes a fair fiberglass duckboat. I give it only a "fair" rating because the boat appears to me to be designed with all-around use in mind—something that will double as a light fishing craft when duck season is over. And any compromise is bound to reduce a duckboat's efficiency.

I feel it lacks sufficient decking for really good camouflage, but it is of relatively seaworthy design and readily accepts an outboard motor. Costs currently run $230, plus shipping.

• A truly fine all-around duckboat for use on big water is the one manufactured by South Bay Boats, Inc., 39 Washington Ave., West Sayville, New York 11796.

The fourteen-foot fiberglass hull is of a whaleback design, with a recessed transom so you can reach an outboard without an extension handle. It will take up to a ten-horse motor.

In many ways, this modern craft incorporates a lot of the features that made the old gunning skiffs great. It has runners so it can be skidded across the ice and an easily camouflaged pumpkin-seed shape, and is heavy enough and high enough to encounter the vilest chop and still remain proud.

While its depth amidships does give it a slightly high profile, this also means plenty of room, and enough vertical rise so that two gunners can shoot from the boat, over open water or a marsh.

The craft comes in two colors: marsh brown and off-white. I think the marsh brown is the best route to go. White would be awfully hard to camouflage with grass, but the brown can effectively be transformed into a floating sheet of ice by sewing up a form fitting snap-on cover of light gray canvas.

The boat weighs 180 pounds; so it virtually must be trailered. But that weight will be welcome in a heavy sea. Another unique feature of this boat, faithfully pegged to the past, is that it's available in a model that can be sailed.

Prices on this duckboat begin at $600 for the basic hull, and climb if you want grass boards and spray shields as part of the deal. The sailing model, with a daggerboard, runs $900.

Building a Duckboat   There is a third possibility should you want a duckboat: building one. It's an exercise I heartily recommend. Like making your own decoys, it helps you stretch out a season, and makes more out of a day on the marsh.

Plans for many of the classics can be obtained from the Mystic Seaport Marine Historical Association, Inc., Mystic, Connecticut 06355. At a dollar each, you can get information on how to build a Halleck-type duckboat, a scull boat, and a Barnegat Bay sneak box. Write to the attention of Mrs. Helen Mark, Curatorial Dept.

Building one of the classics is a labor of love. It requires both savvy slightly beyond my ability and materials not readily available

Author

The South Bay duckboat is a masterpiece of modern design, incorporating many of the features that made classics of the past great.

around my landlocked Montana home. So my solution was to design my own boat. It's neither graceful nor pretty, but it is effective and well suited to the gunning conditions I most frequently encounter out west.

"The Ultimate Weapon," as I've christened my creation, is essentially an adaptation and enlargement of a coffin blind. But coffin blinds were carried on the deck of a boat; my gunning box is designed to function as both blind and boat. Well, barge might be a more descriptive term.

The plans, as listed here, could easily and justifiably be modified. The dimensions of the boat were based on the bed size of my pickup truck; it fits inside perfectly, with the tailgate closed. However, if you choose to make it much narrower, you'll be limited to a one-man box. As mine is constructed, it's a little tight for two big men, but just perfect for my wife and me.

Although The Ultimate Weapon could be fitted with an outboard bracket, my boat is designed with towing in mind, and it tows well. The squared-off barge bow counters most of its tendency to yaw under way. The boat contains enough interior room to hold and haul thirty-five duck decoys and nine geese, as well as life preservers, guns, shells, and such, not to mention my Labrador retriever who occasionally rides on deck.

The double-hinged hatch cover can be put under lock and key if necessary, and it performs a dual function. Folded double-over, and out of the way, it affords easy access to the interior of the boat for reaching stowed decoys, and for gunners when they're ready to slide into place. Once the hunters are comfortable, the cover is then half-folded back, hiding all of the hunters' anatomy except their upper extremities. These, in turn, are partially masked from view when the collapsible blind board is hooked in the "up" position. In cold weather a small catalytic heater keeps hunters and the inside of the boat surprisingly warm.

When it's time to leave the marshes, the four handles on each quarter make loading the boat easy. Two people can lift the empty craft up to car-top carriers and, with a little strain, can swing even the decoy-laden boat up into the bed of a pickup.

As the plans reveal, the boat is simple to build. Using two left thumbs and minimal power workshop equipment, a young friend and I built it in two days for under $80. There are, however, a few tricks I learned in the process that will simplify your job even further.

• Use only exterior or marine plywood, ⅜-inch thick. Interior plywood is held together with a glue that will let go when the wood gets wet.

• Buy clear, straight-grained pine 1 x 4s for framing, and have your lumber yard rip them in half; 1 x 2s will provide all the strength you'll need, so long as there are no knots in the wood.

• Use generous applications of waterproof glue wherever wood meets wood. I used "weldwood" glue, a type of cement that comes in two cans, one powder and one liquid. After five years' hard use, not a joint has let go.

• You'll save a lot of time, blisters, and money if you'll use nails, not screws, to hold the boat together. Make sure, however, to use boatbuilder's nails. They're brass, and they have sharp ripples on their shafts to keep them from ever pulling out. Use one-inch nails for securing plywood to framing, two-inch nails for framing-to-framing joints. Herter's sells these nails, in case you can't find them locally.

• Fiberglass all seams at or below the waterline, including glassing small patches over nail holes. I know that a real boatbuilder can make a watertight seam, but you're probably not a real boatbuilder and neither am I. Then, too, the in-again/out-again nature of a car-top wooden boat is bound to result in expansion, contraction, and an opening of even the tightest unglassed seam.

• Seal all the seams that lie above water—where the deck meets the coaming, the gunwales, etc.—with the type of bathroom caulking compound that dries to a rubbery tough sealer. This stuff is best applied with a squeeze-type (cartridge) gun.

Part of the intrigue involved with old duckboats is the ingenious way in which they were adapted to local conditions. Like the gunners of bygone days, there are still a few contemporary nimrods who are working to model their boats more along the lines of modern gunning.

One gentleman whose work I've long admired in this field is Zack Taylor, the boats editor of *Sports Afield*. He has designed several craft for duck hunters, most notably the "Zackbox," a decked-over grass boat built on an altered semi-vee hull. His boat can handle quite a bit of power; so it's capable of covering good distances in a short time and is seaworthy in heavy weather. Most important, it does a good job of camouflaging the hunter. Plans for this boat are available for $1.50 through *Sports Afield* magazine, 250 W. 55th St., New York, New York 10019.

Duckboats

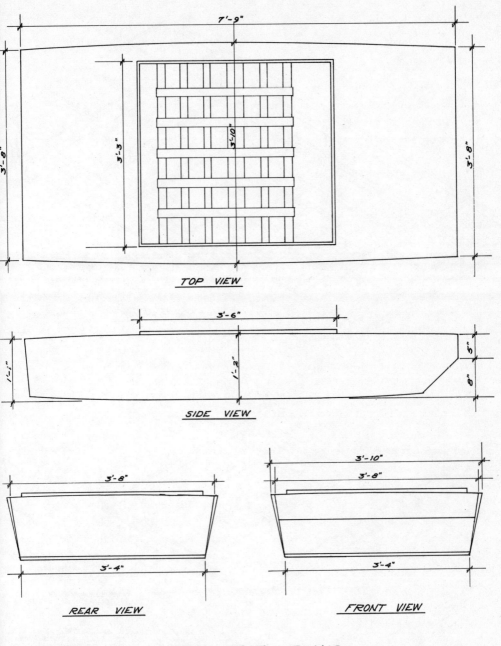

TOP VIEW

SIDE VIEW

REAR VIEW

FRONT VIEW

DUCK BOAT PLANS

The "Ultimate Weapon" is an easy-to-build gunning box well suited to the demands of modern waterfowling. The dimensions of the boat can easily be altered to fit the size of car-mounted roof racks or the bed of a pickup truck.

103

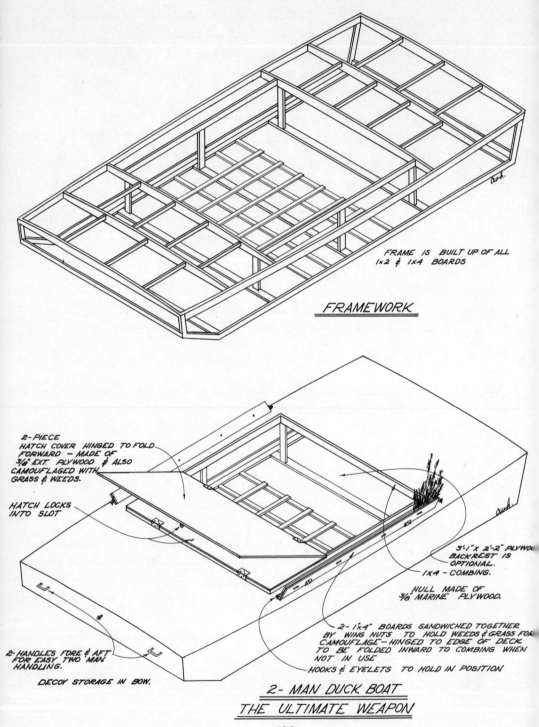

FRAME IS BUILT UP OF ALL
1x2 & 1x4 BOARDS

FRAMEWORK

2-PIECE
HATCH COVER HINGED TO FOLD
FORWARD — MADE OF
3/8" EXT. PLYWOOD & ALSO
CAMOUFLAGED WITH
GRASS & WEEDS.

HATCH LOCKS
INTO SLOT

3'-1" x 2'-2" PLYWOOD
BACKREST IS
OPTIONAL.

1x4 - COMBING.

HULL MADE OF
3/8" MARINE PLYWOOD.

2-1"x4" BOARDS SANDWICHED TOGETHER
BY WING NUTS TO HOLD WEEDS & GRASS FOR
CAMOUFLAGE—HINGED TO EDGE OF DECK
TO BE FOLDED INWARD TO COMBING WHEN
NOT IN USE
HOOKS & EYELETS TO HOLD IN POSITION

2-HANDLES FORE & AFT
FOR EASY TWO MAN
HANDLING.

DECOY STORAGE IN BOW.

2- MAN DUCK BOAT
THE ULTIMATE WEAPON

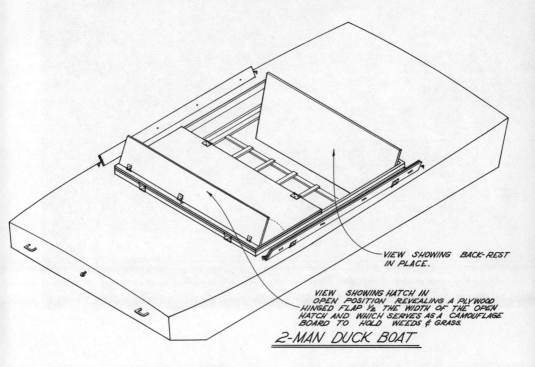

VIEW SHOWING BACK-REST
IN PLACE.

VIEW SHOWING HATCH IN
OPEN POSITION REVEALING A PLYWOOD
HINGED FLAP ½ THE WIDTH OF THE OPEN
HATCH AND WHICH SERVES AS A CAMOUFLAGE
BOARD TO HOLD WEEDS & GRASS.

2-MAN DUCK BOAT

Construction begins with prefabricated sides, stern, and bow being nailed together.

The bottom is attached next; all wood-to-wood joints are glued.

Decking is braced underneath and cockpit is framed in
Decking is applied and lattice floorboards nailed in place.

The "Ultimate Weapon," fully grassed, afloat, and in the marsh.

DUCKBOAT EQUIPMENT

Hunting waterfowl with a boat requires substantially more equipment than merely a good hull.

Outboard motors eliminate the work and save time over rowing or poling. Except when you have broad expanses of rough water to cross, or great distances to travel over water, I favor three-to-five-horsepower engines with pivotal reverse for waterfowling. High speeds are seldom of the essence, and these small engines are light and compact enough to make the work associated with mounting, removing, and hiding your engine negligible. They'll often fit right in most grass boats, tucked under the afterdeck.

These tiny outboards are available in short shaft lengths—a worthwhile feature to consider if you travel in extremely shallow waters. There are also substantial savings to be had when you choose a pivotal reverse as opposed to an outboard with a gearing system.

My only reluctance to make a blanket recommendation arises when you frequently hunt in bitterly cold weather. Because you're turning an entire drive train when you spin these outboards over, cold grease will occasionally prevent the cold engine from turning fast enough to start. With a gearing system, you're only turning over the engine—not the shaft and prop too.

However, if your weather is so consistently cold, chances are you'll take the time to put a lighter grease in the gear housing, and will know and understand the wonders of ether-base starting fluid.

One other feature I strongly recommend on any outboard used for marsh shooting is a slip clutch on the propeller. This is a rubber shear-pin arrangement whereby the propeller shaft can be momentarily disengaged from the prop without actually shearing a pin that must be replaced. Taking into account the shoal nature of marshes, you're bound to bump bottom now and then.

An outboard extension handle for any size motor is a far more important tool than the average duck hunter realizes. On many duckboats the afterdeck is so long that reaching the outboard handle to steer or change speed requires a monumental stretch, if it can be reached at all. An extension handle puts the motor in your grasp, and performs a few other functions too.

In Montana, I use a fourteen-foot aluminum jon boat to tow my duckboat, and on it I mount a five-horse engine. When I drop a bird without my Lab around, I chase it down in the jon boat. Between the weight of the motor and me, sitting far aft, the bow of the boat sticks way out of the water and the boat will not plane. With a handle, however, I can move farther amidships, achieving better weight distribution, and the boat gets up on top and really moves. The handle is also a big plus when I get to where the bird dropped. With it, I can run the motor standing—and get a much better view into the troughs of waves. Should the bird dive when I come close, I have a good angle to see down into the water from this standing position.

A large scoop-type fishnet is a handy adjunct to a duckboat too. Although I think the law insane, in most sections of the country it's illegal to shoot a crippled bird from a powered boat, and a fishnet is the only way you'll be able to snare a lively cripple. A net is just as welcome on dead birds since it means you don't have to get your hands wet.

Anchoring   Except for when you pull your boat right up on the marsh or beach, both grass boats and lay-out boats will have to be anchored fore and aft. A yawing boat alarms birds and makes shooting nearly impossible.

In deep water, and over all bottoms but craggy, sharp rocks, I've found the Danforth-type anchor performs best, and I can think of no duckboat so large that it would ever need more than four-pounders. To anchor, point the boat directly into the wind, drop one anchor, and drift back for a distance of six to eight times as far as the water is deep. Cast the second anchor directly off the stern, and draw yourself up halfway on the bow anchor line. Secure the stern line tight, and you're in place for the day, barring wind shift.

Grass boats are best anchored by driving two steel reinforcing bars into the mud fore and aft, then tying the bow and stern fast to them. If you know, or if you have a friend who knows, how to weld, you can also put together an oarlock-type arrangement that will screw into your bow and stern, and pass the re-bar through that.

Push poles should be carried aboard any grass boat. They're used when the water's too low or too shallow for an outboard and the bottom too mucky to walk on. Push poles should have some sort of lattice work basket, like the bottom of a ski pole, to keep them

111

from sinking in the mud. Herter's sells such a pole for around six dollars.

Lay-out boats should have either a long boat hook or long pole with a snaring notch carved into the end. This is the most efficient way to gather stool and ship them aboard.

Life preservers are required by law on any craft—even a duckboat used in shallow water. When hunting in shallow water, use the cushion type in camouflage color. They make a hard seat or back-rest a little more bearable.

In a lay-out boat I like to bring a cushion for comfort, but always tuck a vest-type preserver under the decking. The water's usually cold and deep when you're open-water shooting, and should you go in, you could never keep a cushion preserver on for any length of time. A vest preserver, on the other hand, will keep a man afloat with his head out of the water, even if he's unconscious.

Camouflage   Lay-out boats can be sufficiently camouflaged with a coat of oyster white or flat battleship-gray paint, the color being determined by the presence of or lack of ice. I've seen hunt-ers go one step further though. They made canvas sheeting that snapped or clipped on to the decking. It lapped over the gun-wales and trailed in the water, the cloth's crinkly, rounded con-tours doing a marvelous job of breaking up the boat's formal, severe outline.

Grass boats require a bit more work. They must first be painted, then covered with native grasses.

If the region where you do most of your hunting remains essen-tially green throughout the season, lay on a coat of olive drab paint. This shade blends in best with a living plant background.

If, however, your favorite marsh melts into the rich golds, tans, and browns of fall, choose a color more akin to that shade. The closest I've come to the color of dead fresh-water bulrushes and salt-marsh hay is Herter's Dead Grass paint. Interlux also makes a good paint for dead marshes, and for lay-out boats too. Though it is usually a special-order item in paint stores, perhaps you can find a place that carries the brand.

Once your base coat is on, it's time to grass. The best way to get your grass is to take your boat right to the marsh you plan to hunt and gather it there. The quickest way I've found to cut it is with hedge shears. A scythe is faster, but it scatters the grass blades, and you've got to line them up before you can put them in place.

Grass boards are the traditional method of attaching grass to a boat. These are strips of hardwood, anchored to the decking, through which pass bolts that point out. Grass is laid along these boards, then a second strip of hardwood is fitted on top, the bolts passing through this board too. Wingnuts or common nuts are then screwed down tightly, sandwiching the grass in place.

Grass boards are a necessity on fiberglass or aluminum duckboats. They're also commonly used on wooden duckboats, though I think there's a better way here.

There is something a bit formal about the way grass lies in a board—a kind of man-made neatness and order that's never a part of nature. To achieve a helter-skelter pattern, I simply staple grass directly to wood decking, using a staple gun.

Just take a hank of grass and twist it twice. Set a staple at the top of the twist and one at the bottom. Continue the process using no pattern at all, and you'll have a grassing job that looks like it grew there. A word of caution, however: the flimsy staples used in a gun rust through quickly when exposed to salt water. The problem would be eliminated if you could locate galvanized staples, but I don't know if such a product exists.

Keeping warm lying flat on your back in a duckboat is no small trick, but one of the most effective aids I've found in this department is a thin sheet of styrofoam, covering the floorboards like a camper's ground cloth.

The styrofoam has excellent insulating properties; it provides a comfortable cushion, and even generates a degree of heat as you lie on it.

6 | Goose Pits

A well-constructed, carefully camouflaged pit is by far the most perfect form of concealment there is. There have been times when I've walked away from a covered pit on nature's call and had trouble relocating it though I knew it was only paces away. When a hiding place blends in that well, it's got to fool waterfowl.

Obviously, and unfortunately, pits do present some problems around a marsh or bay because of water seepage, so they're largely limited to high-and-dry land. Beyond that consideration, they should also be located around established feeding grounds, and in a field of low grass or harvested crops. Waterfowl simply won't land in a place with high cover. Even on a federal reserve that's been closed to gunning for years, I've watched geese and ducks land first in a tilled field, then walk into a standing crop of unharvested corn to feed.

There are five basic pit designs. The first and simplest is comparable to the "portable" duck blind. It's just a cloth covering whose color matches that of the immediate terrain. To use it, you dig a narrow slit trench, lie down, and cover up.

Sil Strung

A well-constructed pit affords near-perfect camouflage.

Joel Arrington, North Carolina Dept. of Conservation

Lying down in a slight depression or slit dug in the earth is the simplest form of "pit," but it's effective only in isolated instances.

While there's a degree of beauty to its simplicity, and it has an effectiveness that will surpass a sloppily constructed permanent pit, a slit trench has a few inherent problems.

First, it's damp, and because you're lying on your back, you're bound to feel that dampness quickly. The same thing is true if the weather's cold. In a half hour a slit trench becomes intolerable. Because of man's fidgety, impatient nature, hunters seldom remain in a slit trench, covered up, for long periods of time. Rather, they'll

116

get up and walk around, planning to slip into place at the approach of birds, and it seldom works out. Either the birds catch you flat-footed, or you just can't get into the trench, well covered and immobile, in time to hide from their approach. Finally, a cloth cover can never afford the letter-perfect camouflage that's possible with other types of pit blinds.

There was, however, one time when slit trenches were the order of the day. Several years ago I was hunting near Devil's Lake, North Dakota, with a friend. We were gunning out of a pit in a harvested grainfield and were frustrated for two days in a row after a flock of two or three thousand lesser Canadas arrived en masse to feed in a field a mile away.

While it's generally unwise to shoot into big flocks, these were migrants who would leave in a few days, and with numbers like they had, they drew every potential flock away from our spread and into their own. They were feeding in a stand of winter wheat, a grain that's planted in the fall and that sprouts to a seedling before the frost sets in. The ground was still soft and the birds were doing quite a bit of damage to the crop, pulling the seedlings up by the roots and trampling the rest; so the farmer who owned the field was glad to let us shoot the geese out of his crop.

The morning of the third day we walked out into the part of the field where they'd been feeding, and in the half-light of predawn dug two trenches parallel to the lines of sprouting wheat. Just before sun up we saw the birds coming on; great lines of them were strung out pencil-thin on the horizon. We slipped into our trenches and covered up to wait.

Although small groups of geese take some persuasion to lure in, when you're dealing with huge flocks that are familiar with an area they consider safe, the normally wary birds pile in like chickens, and that's just what those Canadas did.

The sound of the geese grew to a deafening cacophony as they came closer and closer. Then the lead birds set their wings and quieted down to scout the area briefly. They were a little suspicious of our covered forms; I could see one old gander looking down on me from about thirty yards up. Then one bird broke and dropped in. It was all the invitation the flock needed; the rest of the geese dipped and fluttered down like so many sheets of paper.

Then the great flocks came in wedges that never seemed to end, landing to our left and our right, in front of us and behind us, talking, gabbling, raising an ear-splitting din more sweet to my ears than the combined products of Bach, Beethoven, and the Beatles, and perhaps sounding as that unlikely trinity might if they could ever be organized.

"Ready?" I asked my partner.

"Ready," he replied, and we both sat up at the same instant. For a second you could have heard a whisper from a mile away. I don't know how many birds were there, but every one was silent and stock-still; their necks craned in response to some unknown communication geese have among themselves. Then, in a great rustle of wings and yelps, they were aloft, climbing for the clouds as our guns hammered away at the closest birds.

It was a wild, wonderful moment: the smoky fingers of yellow dawn, the musky smell of the prairie in the fall, and geese, geese everywhere. In the span of a few seconds we had our limits, and in a few more seconds the huge flock of Canadas was a misty, fast-disappearing cloud.

That particular flock would never return to that field during the season; too many birds would remember that hunters had hidden there. So in that specialized case the work of digging a pit just didn't make sense and the ease and speed of locating a slit trench did. But in virtually all other situations a bit more sophisticated hiding spot is the rule for successful field hunting.

One excellent pit with some degree of portability is a type that an old friend from Forsyth, Montana, taught me to build. Eli Spannagel, Sr., is a goose hunter's goose hunter—the kind of gunner who sits up nights dreaming new ways to outsmart geese, and who listens each fall evening for the sound of new flocks arriving from the North. When he hears those plaintive cries under the pale yellow light of a harvest moon, he grabs a shovel and strikes off for the field the birds have chosen to feed in.

The construction of Eli's pit hinges on four brace boards he builds at home. Length isn't an absolute; he puts together two four-foot-long and two six-foot-long boards to produce a pit three feet by six feet that hides two gunners. I've built four-by-eight-foot brace boards that make for a pit of three-foot-by-eight-foot dimensions with enough room for three. Even larger pits could be dug so long as the soil isn't too sandy or unstable.

The boards with the longest dimensions frame the front and back of the pit. Each of these brace boards consists of a six-foot-long 1 x 4 and a six-foot-long 1 x 6. The boards are nailed at right angles to each other; so viewed from the butt end, they look like an L.

The shorter boards shore up the sides of the pit, and each consists of one four-foot-long 1 x 8 and one three-foot-long 1 x 5. The 1 x 5 is nailed at right angles to the 1 x 8, perfectly centered on all sides; so viewed from the butt end, this portion of the blind looks like a T.

To understand how these boards work, imagine them lapped together to make a square. The shorter sides go down first, and the long L-shaped boards lap on top of them, producing a square frame. The leg of the T and foot of the L meet to create a flush lip four inches high around the entire perimeter of the pit.

After you dig your hole, these boards are then set around its rim, and recessed in the earth so the top side of the lip is flush with ground level. Dirt is then backfilled up to the top of the lip, producing a square, stable top to the pit that won't slough dirt into your lap when you climb in and out, and to which any sort of hatch may be attached.

Note, too, the 1 x 8 sides have a 3½-inch lip that juts into the pit. Eli uses these to support six-foot-long 2 x 12s, which he lays across the pit opening when it isn't being used. This arrangement keeps him in the good graces of the farmers in whose fields he hunts; a thousand-pound cow really can get wedged in a pit six by three by five feet, and they'll do it religiously if given the opportunity.

Eli's pit design is advantageous in that it's so wonderfully portable; two gunners digging in soft soil can build one in under a half hour. But this type of pit does have one big drawback: unless you're working with stable soil, the sides will slough in without some interior bracing; and even in stable soil they'll collapse in a heavy rain.

Just that unfortunate thing happened to Eli three seasons ago. He spent the entire week prior to opening day carefully scouting goose movements and digging and camouflaging his pits. A freak rainstorm dropped three inches on normally dry Forsyth the day before opening. We tried to bucket out the pits, but they caved in.

It very nearly brought Eli to tears—and he's a hard-bitten rancher who withstood the worst days of dustbowl and depression without a whimper. I could understand it though—opening day, and all the geese that were around that year. There are some frustrations man will never be able to bear.

One compromise to consider in unstable or wet terrain is the coffin pit. This amounts to a bargelike shallow box, made of light plywood and 1 x 4 bracing. It can be as large or as small as you wish;

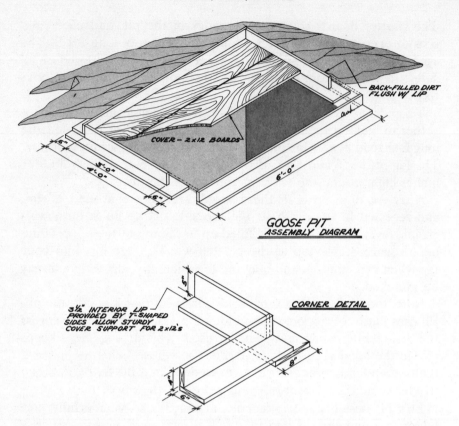

BACK-FILLED DIRT
FLUSH W/ LIP

COVER - 2x12 BOARDS

GOOSE PIT
ASSEMBLY DIAGRAM

3½" INTERIOR LIP
PROVIDED BY T-SHAPED
SIDES ALLOW STURDY
COVER SUPPORT FOR 2x12's

CORNER DETAIL

This top-of-the-pit framing affords the goose hunter portability or permanence. The framing keeps dirt from sloughing in and, covered with 2 x 12s, it will keep cows out.

I've seen them come in dimensions with room for one, up to a giant that held six.

Hunters lie on their backs in these, usually covered by a spring- or rubber-band-loaded door that swings out of the way when they sit up to shoot. Coffin pits are also a blessing in rocky or hard-to-dig soil. They're only around twelve inches deep; so they don't require a lot of deep digging to get them set in place.

A coffin pit large enough for two can be carried in the bed of a pickup truck; so with this type of blind you can be mobile too. An interesting variation on a coffin pit can be constructed from The Ultimate Weapon, outlined in the section on duckboats. All that's needed is the substitution of a spring-loaded door for the fold-back hatch, and you're in business.

One problem that needs to be overcome in the coffin-type pit is getting up. You've got to bend at the waist, like doing a fast sit-up, and with heavy clothes and guns it requires no small effort to achieve momentum. As a result, you lose a few precious seconds in the getting-up process.

One of Eli's gunning buddies tackled that problem during one of Montana's long winters and came up with an idea that has real potential. Essentially, he built a one-man coffin blind with a spring-loaded backrest made from an old tractor seat. The seat was set by pushing it into a locked position, then you lay down on it and closed the doors to wait.

Unfortunately the invention met with questionable success during its first test. The spring was stronger than the inventor anticipated. When he was confronted with a hundred geese drifting into his decoys, he released the lock and was launched clear out of the coffin, eating a mouthful of Montana mud and clogging his gun barrel as well. The design went back to the drawing boards.

Permanent blinds are best when you hunt the same field all season, as is often the case with leased lands and hunting clubs. They're pleasant because their permanent nature allows you to build them quite comfortably inside, with special features that include heating to living-room temperatures.

These pits are commonly of large dimensions; four by eight feet of floor space is rather standard. They're usually sunken in the soil four and one-half feet, affording room to move around with the hatch closed and an opportunity for hunters to see above ground level when standing.

Construction amounts to a little more than for a box; so there's no real need to go into great detail, though I would recommend building them on the same order as is outlined in the section on blinds: prefabrication that can be quickly assembled on the spot.

Another wise move is to use extra-sturdy materials with plenty of bracing: I'd say at least ½-inch plywood, and double the amount of 2 x 2s that will be reinforcing the plywood. When soil gets wet and unstable, it exerts tremendous pressures on the walls of a big pit blind; the larger the blind the more the pressure. Since you'll be using the pit throughout the season and possibly year after year, you might as well put something together that will withstand adverse elements.

Barrels account for the final category of pit blinds. They're nothing more than fifty-five-gallon oil drums, dug into the soil. They'll accommodate one hunter in reasonable comfort and are advantageous in that they don't leak. This is one of the few types of pit blinds useful around marshes and seashores, and I've seen them used with great effect. The neatest barrel blind I've run across was used on the shore of a reservoir that was studded with old tree stumps when the water was down. The barrel was painted bleached-barn gray, it had some driftwood placed to imitate roots around its six-inch-high lip, and the top was the cutaway drumhead. It too was painted gray, and was suspended six inches above the top of the barrel by a single rod on a swivel that allowed it to swing away when the gunner was ready to pop up.

Hatch Covers   Building or digging a pit is a pretty simple matter: nothing more than muscle work and minor bracing. Pit preparations above ground, however, require more than brawn.

A goose, especially a Canada goose, is one of the wiliest birds that fly. They will occasionally be driven by circumstance to do monumentally stupid things, but that's the exception, not the rule. In terms of being aware of danger, and the ability to perceive it, geese seem to possess near-human intelligence; and remember, these birds are viewing your pit from the air.

I once flew over some fields in Utah that had goose pits dug into them, and it was a bit of a revelation. One field was earth brown, with the wispy green hint of winter wheat. The fellow hunting there had simply put some green roofing material—perhaps indoor/outdoor carpeting—over the hatch cover. It stood out square and obvious, a patent fake.

Another gunner had done a bit better job. He'd set up in a row of cornstalks that were knocked down to the earth when the harvester made its first pass at the field. The camouflage on his hatch cover was fair, but when he dug his pit he didn't haul the dirt away. The subsoil he'd unearthed was a slightly different shade from that on the surface, and when he raked the mounds back, the entire blind area took on a plainly different hue from its immediate surroundings. Another mistake he made was setting up in the corn row. Like ducks being wary of thick cover, geese know that the leavings of an old haystack or a line of chaff make for good hiding spots. They'll often land well out of gun range of these places, then slowly walk over to the decoys.

There were other signs of human presence visible from the air—footprints, tire tracks, disturbed earth, and trampled stubble—that were surprisingly easy to pick out. After that flight, I knew a lot better why some of my supposedly best-laid pit plans went awry and why they'll continue to do so unless I've got a little bit of luck working for me too. There's just no way to avoid some of those signs—footprints in soft earth leading to a pit, for instance. But there are some measures you can take to keep the giveaways to a minimum.

Hauling dirt away from the pit you dig is a wise move under all circumstances. Even if you dig your pit well before the season and plant some cover around the blind, the earth might not have a telltale shade to identify it as freshly moved, but there will be a slight mound around your blind. The mound won't be visible from the air; it's too gentle, and waterfowl have very poor depth perception anyway. But if geese or ducks land outside of gun range, they can easily pick out that mound on the horizon and will never come close.

Exquisite camouflage of your hatch cover helps a lot too. Except when pits were located in dense grasses or a line of knocked-down stubble or chaff, I've never seen a hatch whose presence wasn't hinted at when viewed from above. But I have seen camouflage jobs that were at least hard to pick out.

One pit I saw in Southampton, Long Island, had dirt glued to the hatch cover, with lines of green ryegrass glued to the dirt so they lined up perfectly with the rye and furrows in the surrounding field. Another ingenious nimrod made hatch-cover furrows like the plowed field he was hunting in from window screening and plaster of Paris, painting the final product with a mixture of paint and dirt or cornmeal so it had a pebbly texture. I've also seen plywood hatch covers with corn stubble glued on in an upright position so it lined up with the stubble in the field. It's that kind of attention to detail that will pay off in more geese.

It's also wise to make it a practice not to do a lot of walking around a pit area. Walk to it, climb in, and remain inside for the whole hunt. Walking is bound to leave unnecessary footprints in soft soil and trample any cover or stubble. Both disturbances are surprisingly visible from the air.

Hatch-cover design is the final component of a goose pit, and the most simple is a plywood cover or a piece of reinforced, heavy-duty chicken wire, with appropriate camouflage glued, painted, or tacked on, or woven into the hatch.

While this type of lid might fool birds, it presents a problem in that it makes it difficult to get clear of the pit. I've tried to overcome the problem through drills with gunning buddies where we, by the numbers, sit up and slide back; we've even attempted hitting the hatch with Samsonlike strength in hopes of throwing it free, and still other attempts where we slowly rise and try to shoot, the cover supported by our heads. No matter how we do it, that doggone cover always interferes with our swing and costs us precious seconds as well as the element of surprise.

So I'm a thorough convert to mechanized hatch covers that swing out of the way on their own accord.

By far the finest and most foolproof is the drop-away cover. The principles by which this operates are best understood if you'll imagine a pit with a solid roof covering the back half of it. The half-roof runs parallel to the longer dimension of the pit. Another section of roof, the same size, covers the front half; but rather than being permanent it's hinged to the front wall, so the roof swings down into the pit.

The drop-away part of the roof is held in an "up" position by a stick propped under it. When it's time to shoot, you knock the stick out, half the hatch drops out of the way instantly, and you're able to boil out of the pit, gun at the ready, with no preliminary messing around.

One great feature of this kind of cover is that the roof drops down. While it makes a loud bang, there's no initial wild motion above ground to spook decoying birds. Because there's some amount of room needed for this type cover to operate, it's best suited to blinds of large dimensions.

Author

The spring-loaded hatch cover is lightning-fast to open. It is best used on small pits and coffin blinds (pictured here). Note the excellent grassing job; these gunners are real pros.

The spring-loaded cover is better for smaller blinds. This design requires a hatch cover that's split in the middle and hinged at its ends—a bit like saloon-vintage swinging doors. But these doors only open one way. The "spring" is usually provided by heavy rubber tie-downs of the type used to lash gear to luggage racks on cars. Four of them are employed, though you could get by with two on a small blind.

The rubber bands are attached to the outer mating ends of the split in the hatch cover, stretched back away from it, and anchored to a stake driven into the ground behind the point where the covers are hinged to the pit frame. The angle of pull exerted on the closed covers has to be slightly downward, so they're held in a closed position. When you push up on the covers, the point of equilibrium is soon passed and the hatches literally fly open.

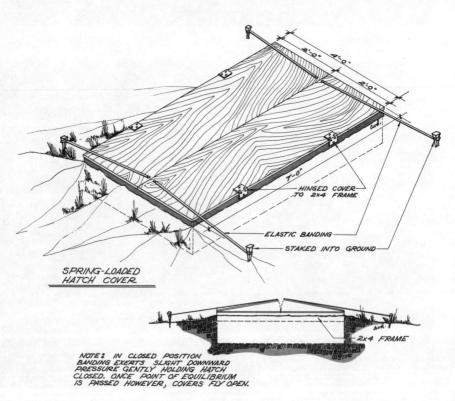

2'-0" 4'-0" 2'-0"

7'-0"

HINGED COVER
TO 2x4 FRAME

ELASTIC BANDING

STAKED INTO GROUND

SPRING-LOADED
HATCH COVER

2x4 FRAME

NOTE: IN CLOSED POSITION
BANDING EXERTS SLIGHT DOWNWARD
PRESSURE GENTLY HOLDING HATCH
CLOSED. ONCE POINT OF EQUILIBRIUM
IS PASSED HOWEVER, COVERS FLY OPEN.

One disadvantage to this kind of hatch is that the flying doors spook birds immediately. And because of the need for the elastic springs to angle downward, they're a bit difficult to build flush with ground level. But they still remain the best answer to getting a hatch off in a hurry when you're hunting from a small pit or coffin.

The plywood cut-out is a type of blind that doesn't fit into any previously discussed category, but is probably best explained here since it's usually used in conjunction with field hunting.

Indians used to sneak up within bow range of geese by hiding behind a horse and slowly working in decreasing concentric circles toward a feeding flock. It still works today—so well, in fact, that, like shooting from sink boxes, using livestock as a blind is illegal.

But phony horses aren't; so in a moment of inspiration and experimentation you might want to cut out a plywood facsimile of a horse and take a whirl at jump-shooting geese this way.

It does work. Just last year, Eli cut out a huge plywood horse, without its legs, and decorated it with a flowing mane and tail made from frayed rope. He bolted a handle to the neck and one near the tail, so two hunters could maneuver the "blind," their legs appearing to belong to the horse.

It produced some unusual effects, and not just on waterfowl. Eli first unveiled his creation in his ranch yard, walking the horse over to several goose hunters who were gathered there, and created near pandemonium. Cows bellowed and ran from the sight of it, chickens didn't lay for two days, and a horse in the corral flared his nostrils, pawed the earth, and cleared a five-foot fence. My Labrador retriever also responded. He came very close to biting Eli on the leg.

But the crazy thing worked! On a test run, we walked right into a flock of sandhill cranes, and Eli has since told me of walking up on geese as well.

Another invention of Eli's that might seem equally dubious at first, but in fact makes good sense, is his "hatch-cover periscope." This is a goose field decoy of the shell type, with two thin slits cut out of the sides. Perched on top of a pit with a permanent roof that's been cut out to accommodate a hunter's head, the decoy makes a prefectly camouflaged observation point from which to keep track of the progress of incoming birds.

PART THREE

DECOYS AND HUNTING

7 | The Art of the Decoy

The technique of luring waterfowl to decoys is as old as America and indigenous to this country. This is where the decoy was born, grew, and prospered.

The first waterfowlers to use decoys were Indians. A cache of canvasback stool, nearly letter-perfect in conformation and excellent in detail, was found in a Nevada cave in the 1930s. Anthropologists dated their manufacture to 1000 A.D.

Decoys were also used by the colonists. Samples of their crude attempts to imitate a duck are in museums and private collections today: chunks of wood with a knotty root for a head, and pieces of discarded planking shaped in the outline of a shorebird.

Around the turn of the century, decoy-making was raised to the status of an art by carvers like Corwin, Dudley, Ward, Purdew, and Wheeler. Their carefully hewn, well-engineered blocks were then in demand by market gunners and genteel sportsmen, and are prized by collectors today.

Europe, in so many ways our cultural progenitor, knew nothing of the decoy. The few that appeared across the sea were imitations

The technique of hunting ducks over decoys is as old as America and indigenous to this country.

Manitoba Department of Tourism

of American products and seldom used. There they had a "shoot" when they wanted ducks—birds driven by beaters and gamekeepers. Here ducks were truly hunted: with stealth, cunning, intelligence, and, as the decoy testifies, art and love.

It is partly this heritage, I think, that motivates waterfowlers. Keeping a rig in good repair, maintaining a duckboat, arising at three in the morning, and subjecting yourself to the worst weather nature can dish out is hard work—certainly more work than today's low limits would justify, if killing a duck were at the center of a waterfowler's universe. In that chunk of wood or cork that is a decoy lies man's attempt to imitate nature, to fit in with her schemes so perfectly that a beautiful, wise, wild creature will be lured to a hunter. More than any other symbol of waterfowling, the decoy is the essence of its charm and intrigue.

WATER DECOYS

Commercial Decoys   The most popular decoy in America today is the commercial, machine-produced block. Materials used for construction of these stool include papier-mâché, hard plastic. styrofoam, cork, rubber, soft plastic, and wood.

• The papier-mâché decoy is the cheapest decoy you can buy and, according to that old maxim about getting what you pay for, the least desirable afield. I've never seen a paper stool that really looks like a duck on the water. There's something about every one that's ever been molded that's too ornate. In addition, papier decoys simply don't stand up. Bills and heads break off, and in hard use they often turn into a pulpy, messy mass.

• Rubber decoys are a good idea that never seems to pan out in practice. They're completely collapsible and self-inflatable; so transport is no problem. Just drop their heavy ringed bottom into the water and they pop into shape; but again, that shape just doesn't look like a duck. They're always either too puffy or too droopy, and of course a stray pellet totally and literally knocks the wind out of them.

• Soft plastic decoys made of material roughly the consistency of the rubber floor mat in a car are good. I once had a set of mallard stool made of this stuff. They had an admirable ducklike shape that retained the detail and attitude around the neck and bill. What I liked about them, aside from the fact that they looked real, was that their colors were impregnated into the material, and no decoy ever needed painting. I'd recommend these as one possibility for the nimrod who doesn't want to spend a lot of time caring for his stool, at the same time pointing out that other types have pulled me more ducks.

I might also mention that there's currently a product on the market made of soft plastic that I don't think is worth a duck hunter's damn. It has every feather on a duck's body detailed into the plastic—an admirable idea, possessing a potentially great effect. But there's something about this decoy that just doesn't look right on the water—that ornateness I perceive in paper stool, as if the guy that designed them used to carve gargoyles. And, if you hunt under icing conditions, the feather detail holds ice like a vice.

• Hard plastic: while I'm not too enamored of hard-plastic decoys, feeling they glare too much, don't hold paint well enough, and crack too easily, I do recommend this type if you don't have much money to spend and plan to rig for pintail. The long slender contours of a pintail's body can't accurately be cast or worked into other cheap body materials without inviting frequent breakage of bills, necks, and tails. These will break even on plastic decoys, but not so often. In addition, plastic decoys are delightfully light and cheap—often available through mail-order houses for under $25 a dozen.

• Styrofoam is a construction material I lean toward heavily. It's cheap to manufacture, relatively tough, quite light, and its pebbly surface resists glare better than any material I know of, except perhaps cork. And, like cork, it will absorb shot until it sinks from the sheer weight of lead. While bodies are best when they're styrofoam, I don't recommend it for heads. Styrofoam has a resilient kind of toughness, but only in a large mass. The bill or neck of a decoy would quickly crumble if it were made of this stuff and subjected to only the minor stress of being carried in a gunny-sack.

The best arrangement I've seen on a styrofoam decoy is a separate, hard-plastic head, attached to the body by way of a long eyebolt threaded through the body. The heads are replaceable in the event of breakage. Remember, too, to steer clear of graceful tails in styrofoam decoys.

• Balsa, cork, and wood decoys have a lot in common. First, they *can* be the finest stool you can buy—but when they're mass-produced they seldom are. Second, if they *are* good decoys, you can bet you're going to pay a price; $60 a dozen is as cheap as I've found.

There are several features to look for in a good natural-material decoy—any decoy for that matter—and, since you'll be paying quite a price, you'd be wise to demand those features because they are what make their purchase worthwhile.

There is no right or wrong body shape for all conditions; rather, this is a matter of regional circumstance. If you're gunning on small ponds or in the protected swamps of the South, look for a decoy that comes very close to a mirror replica of a duck, with a slightly narrowed breast, rather slim body, and a high visible profile.

On the other hand, if you're gunning the Atlantic or Pacific tidewaters or large open lakes, demand a low-profile, fairly squat decoy with plenty of bottom board in contact with the water.

This type of decoy is the only design that will ride well in the heavy water you can expect when gunning open areas. The pond or swamp decoy will pitch and roll badly under these conditions.

A self-righting feature is another necessity when you're gunning over big-water decoys. Waves and winds are bound to tip your blocks over. They must be counterweighted so they will always return to a right-side-up position. This counterweighting is always of the finest quality when the lead is sunken into the body or keel, rather than tacked on. That way it won't interfere with your decoy lines.

If the section of the country you hunt is subject to icing, look for decoys with wide, fully rounded breasts and counterweighting slightly aft of center. This helps prevent ice buildup on your block. Look, too, for bills that aren't dipped too close to the water. If they are, the bills will build up a ball of ice that will throw your block out of kilter.

In terms of wood decoys, no quality product should have any evidence of lathe marks (though many of them are turned out on lathes). This includes corrugationlike gouges around the decoy's body, and starlike indentations at front and rear center of the block. Corrugations present a practical problem—they make hell of a painting job and hold ice tight. Like jig clamp marks, they also offend any serious waterfowler's artistic sensibilities, and I suspect any self-respecting duck's as well.

Commercial natural-material decoys I've either seen or used, and liked, include those made by L. L. Bean, Freeport, Maine 04032; The Orvis Company, Inc., Manchester, Vermont 05254; Great

South Bay Decoys, 284 Durkee Road, East Patchogue, New York 11772; and Wildfowler Decoys, 1309 Bay Avenue, Point Pleasant, New Jersey 08742.

FIELD DECOYS

Because they're simply propped up in a dry field, field decoys don't require the exquisite engineering—or careful appraisal on the part of the buyer—that water decoys do.

It's a pretty safe rule of thumb that if the decoys look good to you, they'll look the same way to waterfowl. There are, however, a few things to consider when purchasing a field rig.

Construction material looks the best and lasts the longest when it's either plastic or styrofoam. Papier-mâché just doesn't stand up, and I've yet to see a really good-looking papier field decoy. To my knowledge, there are no other materials used for field decoys by commercial firms.

Styles of field decoys fall into three categories. The nesting-shell type, the full-bodied type, and the silhouette.

• Silhouettes have proven worthless for me. They just don't draw today's smart birds. They might be used on shore as a confidence decoy in a duck rig, but geese seem to recognize them as fakes from way outside gun range. Silhouettes might draw geese near, but they'll never come close enough for a good shot, except, perhaps, in the confusion that is opening day.

• The nesting-shell-type decoy is the choice to make if you do a lot of moving around when you field hunt. These decoys have removable heads and the bodies fit one on top of the other, so that a dozen of these stool require about as much carrying room as a bushel basket. They're also light. Twelve complete goose decoys weigh less than fifteen pounds; so it isn't out of reason for two hunters to handle a rig of forty to fifty geese.

• The full-bodied decoy is certainly a better lure than the shell type, by mere virtue of the fact that they show an entire body, not just a back. But they're quite bulky and expensive. These are the decoys to use if you've got a permanent blind where you don't move around with the flocks. The most practical full-bodied field stool— taking price into account—is made of styrofoam.

By far the best full-bodied decoy is a stuffed bird; though at today's taxidermy prices you virtually have to learn how to do this yourself. But if you like to shoot ducks and geese, you'll find the effect astounding.

Todd Conningby and Tom Stachecki gun the geese around Southampton, Long Island. As goose hunting goes, the birds in that area are probably some of the best educated in the United States, but both these gunners regularly limit out.

How? They've put together a phenomenal rig of 120 stuffed Canada geese! I hunted with them once, and there was simply no contest. Every Canada within eyesight dropped in with supreme confidence; at one time we had over four hundred birds walking around the pit, with more arriving every moment. I could feel their wingbeats on my face as they landed close by, and one goose even cocked his head and peered down into the viewing port, looking me square in the eye! It was, indeed, the kind of day you recall the rest of your life.

But full-bodied stuffed stool aren't without a few problems. You can't hunt them in a rain because the water will mat the unoiled feathers. Rodents raise hell with them, and of course it takes a lot of time, a lot of knowledge, a lot of dedication, and a lot of geese to put a rig like that together.

BUILDING YOUR OWN DECOYS

Although outright purchase of your decoys is the shortest route to owning a rig, it's not the most sincere or satisfying way to hunt. Hand-making your own stool adds a whole new dimension of pleasure to days on the marsh.

In a decoy of your own design and manufacture you not only have an effective way to lure a bird into gun range, but an example of your collective ability as artist, craftsman, marine engineer, and natural scientist. The net result is a kind of intimacy with nature that bought blocks can never achieve, and pride—pride of ownership, pride of creation, pride in a job well done.

Decoys are currently being produced in home workshops using three materials: styrofoam, cork, and wood. My first reaction is to play down styrofoam as a mere money-saver; but cork is getting tougher and tougher to find, and this synthetic is the closest thing to it I know of.

138

Stuffed birds are the ultimate decoy, though they are not without their problems of use and manufacture.

I've tried "carving" styrofoam from the sugarlike blocks used for decorating around Christmas time and for flotation in boats, and had little success with it. The quality of this stuff is inferior for decoys—it just doesn't hold together.

On the other hand, I've made very sturdy decoys using the heat-mold method. This technique involves either making or purchasing a female mold of the species you want to cast, filling it with styro-foam "seeds," and baking it in the oven. The styrofoam swells and expands to fill every recess in the mold, and, when you crack it, you've got a decoy body ready for painting and weighting.

Decoys Unlimited, Box 69, Clinton, Iowa 52732, sells a complete kit: mold, chemicals, and necessary hardware. After the initial price of the basic equipment to cast decoys (approximately $50), you can make them for under a dollar each.

Cork makes for a wonderfully interesting decoy body; it is light and easy to shape and work; its rough, pebbly texture does an excellent job of simulating feathers.

Cork comes in two types—natural or pressed. Natural cork is just as it came off the tree—a solid piece of material. Pressed cork is small cork scraps that have literally been pressed together to form a solid sheet. Of the two, natural cork will stand up best under hard use, but it is more difficult to obtain and the more expensive to buy.

Natural cork can occasionally be purchased through lumber yards and boat yards. Another way to find it is to zero in on some cork products—a bottle cork, life preserver, or flooring—and start tracing down the source of the manufacturer's supply by letter and phone. Natural cork can occasionally be beachcombed; look for it to wash ashore after a storm.

Pressed cork is a little easier to come by. It is currently used as a creative material by artists and interior decorators, and was once the standard insulation material for refrigerators and refrigeration units.

Never overlook an old refrigerator in a dump—it might hold a dozen potential decoys. And one time I hit upon a real windfall. I drove by an old building being wrecked, to discover it had once been an ice house. The wreckers surely thought I was crazy, because once I got permission to take all the cork I wanted, I took all the big pieces they had: fully three pickup loads!

Once you find cork you've got to build it up or cut it down into rectangular chunks roughly twelve inches long by four inches high by five inches wide. This is the approximate size of a live mallard or black duck. If you want to make oversized stool, cut bigger chunks.

Most pressed cork comes in two-inch thickness; so getting the proper height will require gluing two pieces together. The best "glue" I've found for this job is the type of roofing tar known as "lap cement." Cover both surfaces to be joined (join the smoothest surfaces) with a coat of the stuff, lay the two pieces of cork on a table, and weight them down with a flat board and some iron or lead. The lap cement will set up in twenty-four hours at room temperature.

Bottom boards are necessary with cork—they give cork extra strength to hold together under heavy use, and provide a place to attach your decoy's head and keel. A bottom board can be made of one-inch clear pine stock or, better yet, ⅜-inch marine plywood. The board is cut in the precise shape the finished decoy will assume and is initially attached to the cork by gluing with lap cement.

Once the cement sets up, shaping the body comes next. For this job I've found nothing so efficient as an electric sabre-saw, a modern blade-type rasp (the commercial name of this tool is a "Shur-form"), and coarse-grit production paper.

The sabre-saw can be used as a chef would carve a beefsteak with an electric knife. Any size chunk can be lopped off here and there to form the general body conformations. As you work and shape, keep in mind the type of decoy you're fashioning. If it's a puddler, don't take any cork from the upper tail area, and very little from the upper mid-body section. These are the highest floating portions of a puddle duck's anatomy. If you're working with divers, be careful how much you remove from the entire mid-body section. With their wings folded over their backs, divers appear highest and widest through this region.

Rough edges can be smoothed out with the rasp. These rasps have interchangeable blades, one flat, one round. Use the flat blade first to work the decoy down and round off the square edges; then use the round blade for details like tail shape and the slight depression that runs down the middle of a duck's back, created by the two folded wings.

The production paper provides the final sculpturing touch and will remove any fuzzy shards of cork. Do not, however, sand the decoy smooth or you'll defeat one of the reasons for using cork— that textured suggestion of feathers.

One of the drawbacks of cork is that it isn't a structurally sound material; so if you've made a long, graceful, upswept tail, I'd recommend reinforcing it with dowels. Sharpen one or two quarter-inch dowels on one end, and drive them from the tail well into the body. This will reduce the chances of the tail breaking off.

Dowels are also used to more firmly attach the cork to the bottom board and affix the keel to the decoy. Keels should be of clear pine, one-inch stock, and an inch and a half deep. They should run nearly the length of the bottom board and have a hole drilled in their fore-end for attachment of the decoy line.

To attach the keel in the rear of the decoy, drill a ⅜-inch hole

Cork pieces are glued together with a roofing tar known as "lap cement."

through both the keel and the bottom board, and push a sharpened ⅜-inch dowel through the hole until it reaches a point just under the decoy's back. Although expansion should lock the dowels firmly in place, I like to glue mine just to make sure. Nothing beats epoxy for this job.

Attaching the front of the keel amounts to essentially the same job, *except* the dowel used for this job will also hold the head in place. The hole must be perfectly centered and aligned, with the head in mind, and the dowel long enough to reach two to three inches beyond the body into the neck.

After the head is in place it's time to paint. Another plus with cork is that, if you're making black-duck stool, painting the body is largely unnecessary. Just give the cork a quick once-over with a blowtorch and you'll achieve that smoky/burnt umber color of a black. This is one reason why cork stool prospered so on the eastern seaboard; it was the easiest way to imitate their most prized duck.

On other species, however, I'd recommend some undercoating on the cork. It helps to hold it together and deter rotting. For this job I've yet to find anything that beats another roofing material: a fibrous, tarry, silvery substance that goes by the trade name of Alumination. Using this stuff, I've had decoys in regular use for ten years and not one of them has deteriorated.

Wood decoys are a bit more time-consuming to build than cork, but, by virtue of their strength, it's possible to work quite a bit of exquisite detail into the bodies. I must confess my working stool are all cork, but I have built wooden decoys for my friends' mantels.

It's preferable to build hollow stool—I'd say essential if they're going to be used afield. The hollow bodies are lighter to carry and bob in a far more lifelike way when they're afloat than do heavy, solid stool.

The best material to use—taking availability, expense, and practicality into account—is clear white pine. Use both one- and two-inch stock, using the two-inch-wide material for the center of the body and the one-inch stuff for the top and bottom boards.

The actual construction is a matter of lamination, with those woods making up the mid-body section hollowed out with a sabre-saw. The top and bottom pieces of wood seal off the hole and make the body watertight.

Each section of laminate is first roughed out from a pattern with a

Decoy bodies are roughed out with a power sabre-saw (see body and head patterns, p. 147).

Once the cement is hardened, bodies are worked into final conformation with a rasp and covered with a protective coat of Alumination. Drilling the hole and affixing the head are the final steps.

sabre-saw or scroll saw. The pieces are then lined up, glued, and clamped. Again, no glue is better than epoxy for this job.

Roughing and shaping is done with a wood rasp of the same type used on cork. You can also save a lot of work by buying a power rasp attachment for an electric drill.

Sanding, as on cork, should be done only to smooth off rough edges and round off prominent corners. The rougher the texture of the wood, the more it will appear like feathers and the less it will glare in the sun. Standard wood-carving tools are used to work in feather detail if you choose to go this far with your creation.

When constructed this way, bottom boards of the type used on cork are unnecessary. Keels can be screwed directly to the bottom of the block with brass screws. It's still best, however, to attach the head with a dowel through the wood, slid into place from the bottom up. Remember this when hollowing out your middle laminates, and don't make the hollow so large that your head dowel passes through the cavity. It weakens the head and could cause the stool to leak.

Heads are an art unto themselves and deserve extra-special care and attention to detail. I'm firmly convinced that birds are far more likely to decoy to a top-notch head on a so-so body than to a block constructed the other way around. And from what I've seen of other duck guides, I have company in that assumption. Hunting with some of the guides in both Shinnecock and Chesapeake bays, I've noticed their huge rigs of one hundred to two hundred decoys have rough-hewn bodies, truly "blocks" that look like they were carved with an ax. But the heads were letter-perfect in every detail.

Heads are different in shape for each species, with the exception of black duck and mallard. The head profile on those two birds is, for all practical purposes, identical. In addition, it's also wise to make a few of your decoys "sleepers," an imitation of a bird with his head turned full around, either sleeping or preening his feathers. This means that you'll need two head patterns for every species of decoy you plan to carve.

The best material for a head is clear straight-grained pine, two inches thick. This is a bit thicker than is necessary for any head but the goose, but one-inch stock is too far on the thin side.

When outlining your pattern, always remember to align the bottom side of the bill perfectly with the grain of the wood. If you don't do this, the bill is sure to break the first time you carry the decoy in a gunnysack.

DECOY HEAD PATTERNS

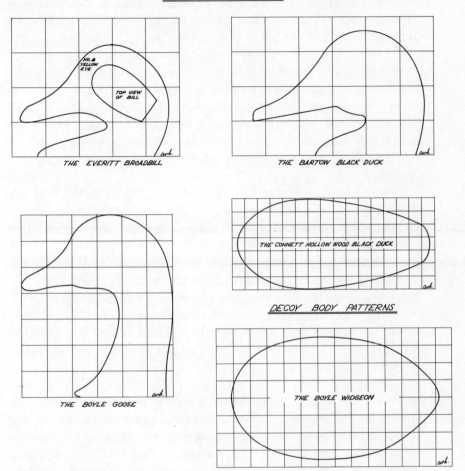

THE EVERITT BROADBILL

THE BARTOW BLACK DUCK

THE CONNETT HOLLOW WOOD BLACK DUCK

DECOY BODY PATTERNS

THE BOYLE GOOSE

THE BOYLE WIDGEON

A few decoy patterns recognized as all-time greats. The squares on the larger patterns all represent one square inch, reduced for purposes of reproduction.

When I shape a head, I prefer to begin with the bill. The bill will be the place where you stand the greatest chance of miscarving or splitting wood. When the rest of the head is unworked, it doesn't take much fortitude to throw the mistake away; but when you split a bill on an otherwise letter-perfect head, casting off your total effort is difficult. You tend to make allowances—glue here, reshape there—and end up with a second-rate job.

Until you get the feel of carving a head, go slowly. You can always take wood off, but once you've carved too much away, you can't put it back. While it would be impossible to define each step in head carving for each species, here are a few tips about roughing out heads.

• The narrowest part of most duck heads will be at the very top of the head and the bill. These widths are roughly the same.

• The thickest part of a duck head is the rounded "cheek" that flares out just below the eye.

• Intermediate thickness is in the neck, though it should flare out to nearly the width of the cheek where the neck will join the body.

Further detail is up to you, and I think you'll find "further detail" to be the most important part of your decoys. The feathers you choose to carve in, and things like the bill nail, nostril holes, and so forth, are your interpretation of what a duck should look like—your creation; your art.

Eyes I once had a friend who was a very good artist. She painted in oils, and portraits were her love and pride. She once did a portrait of me, and I watched the whole process as she worked—the ghostlike emergence of my image. When I thought she was finished, the likeness was very good, very complimentary. But she said she wasn't quite done and told me to watch carefully. She took a minute bit of white paint on a feather-fine brush and put one tiny highlight in the pupil of the eye. The image that had been merely an excellent reproduction caught life and animation with that single simple act. Even from across the room that tiny dot sparkled.

That same breath of life is achieved when you put a glass eye in a decoy—it's a magic, necessary touch.

Glass eyes are available from taxidermy supply houses, Herter's being one of them. Generally, divers have golden eyes, puddlers reddish brown eyes. The glass is cast on both ends of a wire. To install the eyes, predrill an eye hole of the same diameter as the eye you'll mount in the decoy's head. Don't go too deeply; a quarter inch is just about right.

Next, fill the hole with Plastic Wood, or a similar quick-drying wood filler. Clip the wire one-half to three-fourths of an inch away from the eye and press it in place, pushing the wire into the wood. Clean off the excess filler that will ooze out, and the eye will remain in place for the life of the decoy.

Attaching the head is next. The head dowel should already be in place on your body, so use a drill of the same diameter as the waiting dowel.

Center the head upside down in a vise (wrap the head in cloth to keep it from being marred in the vise's jaws) and drill straight and squarely down the center of the neck. Bore the hole at least two inches deep.

Use epoxy glue liberally, spreading it both on the dowel and on the flat base of the neck where it will join the decoy body. Seat the head firmly in whatever position you wish.

At this point your wood or cork decoy is nearly finished. If there are some rough spots or gaps where the neck joins body or at a point of lamination, or a carving mistake, you can rectify them by using epoxy like putty. Let it set up to a point where it won't drip or run, and press, push, and smooth it into position with your fingers. Once it hardens, it can be reworked like wood if necessary.

Weighting is the final step in construction. Unless you're extremely skillful or downright lucky, your decoy won't float on a perfectly even keel but will list one way or the other. Lead must be added in just the right spot to achieve an even keel. The decoy should also carry enough lead so it will always return to an upright position when overturned. Even if you're hunting on calm ponds this is a valuable feature, since you can literally throw your stool into position and not have to worry about righting it.

The best way to get correct weighting is to experiment by tacking lead in appropriate spots until you achieve the balance you want. Once you know the exact place and amount, melt the lead down in an iron ladle. If you let it harden and cool in the ladle, you'll have a dish-shaped chunk of lead that can be screwed into the decoy body so the edges are flush against the wood. In that position they won't interfere with your lines.

An even better way is to drill out the wood in the correct spot, and pour the hot lead directly into the hole. Get the hole soaking wet first, so the hot lead doesn't burn the wood to the point where it will fall out.

Decoy painting comes next, and this pastime is bound to have more adherents than carving by mere virtue of the fact that any decoy, commercial or hand-carved, is going to need touching up regularly.

When you actually do that touching up is important. The temptation is to do it either as an exercise to shorten a long winter or as a prayerful prelude a week before duck season. The problem with this approach is that you then end up with bright, fresh-looking decoys at a time when the real birds look dowdy and dull. The gaudy colors you think of when someone mentions "mallards" or "woody" don't occur until late November or December; so I think it a wise move to delay painting your stool until then.

The use the block will get during the rest of the season will scrape and scuff it up a bit, the sun will dull it, the water will chip it, and you'll go into the next season with slightly beat-up birds that look very much like their natural counterparts.

Another common practice I don't agree with is painting the majority of your stool as drakes. There's theoretical and artistic justification for making mostly drakes; supposedly they show up better, and certainly they are pretty to paint and behold. But the drake, visually, is the best-defined of the species. You could never miss spotting the difference between a drake mallard and a drake black, or a drake whistler and drake broadbill. However, the hens are a different matter. Rather subtle differences exist between hens of all the species; so when you include mostly hens in your rig, it's bound to have a broader appeal to a wider variety of ducks—and you're sure to enjoy more shooting as a result.

Whenever you're ready to paint, you'll need a model; and there's no better model than the feathered carcass of a duck you recently shot—another reason for painting stool in the middle of the season.

Another way to find a model is to buy a hand-carved and -painted replica of the type of duck you use in your decoy spread. They make the most attractive mantel pieces, and collecting them is a fast-growing pastime among waterfowlers. One of the best carvers I know of is John Kouchinsky, 284 Durkee Lane, East Patchogue, New York 11772. His birds are quite reasonable; an average duck costs around $30.

A third way—the easiest, but not necessarily the most rewarding—is to buy a decoy paint kit. Separate kits, with all the colors you'll need for both hens and drakes, are available for major species of ducks and geese. Most companies that put them together also provide a paint-by-the-numbers chart so you have an excellent idea of what goes where. Herter's Inc., and Cabela's, 812 13th Avenue, Sidney, Nebraska 69162, are two dependable suppliers of quality paint.

Without a paint-by-the-numbers kit you'll have to mix your own paints, but for me, and most other gunners I know, the effort is surely worthwhile. The product is more truly yours, and there's an element of build-a-better-mousetrap inventiveness: that one dynamite color mix that will consistently pull ducks like hungry boys to hamburger stands.

Although some painters still favor oil-base paints, I'm a recent and thorough convert to acrylics. These latter are completely weather- and waterproof, and are far easier to find in stores than flat outdoor oil paint. Another fine feature of acrylics is that they don't hold ice as tightly as other paints—a real blessing if you'll be hunting in cold weather. But most important, acrylics dry fast—in a half hour in a warm room. This means you can do an entire set of decoys, from base coats to final feathering, in a day.

I get the best results by buying a quart of black and a quart of white, and then working from tints to mix specific colors. There are some exceptions, however: I mix up a full quart of an off-brown for a common base coat on several species of hen birds, for example.

As you blend colors to imitate a particular shade on your model, remember that the paint is going to be of a slightly different shade when it's dry. To test that shade quickly, rub it on a neutral background like common cardboard with a cloth. Apply it thinly, then hold it close to a light or in full exposure to the sun. It will dry in a matter of minutes, revealing the precise shade your decoy will become when dry.

Another pitfall when painting is artificial light. Ideally, you should test your colors in sunlight. If this is impossible, use only incandescent lighting around your work area. Fluorescent lighting is strange stuff, and it won't give you an accurate color reading. I once painted the bills on forty-eight broadbill stool under this type of light. The color looked perfect as it went on, but when I rigged the stool in sunlight those bills turned out to be the brightest, most un-duck-like robin's egg blue I've seen then or since! Dick Freidah dropped by the blind that day, took one look, blinked, and muttered diplomatically, "I know broadbill are also called bluebill, but don't you think you went a little far?"

The technique of painting decoys generally involves a thick base coat that roughly approximates the main colors on a particular bird. Black duck, for example, receive a coat of yellow brown on the head, and a smoky, burnt umber body (assuming they're not natural cork). I also feather in a dark brown stripe along the top of the head and back of the neck with my finger. A drake broadbill gets an entire coat of dark, smoky gray, a lighter gray on his back, and an oyster-white side.

Next comes feather detail. There are as many ways of achieving this as there are species of duck.

• The easiest way to create an impression of feathers is to take a near-dry brush and lightly sweep it across the area to be feathered. Use slightly lighter paint than the base coat. It creates highlights, much as feathers do, and is particularly effective on natural cork stool. This technique is most often employed when you're in a hurry or have a hell of a big rig—100-plus birds. When you're doing that many decoys and try to work in any kind of detail, you're bound to run out of patience at around the thirtieth one and revert to the easiest method anyway.

• Another wild way to achieve basically the same effect is to mix a light-color acrylic with a dark-color oil-base paint. On the drake broadbill, for example, the back should have some feather detail. If you take a light gray acrylic and stir in some dark gray oil-base paint, the paint won't mix; but the oil-base paint will break up into little globs, separate and distinct from the acrylic. It will paint on the same way—in tiny polka dots. The acrylic will dry first; so then all you need do is take one swipe with a folded cloth and you'll smear the still-wet oil paint so it looks very much like feathers. Always brush the cloth in the direction the feathers would normally point.

• Combing is a more detailed technique that, taking time and effort into account, is the most desirable for the effect I hope to achieve in a decoy. It involves the initial base coat, then a fresh coat of darker paint over the base coat. For example, on a black duck or hen mallard head, your base coat is a brownish yellow, and the second coat a darker body brown. Let that second coat begin to set up, just to the point where it's tacky to the touch, and then take a comb and rake featherlike patterns through the paint. The tooth marks reveal the undercoat, creating both a texture and a feather-like appearance. For delicate head-feather detail, use the fine part of a comb. For thicker body feathers, use the coarse teeth.

• Individual feather painting is tedious and time-consuming, but is it pretty! You need an extremely fine brush, and will have to thin down your acrylics a bit to keep the paint flowing smoothly. I'm firmly convinced such detail looks every bit as good to an incoming duck as it does to a human, but such artistry isn't without its price. You can bet your last shotshell that when you make working stool so detailed, they're going to be begged, borrowed, bought, or stolen from you by admiring friends for mantel pieces. So I save those labors of love for Christmas presents and keep my working stool a bit on the homespun side.

Fine details like the speculum, contrasting feather borders, and nostril holes are the final step when you're painting a decoy. Some gunners ignore the real detail, like nostril holes and the nail on the end of some birds' bills, but I always paint them in. The more your decoy looks like a real duck, the more ducks it's bound to fool— and those little touches satisfy the repressed artist in me.

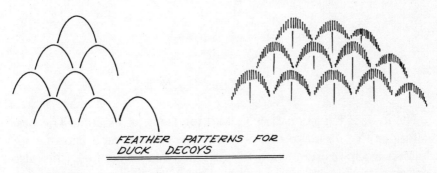

FEATHER PATTERNS FOR
DUCK DECOYS

Drawing in each individual feather is tedious, but beautiful to behold. Here are two feather patterns in common use.

Rigging Decoys   You should always check out your lines and anchors twice a year: around midseason and before opening day. A few seconds retying a worn knot or replacing a rotted line is a much wiser investment in time than buying or recarving decoys you lose.

Not just the best but the *only* line with which to rig a decoy is nylon. It won't rot, it's resistant to wear, and it packs phenomenal strength into a very small diameter. My favorite line is parachute cord, testing out above two hundred pounds of strength. I never cease to be amazed at how quickly a three-pound decoy in a light breeze can chew through most lines, and this is the only stuff I've found that will stand up. When it is ready to let go, it is so frayed that you can't help but notice the weakness—still another plus. Use only green or, better yet, olive drab lines; any other color shows up readily when viewed from above. Both Herter's and Cabela's stock these lines.

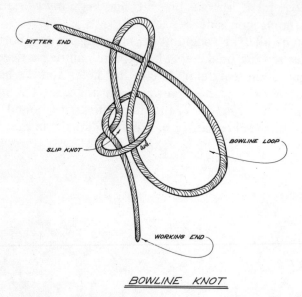

BITTER END

SLIP KNOT

BOWLINE LOOP

WORKING END

BOWLINE KNOT

Nylon does have one drawback: it tends to slip its knot. The best solutions I've found to this problem are 1) burn each end of your line so a slip-resistant blob of melted nylon is created (this also prevents fraying and unraveling); 2) wrap the line twice around the handle you're tying on to; and 3) tie only bowline knots. The quickest way to tie a bowline is to make a common slip-loop three inches below the end of your line. Thread the working end through the decoy or anchor twice, then pass the end through the hole of the slipknot. Pull the slipknot tight, and you've got a bowline.

Anchors   Like lines, I have definite opinions about anchors too. Chasing decoy anchors that are bottom-bouncing in the teeth of a strong wind or stout tide ages one fast, and the only anchor I've found that will hold bottom under these conditions is the mushroom type. Although commercially produced mushroom decoy anchors are available in steel, I prefer to cast my own of lead. By virtue of its weight, lead is more efficient than steel.

To make the anchor, I pour six ounces of melted lead into a muffin tin (I use twelve ounces for a goose decoy). While still molten, I inset a heavy copper wire into the lead, bent into a fist-sized half-ring roughly comparable to the shape of the Greek letter omega. Such wire can be bought in any electrical supply house.

In use, the weight not only has that efficient mushroom shape, it also can be slipped around the decoy's head after the line is wound around its body, helping to hold the line fast and discouraging tangles.

Cabela's Inc. sells this type of weight commercially. They also stock a rather ingenious decoy anchor that looks a little like a minia-

Author

A sampling of commercial decoys and types of anchors. Clockwise from the top: Victor mallard with homemade mushroom anchor; Trend-D-Coy Canada goose with commercial ring-type anchor; Herter's broadbill with home-cast ring-type anchor; and Herter's black duck with commercial grapple-type mushroom anchor.

155

ture bucket, with the bottom cut out. The bucket/anchor slips over the decoy's bill and is held fast by a rubber band attached to the anchor that runs around the back of the head. This is the only type of anchor I've found that will never unravel your decoy line during transport, but it doesn't have quite the holding power of the mushroom. It's sure a blessing to use in protected waters though.

Line Length   The amount of line you rig on a decoy should be a function of the depth of the water you're hunting over. Except in small ponds where there's no current or wind, you'll need a line at least three times as long as the water is deep. This length line then results in an angle of pull sufficient for the anchor to get a purchase on the bottom.

In the case of divers, often gunned in ten feet or more of water, the above rule of thumb can result in anchor lines longer than a Kansas well rope; so a few words about wrapping tricks might be in order.

Wrapping line across the back, from head to tail in a figure-eight pattern, is the most efficient wrap. It gathers line up quickly, and when the anchor is slid around the head, you've got a tight fit that won't unwind in a gunnysack to create a mind-boggling tangle.

But most diver decoys don't have that handy upswept tail to latch on to. With them, you have to wrap the line around back and belly — a slightly slower process but handy when it's time to rig out. Just hold the decoy by the head with the tail facing the water and throw the anchor. The line twirls off the decoy like monofilament from a spinning reel.

When you're dealing with truly long lines, or are in a real hurry to get wrapped, double your lines. This is a technique I've seen used when I've been punty shooting on Long Island's Great South Bay. When it's time to pick up the stool, the party boat, usually a thirty-to-forty-foot cabin cruiser, lies upwind of the rig. The wind then pushes the boat down through the stool, and two men with long boat hooks snare decoys and ship them around. Wrappers have to keep pace or face an impossible tangle, and they do this by first slipping the weight over the decoy head, then winding the line around the body doubled. On the last turn of line they throw a half-hitch, loosely securing the line in place. While the line would never remain wrapped if the stool were carried in a sack, it's a fully functional method when the decoys are merely tucked in a cabin and left there.

Decoy Transport   The best way to transport your decoys is in a tender or, more realistically for the bulk of this country's gunners, in a "trailerable" duckboat. They don't get much banging around when carried so, and have a longer life span.

Of course, circumstance often dictates a different arrangement: namely, humping across the marshes with your stool in a bag. I've seen many ingenious devices for making this job easier—racked boxes, special duffels, even an apron arrangement with pockets for individual decoys; but nothing so far has beat two burlap bags, tied together.

Just lash a small portion of the rim of one bag to another; fill both bags with an equal weighting of decoys and sling them over your shoulder, one bag in front, one in back.

Using this method I've carried fifty stool in four bags, together with my gun and my shellbox, covering nearly a half mile of marsh without dropping so much as a decoy. But I must admit the trek involved rest stops too numerous to mention and badly bowed legs by the time that particular day was done.

Antique Decoys   As the crafts associated with waterfowling have prospered in recent years, so has interest increased in objects associated with duck-hunting antiquity, most notably old decoys.

I've seen some outrageous shams labeled "antique" decoys. On a recent trip to the East I walked into a chi-chi Delaware shop and discovered they were selling Herter's tenite black-duck stool, circa 1956, as antique decoys—and at fifteen bucks a crack!

For all practical purposes, no mass-produced decoy is worth more than a buck or two. Plastic and paper stool are easy to identify as such, but wood is sometimes more difficult.

Corrugation in the body—little humps and dips like the corrugation in packing board—is a sure giveaway the block was chipped out on a lathe. If you see no corrugation, look then for jig marks, usually starlike lines a half-inch long, that radiate from a center hole. The jig marks will appear in the front and tail end of the decoy, at a point in the very center of the wood. Realize, too, that these jig marks can be covered over with paint or wood filler, but close scrutiny should show some signs of their presence.

Another truism is that no freshly painted decoy rates as an antique. Any dealer who knows his business is aware of this, and would never paint a decoy himself or buy one in that condition. Duck hunters, however, might well have some venerable block in their rig that they regularly paint, so keep a weather eye peeled in that direction. I once allowed myself to be talked out of a beautiful sleeper by a collector who happened by my blind.

Repairs of any nature usually render an antique worthless too; bills are the easiest part of a decoy to break, so check there first.

On a more positive side, there are some signs to look for that will point in the direction of a real antique. The type of bird the block depicts is one.

With the exception of snipe, shorebird hunting has been illegal since the turn of the century; so any shorebird that wears age is bound to be of value. Swan decoys are priceless for the same reason.

Solid cast-iron duck decoys rate highly with collectors too. These birds were used to weight down the outboard wings of a sink box. Several years ago a friend of mine dredged up one of these iron birds with his clamboat, and sold it for $60.

Duck and goose decoys, because there have been so many of them made, are the least valuable as a category. But individuals can be worth a great deal.

Aside from signs of sheer age, look for uniqueness in a decoy: some unusual adaptation, design, or origin that might set it apart from the ordinary.

Unusual head positions—sleepers, preeners, and underwater feeders—are much more valuable than an ordinary head. John Kouchinsky, a good friend, bird carver and decoy collector, recently showed me a most interesting goose stool that had a stabilizer carved into its body. The stabilizer amounted to an extension of the decoy underbody that flared out like a squared shingle beneath the carved tail, exposing more flat surface to the water and dampening any tendency to rock in heavy weather. That kind of old-time ingenuity is worth a lot of money to collectors.

Malcolm Fleming, one of the foremost authorities on decoy collecting in this country and a waterfowl artist of wide repute, once showed me a sandhill-crane decoy from New Mexico that had graceful, gentle lines on a par with a fine abstract sculpture like "Bird in Flight."

Construction materials can add value to an antique too. One of the most beautiful decoys I've ever seen was a piece of driftwood fashioned into a duck's body. Some bayman found the piece of wood, recognized its potential, and slapped a head on it. The wood was a knotty hunk of pine, and the wear the softer wood endured made the knots protrude, closely resembling feathers. Decoys' heads made of roots are another feature high on collectors' lists.

A name stamped in the bottom of a decoy increases its value too; especially if it's the name of one of the great decoy carvers of old: a Corwin, Crowell, Wheeler, Smith, or tidewater artisan of similar repute. However, most of the decoys carved by the recognized greats have already been snapped up by collectors; so view any "find" you might make in an antique shop with a jaundiced eye.

How much are these decoys worth? I'd say a genuinely old, hand-carved, but otherwise nondescript decoy in weathered, broken, or cracked shape should bring around fifteen bucks. The price then increases as you approach mint condition, and that state of grace will probably cost you sixty to seventy-five dollars.

Unusual features on the same decoy will, of course, bring more, and the rarest and best examples of past waterfowlers' art have commanded prices in the thousands of dollars.

8 | Setting Decoys

The waterfowler who lures birds to decoys is like a painter, working his canvas in the half-light of morning to create an illusion of nature and life. His raw materials are water, marsh, blocks of wood, and a sense of proportion.

"This decoy goes here" is the unspoken decision, born of careful observation and past experience.

Line, anchor, and hand-hewn block of cork or wood sing through the chill air like the broad stroke of a brush, landing with a splash. The decoy bobs upright, then swings into place as it's snubbed short by the tightened line. It yaws in a puff of breeze, suddenly alive.

"Now another over there, and one by my feet."

Slowly the picture takes shape. The placid gray water gains dimension and depth as decoy after decoy is placed, carefully gauged to complement the whole.

Hummocked tufts of marsh grass mark the borders; the rich golds and soft reds of dawn begin to creep across the sky and are mirrored in the calm. The last ripple from the last decoy drifts outward and dies.

"Not quite right," is the critical judgment. A decoy just beyond good gun range is pulled in a bit closer, and another that has lost its balance weight and rides awry is retired for the day.

A soft breeze again stirs the incredible stillness of the marsh. You smile, suspecting it will blow the rest of the day, and watch as it sets the stool to motion, swinging on their lines. It is so like a flock of real birds that you do a double take, just to make sure a black didn't sneak into the rig when you weren't looking.

Not to shoot—it's still before gunning hours. But a bird coming in while you were still in the rig would be the finishing touch, and a good omen.

You go back to the blind to admire your creation over a cup of coffee; a few puffs on a smoke, and the cold muzzle of your Lab nudging your hand. The dawn explodes in rainbow hues. It's the prettiest time of all; those last few introspective moments before the gun.

In the final analysis, setting a rig of decoys is an expression of personal style, taste, and experience. There's a hunch factor that operates among decoy hunters: that if you put a certain decoy over here or two way out there, the rig will draw birds more effectively. Balancing the configuration of your stool against things like locale, weather, wind velocity, and waterfowl behavior creates more possibilities of design. Consequently, no two sets are ever exactly alike.

There are, however, some rules that apply to all decoy rigs, rules that provide at least a frame for the picture you paint.

• Waterfowl will be attracted most readily to their own kind. One of the few constants of decoy hunting is that you must use diving-duck decoys if you're after divers, and puddle-duck decoys if you're after puddlers. This caveat has further subtleties of individual species too; a black duck will come to black-duck stool more readily than mallard stool, though because of similarities in habit and food preference, both feel rather free to drop in on one another. Chances get slimmer, however, when you try to lure a black to pintail decoys or, less likely, woody or widgeon stool. This same tendency is exhibited by diving species, but I haven't found it quite so critical as with puddlers.

• Diving ducks want a lot of open water for a landing spot, open water that should be engineered into your decoy pattern. Puddle ducks will be glad to flutter down into a rather tight space right among the decoys. Generally, you'll find you can anticipate the spot where a diver will land; puddlers will be less predictable.

• Spacing of individual blocks is dependent on the weather. Dur-

The waterfowler works his canvas in the half-light of morning to create an illusion of nature and life.

Ted Collins, Browning Arms

ing pleasant weather, spread them out. In bad weather, bunch them up.

On bluebird days, ducks and geese are at their leisure. They feed at will and bask in the warm temperatures. As a consequence, birds tend to spread out—not individuals equidistant from their partners, but in loose groups of two to five birds, one group here, one group there, the entire configuration of scattered individuals making up the flock. Placement of decoys should reflect this tendency.

In cold blustery weather you should pull your decoys into a tight knot. This copies the behavior of the real birds, who develop a sense of urgency about them. They become agitated and nervous, feeding amid the protection from wind and waves provided by their partners.

How close is close? I've seen rigs with some blocks no more than six inches apart, though a foot or two is more my idea of right. This close proximity seems to violate a universal caveat about decoy hunting, that no block should touch another; but that rule is misunderstood.

When a decoy hangs up with another—gets it's anchor line entwined or otherwise remains glued to a neighboring block for minutes at a time—that's bad, and a detriment to your rig. But when decoys bump into each other as they yaw on their lines, then quickly disengage, that's perfectly natural and even desirable. Real birds in real flocks are doing this all the time. They get into fights or they try to steal another's food. I once watched a black duck get into a fight with, of all things, a decoy!

John Kouchinsky and I were rigged out in the spring, shooting with a camera, and an incoming black tolled the tail end of the stool, then started preening. With his head buried in his back feathers, he didn't see the approach of a decoy as it swung on its anchor line. He very nearly shot out of the water as he was bumped. It looked like the duck had been goosed. He turned in fury, pecked at the decoy's head and back and, apparently satisfied that he'd won, indignantly swam another ten feet toward the head of the rig before he resumed preening.

Bunching up your blocks occasionally will be in order even on bluebird days. If there are plenty of ducks in the air and they're ignoring your well-distributed spread, pull your blocks in a little closer. No matter the weather, ducks always sleep and rest in close proximity, and you might be hunting during a resting rather than a feeding period.

• Oversized blocks. These are decoys larger than life-size. Because they're so visible, ducks can see them from far off and they have good drawing power. But there's a fine line to tread when choosing to use or not to use oversize stool. Ducks also feel there's safety in numbers; so the more oversized blocks you use, the more room they require for transport and the smaller total number of decoys you'll be able to carry and rig.

When I'm limited in the bulk of decoys I can lug around, I usually bring a half dozen or so oversized decoys, and keep the rest of my blocks natural size. The oversized stool then provide maximum visibility when waterfowl pass by at a distance. As they come in for a closer look, they then pick out the smaller blocks and, lured by their numbers, decoy freely.

• When rigging mixed-sized blocks, always place your oversized decoys where they can most easily be seen by waterfowl on the wing.

• "Confidence" decoys are imitations of species that you don't necessarily wish to shoot but that are normally found among a contented flock of waterfowl. I've occasionally seen seagull decoys used as confidence stool, but coot and, especially, geese are more commonly used. Geese have two attractive features as confidence stool: they're wise birds, so their presence in a rig indicates all is A-O.K., and their large size allows them to function as an oversized decoy.

Confidence decoys have another function. Because they're plainly different from your other blocks, you can use them to mark distance from your blind or boat, thereby providing an accurate gauge of ranges.

• LOCATING THE SET. You'll get the most birds to decoy if the wind is blowing across the blind, slightly quartering your back.

This is one of the most common mistakes I've seen on the part of waterfowlers; they set their rig in relation to their blind so the wind blows directly from them to their stool. Waterfowl decoy right into the wind, and such a blind location then has incoming birds looking right down your gun barrel.

If they don't spot you before touching down, they'll flare as you rise to shoot. Waterfowl coming straight at you also give the illusion of taking the entire season to get into gun range, tempting the unknowing hunter to shoot early. And they'll often sit down on the far edge of the rig, rather than coming in close.

In terms of divers, there's also a "safety" factor inherent with a crosswind. Open water, to a diving duck, is the same as safety. When your rig is engineered to draw a bird directly to shore, his approach zeros him on land, a thing he likely associates with danger. A wind blowing parallel to land, on the other hand, gives the illusion of plenty of water ahead of the spread. Even though land might be quite close to the bird's left or right, that open water ahead is a persuasive hint at a safe harbor.

But these pragmatics aren't without their price. Even though they cost you shots, a straight-on toll holds a reward all its own. In this set, waterfowl come in breast exposed, wings fanning the air, and legs extended in anticipation of touchdown.

The looking is far more important than the killing when you're hunting with decoys, and a bird tolling directly to you is one of the most beautiful sights in the out-of-doors.

A wind blowing toward you is unworkable in most situations since incoming birds must swing over land and you to approach the decoys. As a matter of fact, there's an old saying about the man who hunts ducks with the wind on his face: he should be hunting with someone else.

• WATERFOWL VISION. Knowing something about what and how waterfowl see is of immeasurable help when decoy hunting. The visual acuity of ducks and geese is an old subject of controversy and myth-making. I can remember reading an article where a guy painted "fake" and "traitor" in bright red all over his decoys, and supposedly brought birds in. Yet you hear so much about the necessity of camouflage. Where, then, lies the truth?

In fact, waterfowl have poor eyesight by one set of human standards. They lack our degree of binocular vision.

The close-set position of human eyes allows us to focus on an object using both eyes at once. The triangulationlike view we get of that object, coupled with the blurred areas in front of and behind the focal point, allow us to perceive depth and distances rather accurately. Put a pencil in the ground five feet away and an identical pencil twenty feet away and we can quickly judge both to be about the same size; though if you measured them with a yardstick held at arm's length, the distant pencil would appear far smaller than the near one.

Waterfowl, on the other hand, have their eyes set in the sides of their heads. If you look at a duck's profile, the entire eye, pupil and iris, appears nearly on a flat plane. Look at the same bird full-faced, and very little but the cornea is evident.

This difference constitutes an evolutionary adaptation for protection. With this type of sight system, waterfowl literally can see from the back of their heads. Sitting on a pond or lake, or in a close-cropped grainfield, any predator would be quickly discovered. But it also limits waterfowl to looking out of one eye at a time, which robs them of binocular vision.

Think back to the last duck you saw pass overhead. When waterfowl want to examine something, they cock their heads to one side, viewing it with one eye rather than looking straight ahead. Now you try the same. You'll note that you now view the world on a single plane—two-dimensional instead of three.

Ducks Unlimited

A duck's wide-set eyes rob him of much of the human's binocular vision, but they allow him, literally, to see "out of the back of his head," and provide a detailed view of the world around him.

Without the ability to judge depth, the ability to judge speed and distance is also altered, explaining, in part, why waterfowl so regularly have collisions with telephone wires, buildings, and aircraft. They simply don't have the mechanisms needed to determine how fast these things are looming up. The same limitations will be revealed if you carefully watch a duck land. Waterfowl bumble into a landing, with much hovering and a slow descent as the ground comes up to meet them. At the last moment they simply abandon flight and splash down. This will be most obvious if you're ever fortunate enough to witness the circus that occurs when a flock of ducks or geese attempt a landing on ice. They'll skid, slide, lose their balance, and, more often than not, end up flat on their stomachs, wings askew, like some portly squire's first adventure on ice skates.

Contrast this, then, with a bird of prey: a hawk or an eagle. The latter are capable of pulling out of a hundred-mile-an-hour dive to skim over land closely enough to snare a mouse that is surely hugging the ground in the bargain. Birds of prey are masters at judging distance, and their eyes are set quite close together.

Granting a waterfowl's characteristically poor depth perception, then, the relative size of things and their spatial relationships aren't too important. An oversize decoy can be seen from afar more readily than a normal-sized block, but, as the bird approaches, any difference in proportions makes little impression because it isn't that perceptible. The same is essentially true of your rig's distance from your blind or boat. Some gunners I've hunted with have theorized that birds weren't coming in because their rig was too close to shore, and moved the whole set out five yards.

While it's certainly true that heavily gunned birds will get shore-shy, jackassing the rig out a few feet isn't going to do any good because the birds are incapable of determining or assessing such a critical "safe" distance.

There is, however, another side to the coin. Look again at that one eye that will be looking at you. The pupil is quite large, and the eye itself is, in proportion to the duck's head, far larger than the ratio that exists in humans. It's a good bet that a duck does a better job of perceiving detail than a human. He lacks depth perception, but on that flat-plane view of the world around him he's better equipped than you to pick out a spent shell casing, a badly painted decoy, or the sunlight glinting off an upturned face.

RIGGING DECOYS FROM SHORE

Puddle ducks are creatures tied equally to land and water. Their legs are set close to the middle of their body, for walking on dry land as well as paddling, and their broad wings allow for slow, precise flight. They can thread their way between towering trees to flutter down on a quiet pond, or follow a twisting riverbed with swallowlike grace.

Coves, cuts, backwaters, sloughs, and small ponds are the places to locate a puddle-duck decoy spread. It's there the birds go for feed and sanctuary.

• Coves and river backwaters that open onto big water are generally my first choice when choosing a place to set puddler decoys. These places not only afford the natural protection puddle ducks normally seek—they open onto probable flyways where birds trading over open water can see the rig.

The most popular configuration for hunting a cove is the C. This was the first pattern I ever learned, shown to me by a kindly old gent who used to walk the marshes every morning.

After passing by my blind a half dozen mornings or so, he stopped to chat one day and, in the course of our conversation, informed me that my black-duck decoys, set off Hollins Point, could be complemented by "steamrolled corn and oats, advertised on an electric caller," and I still wouldn't get any respectable black within gun range.

It was a tough decision to make; the location of my blind faced seaward on a long spit of land, and there were so many birds trading back and forth out there! But I tried his advice, pulling my blocks back from open water and into a small cove the next morning.

I didn't see how the rig would work; hell, passing birds could barely see me in this spot. But I cleaned house that morning with my three-bird limit, sweet success indeed for a fourteen-year-old kid and a bolt-action shotgun.

There are two variations on the C rig: one for pleasant weather, one for bad weather. On bluebird days, open the letter way up, with your farthest stool just inside gun range, and blocks arranged in loose groups of three to five birds. If trading waterfowl don't respond, or you're hunting a storm, tighten up the rig so the majority of decoys lie to one side of the letter—the side closest to your blind. The C then begins to assume a J shape.

In the C configuration, incoming birds should toll to the center, to the open-water portion of the letter. As you pull stool closer together, they'll tend to fly directly over the bulk of the stool, and will look to land toward the upwind half of the main concentration.

• Drainage sloughs and natural cuts in a marsh are my second choice as a place to rig out. Puddlers often follow these riverlike ribbons of water for miles, like a hiker follows a trail. In most circumstances your rig won't be visible from afar due to obscuring vegetation. The duck will suddenly find himself on it, and won't have a lot of time to decide if he wants in or not.

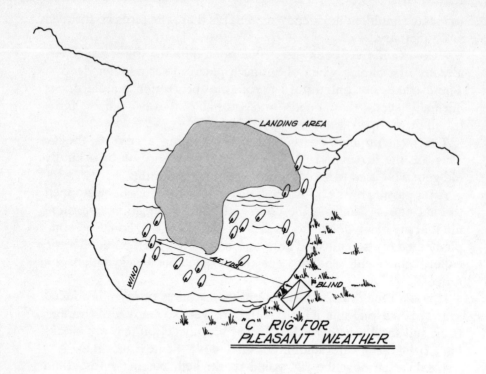

LANDING AREA

45 YDS

WIND

BLIND

"C" RIG FOR
PLEASANT WEATHER

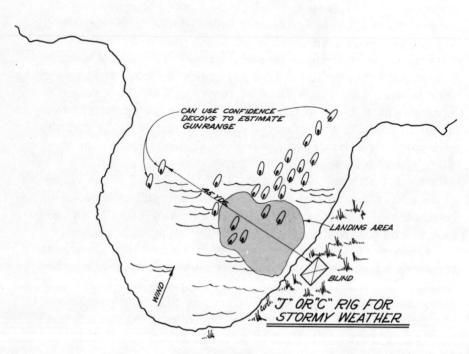

CAN USE CONFIDENCE
DECOYS TO ESTIMATE
GUNRANGE

45 YDS

LANDING AREA

WIND

BLIND

"J" OR "C" RIG FOR
STORMY WEATHER

For this reason, I like to prepare incoming birds for what lies ahead by rigging one or two oversized stool between one hundred and one hundred fifty yards downwind. Don't set out more than this or you might find birds landing there. Place these decoys close to the shore you'll be hunting.

The type of rig you set in front of your blind should be largely a function of the width of the cut. If the opposite shore is within gun range, run your decoys in a half-moon pattern, with the bulk of the blocks close to your blind. This will have a braking effect. Even if the bird doesn't particularly want to drop in, he will slow up, affording a good pass shot. If he does choose to drop in, he'll probably do so at the very head of the stool.

Because birds will happen on this decoy spread quite suddenly, even the presence of those two decoys one hundred yards downwind might not be enough to prepare them for touchdown. They might want to make a second pass before setting in. If, however, they still fiddle and fidget around on the second pass, dump them at the first opportunity; they probably won't toll right anyway.

Wide expanses of water, where the opposite shore is outside of gun range, require a decoy configuration that assumes a tadpole shape. Arrange your blocks so the head and body of the tadpole are in front of your blind, with the tail curving slightly out from shore. This should result in a corralling effect, with the incoming bird picking up the tail and sticking to the inshore side of it. The landing area will be between shore and the tail, or in the very middle of the bulk of the blocks; so it's wise to leave a landing hole in the head of the tadpole.

• PONDS. This category can be the least productive or most productive place you'll ever set a decoy. If a pond is merely one of many in an area, without any special food or attraction, or if it's close to lakes, bays, or rivers and the weather's pleasant, chances are it will be a poor place to put a blind.

But if it's the only water around in an area rich in grain or other foods, or if it provides a haven from churning waves on larger bodies of water, a pond can provide the fastest gunning of your life.

Placing a decoy spread in a pond involves essentially the same patterns and precepts as those you'd use in a cove: a C configuration set somewhere near the leeward shore. Scatter your decoys when the pond is used for water and rest after feeding periods, and tighten them up into the J when the storm chases birds off big water.

One exception to this rule involves larger ponds that are surrounded by obscuring cover. Make every effort to determine the direction from which the majority of birds will be approaching, and place your decoys so the rig is the first thing incoming birds see.

One of my most frustrating experiences involved my failure to do just that. Bob Yaskulski and I were hunting a marshy cove that faced into Moriches Bay. A sudden storm came up, blowing hard from the north, and we lost our lee. Lousy luck, but we theorized that, if the blow continued, ducks would soon tire of fighting the weather and pour into a fresh-water pond we knew of a half mile behind us.

Although we were correct in our prediction, we failed to recognize that the ducks would take the shortest route to the pond rather than approaching the place by flying into the wind. That shortest route found them flying over the tallest stands of vegetation around the pond—vegetation that obscured our spread from that direction. As a result, the birds plopped down in open water, *then* they noticed our stool. A few ducks made a half-hearted attempt to swim over, then started building into a raft, remaining at the opposite end of the pothole.

One of the toughest decisions in the world is to start messing and moving around, changing your rig when there are birds in the air. You always hope, and half expect, at least a few birds will choose you to drop in on. So we elected to wait it out—and didn't get a shot.

The combination of long-range visibility and the undeniable pulling power of live "decoys" brought every bird into that real raft. By rights, we should have moved the whole rig near to where they were resting, even though we would have had the wind in our face and spooked birds in the bargain.

Rigging Puddlers from a Point   While puddle ducks are ordinarily attracted to marshy inland areas, this rule has exceptions like any other. When birds are so heavily gunned that they become shore-shy, you can occasionally get good shooting if you'll rig off a point. Open water is the reason: like divers the puddlers become accustomed to its safety, and decoys rigged off a point jutting out into a bay or lake create that safe illusion of open water.

When setting out stool in this situation, the I formation usually draws the best. This pattern is nothing more than a long, narrow grouping of closely spaced stool. I favor bunching up the blocks whenever shooting off a point, nice weather or not, and I like to use lots of decoys—thirty to forty if possible.

The placement of the configuration is rather important. On any

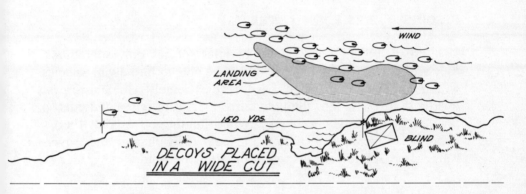

WIND

LANDING AREA

150 YDS.

BLIND

DECOYS PLACED IN A WIDE CUT

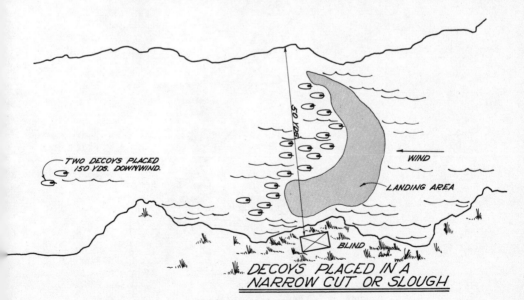

TWO DECOYS PLACED 150 YDS. DOWNWIND.

150 YDS.

WIND

LANDING AREA

BLIND

DECOYS PLACED IN A NARROW CUT OR SLOUGH

point, whether it's in a lake, river, or salt water, there's going to be a lee, an area where wind, waves, and currents are cut off by the jutting land. Rig that I right along the line of the lee, the place where large waves or strong currents sweep by the calmer protected waters.

Place your decoys remembering that birds will swing over this spread from tail to head and, if they are sufficiently fooled, that they'll land toward the middle of the configuration. If they hop-scotch across this portion of your set without dropping in, the odds say they'll pass by the front half entirely, and either make a second pass or head for other climes.

RIGGING DIVERS FROM SHORE

Although points are good for puddler species only sometimes, they are the only place you'll regularly be able to lure diving species within range of a shore blind. Divers are extremely reluctant to pass over land or come into the tight surroundings of coves and cuts so favored by mallards and blacks. When hunting off a point there's good odds that you'll be able to engineer their characteristic over-water approach to your decoys, no matter the wind.

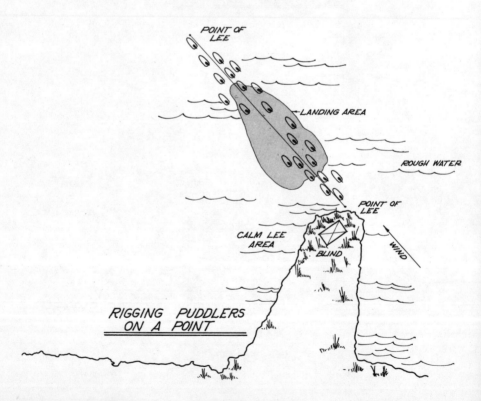

RIGGING PUDDLERS ON A POINT

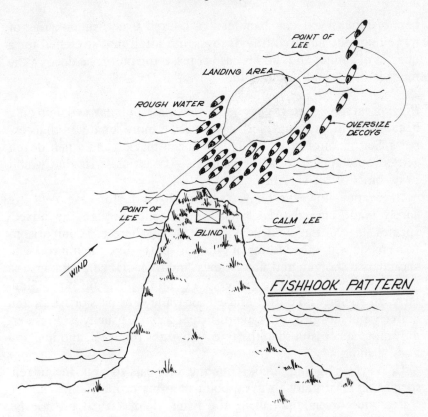

The pattern to use when point-shooting divers is the fishhook. This classic configuration, also known as the stovepipe, finds a half-moon of decoys set in front of the blind. The inner portion of the half-moon should be within good gun range, for this is the place tolling birds will look to land.

Once the half-moon is set, run a tail or line of decoys off the in-shore side, curving it out toward open water. Space decoys on the tail wider and wider apart as you move away from the blind.

This tail functions like a path to lead birds into the main part of your decoys. Ducks trading back and forth over open water will pick the tail up and show interest in it from a mile out; so it pays to have readily visible oversized decoys there.

Set the fishhook so it lies along the rough-water/calm-water point of lee, and use a lot of decoys. I'd say thirty is a bare minimum, with forty-five better still, and the outside limit being set only by the numbers of blocks you can handle. I've hunted over fishhook rigs of more than one hundred fifty decoys, with a tail that stretched for a quarter of a mile; and, in this case at least, the more the decoys, the merrier I've found the shooting.

Rigging mixed species is probably the most popular set, but only because, as in any endeavor, there will be more amateurs than experts. Setting out thirty broadbill, a dozen blacks, and a half dozen geese would appear to be the panacea—the ultimate rig that would draw birds of all varieties.

In practice, however, I haven't found this to be the case. And I've surely made enough trial runs, having gone through the mixed-species stage of rigging decoys myself. I feel there are comparisons to be made with other forms of outdoor sport—like the nimrod who shoulders a shotgun and simply goes "hunting." He seldom bags the game that the fellow who centers on quail or pheasant does. Similarly, an angler who outfits himself for walleye or bass or trout, and actively pursues just one type of fish at a time, usually is considerably more successful than the tyro who grabs rod, reel, and line and goes "fishing."

If, however, going "duck hunting" appeals to you, the mixed-species rig is virtually always a point-shooting proposition.

Rig your divers first, using the fishhook described previously. Set the configuration downwind from your blind but close enough so that the inner half-moon area falls within good gun range.

Although logic would seem to dictate otherwise, set your puddle ducks well in front of the divers, and well defined from them by open water. Set your geese inside the puddlers, closest to shore.

I realize that this puts your geese and puddlers—two calm, shallow-water-loving species—out in the brunt of any wave or wind activity, that the big geese should rightly go out in front to act as oversized decoys, and that any sane duck or goose should rightly stool to the quiet water of the lee; but I've hunted over just that kind of "sensible" setup and done nothing on puddlers (though divers came in pretty well).

Ever since a seventy-five-year-young guide on Shinnecock Bay named Captain Downs showed me this perfectly unnatural and ridiculous way to rig for mixed species, I've persuaded my gunning buddies who insist on going for everything that flies to try it. Doggoned if it hasn't worked better than any other, though personally I'm still a fan of outfoxing one type of waterfowl at a time.

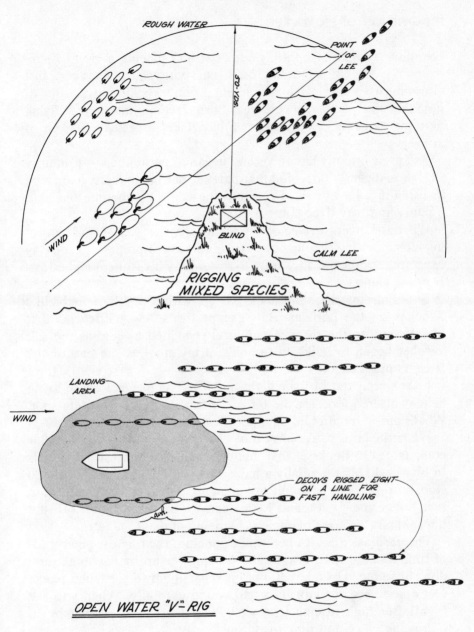

ROUGH WATER

POINT OF LEE

50 YDS.

WIND

BLIND

CALM LEE

RIGGING MIXED SPECIES

LANDING AREA

WIND

DECOYS RIGGED EIGHT ON A LINE FOR FAST HANDLING

with

OPEN WATER "V"- RIG

RIGGING ON OPEN WATER

Location   Setting up a lay-out boat and placing a rig of open-water decoys has subtleties on a par with shore gunning. Just choosing a spot at random seldom produces shooting worthy of note because diving species establish feeding lanes and flying patterns that render portions of a bay, lake, or estuary barren of activity.

As I grew into my late teens and began to earn money—primarily as a clam-digger—I decided that part of that income just had to be invested in a lay-out rig. I ran into the deal of a lifetime one fall: a punty and fifty decoys for $150.

When the divers arrived on the scene later that year, I spent morning after morning rigging out in the darkness of predawn, each day expecting action and adventure to reward my investment and effort. It never came.

Broadbill by the thousands passed within sight, amoeba-like bunches on the horizon. But, except for a few bufflehead that blundered into the rig, my gunbarrel remained as cold as the salt ice that began to build on the bills of my stool as the end of the season approached.

I was simply out of their flight pattern. The places I chose to rig neither offered food for the birds nor functioned as a resting spot. What's more, it didn't lie on a path between these two areas.

When the birds you're after travel in the thousands, or are familiar companions to flocks of that number, trying to interest individuals to break what is essentially a habit with a piddling rig of 50 to 100 stool is futile. They're simply not going to alter their daily pattern to swing over you. If you had 1,000 decoys, you *might* pull it off, but it would take an army of gunners to maintain that kind of rig.

The cardinal rule of open-water gunning, then, is to spend a lot of time looking first. Forget about being set up by daybreak, and don't be seduced by a handful of birds passing by a particular place. Get a good set of binoculars and watch carefully. When you see flight after flight tolling to a well-defined area, or passing by it, *that* is the place and time to rig out.

Easily the best open-water gunner I know is Joe Arata, a friend since boyhood, and I still hunt with him and his buddies whenever I visit the East during duck season. We kid Joe a lot. We even bought him a bus driver's hat for his "tours," because a typical day of gunning with Joe involves about five hours in a car, visiting different spots along the shores of Long Island. Joe will stop along some sandy beach or marshy point, gaze out to sea for five minutes, then say, "Not here—let's try the Sore Thumb," or, "Maybe they're tending to Oak Neck," and we drive some more.

Sometimes we don't have our rig in the water until two or three in the afternoon. But when Joe says, "This is the place," we always get more than good shooting; we get great shooting. Joe really understands the importance of, and how to identify, the flight patterns of diving ducks.

Beyond the powers of observation, there are a few other things that hint at good places to rig for divers. First, they tend to fly along the "edge" of anything.

During a fog, they'll often follow the shore. If there's a partial sheet of ice on a body of water, they'll follow the edge of it. Should that ice be broken into slush, or the water be "making ice," and it's pushed into a slushy broken line by wind, currents, and tides, divers will follow that too.

If a shoal, shelf, or drop-off is visible from the air—even if it's no more than a matter of a slight difference in water coloration—they'll follow that line. Likewise for a line created by the conflict of wind or bottom contours with moving water.

Note again the effectiveness of a long tail of decoys stretching out into open water when you're gunning divers; you're creating that path, that line, that "edge" they love to follow.

Food is another drawing card. If you know a lake or bay contains extensive clam or mussel flats, or beds of wild celery, eel grass, or any other type of favored food, the chances are better than good that spot will be visited by ducks sometime during the day.

When you can find those things occurring simultaneously—a flight path that follows some sort of an "edge" near feeding grounds —a lay-out boat with fifty decoys will still produce the kind of gunning that makes bag limits more than mere pipe dreams.

• The V rig is the setup I've seen Joe Arata use most often. It's nothing more than arranging fifty to eighty stool in a V configuration with the boat at the crotch of the letter.

The V is easy to set because up to ten decoys can be put on one long line for quick handling, without appearing unnatural and soldier-straight on the water. This is a problem with some of the other rigging patterns because of their graceful curves and S's.

Another plus to the V is that it's perfect for two shooters. Other designs find the boat lying to the side of the landing area and one

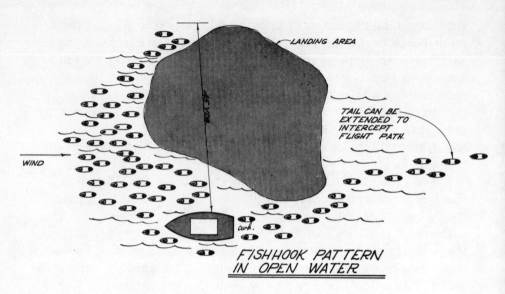

FISHHOOK PATTERN
IN OPEN WATER

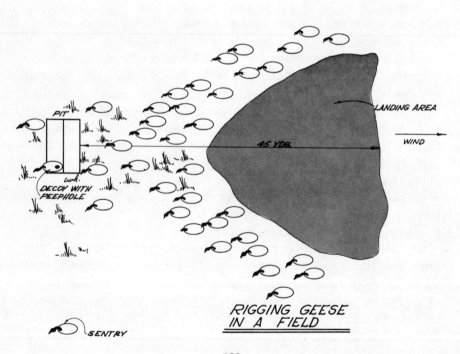

RIGGING GEESE
IN A FIELD

hunter shooting across the other.

One disadvantage of the V is that decoying birds tend to the head of the rig, and suddenly discover you're there. You seldom get a perfect, classic toll. But you do get easy wing shots as decoying divers will pick up one wing of the letter and slow way down as they look for a place to land.

• The fishhook draws ducks over open water as well as it does near shore, though it creates some problems when you're setting it up or bringing it in.

When your decoy configuration involves essentially straight lines like the V, setting them out and picking them up is easy—nothing more than a matter of drifting with the wind.

Curved patterns like the fishhook require a lot of jockeying around to set them, and aside from the extra work involved, there's always the chance that you'll wind an anchor line around your prop—cussed luck at best, and conceivably a very dangerous situation in heavy seas and frigid water.

Fishhook configurations and patterns like it are particularly effective over open water because of the tail. If you find you've misjudged flight patterns, you can extend a line of decoys to the right or left to intercept the passing birds.

• Mixing divers and puddlers is seldom done in open-water shooting. It just isn't that productive.

Occasionally goose or brant decoys are included with a diver rig when these birds happen to be in that area. These decoys are set apart from the main configuration of blocks, up toward the head of the pattern and within gun range of the lay-out boat.

They should be placed with some sort of design in mind, the simplest, and the one I most often use, being a half-moon configuration.

SETTING FIELD DECOYS

Setting out decoys in a field largely involves goose stool. Puddle ducks will freely decoy to a flock of geese; so aside from a few confidence mallards or pintail there's no real need for lots of field duck decoys.

Choose a place to set the decoys that has low or virtually no cover. Geese are reluctant to land anywhere that could hide a hunter.

The same caution is true of a field surrounded by tall timber or thick brush; set your stool in the middle of such a field. If you rig too close to the borders, birds will come in sky-high and will be reluctant to land.

The best blind location in relation to the decoy configuration is among the decoys at the head of the spread. The presence of decoys in close proximity to the pit helps break up revealing outlines, and you have the "peep-hole" option of a slit-sided hollow-bodied stool on your hatch cover as was described in Chapter 6.

The only disadvantage to this pit location is that birds will occasionally land behind you, making for a tough shot. But all in all, I think the credits far outweigh the debits here.

Geese generally want a much bigger landing spot than ducks. If there are none provided, they'll land outside of the stool, usually toward the front half of the flock. Like water decoys, field decoys should face into the wind. Be very aware of wind shifts, too. A drifting decoy will align itself naturally, but a field decoy can't.

Another pitfall common to field hunting is frost. Just before sun-up on cool mornings, check for frost on the backs of your decoys. If you find it has formed, take the time to dust it off with a whisk broom; even the lightest touch of frost appears white and unnatural from the air, and when it melts, the wet decoy backs will shine like polished glass.

• The V formation is the field rig I usually set for Canadas and their subspecies.

This configuration requires between fifteen and fifty decoys, with the pit located in the crotch of the V. The open end of the V affords plenty of landing room, and birds will tend to this spot, offering the best shot in the business.

It is common practice to set a gander in the alert posture, ahead of and slightly off to one side of the V configuration, as all real flocks of feeding geese post at least one sentry.

Occasionally, goose hunters like to set five or six more stool in a separate block to the side of the main body of decoys, but I find this practice questionable.

It is designed to give the illusion of a newly arrived knot of birds that haven't yet had time to join the main flock—sort of a confidence setup—but I've found it serves to encourage incoming birds to land in back of the pit. Jumping up, swinging around, locating and tracking birds behind you adds up to tough shooting.

If you have trouble with high-flying geese that don't want to come down, set a small bunch of stool one hundred yards or more downwind of the main spread. Approaching birds see these decoys first and are encouraged to drop down for a closer look at what lies ahead. This then puts them in a more willing position to decoy.

Be careful about the head positions on your stool; too many sentries will give indication of a nervous flock. In a rig of forty decoys, set no more than nine heads in the alert position, an equal number of sleepers, and the rest feeders.

Field duck decoys, if you choose to use a few, should be bunched together and distinct from the main body of geese. Geese will harass smaller waterfowl in a feeding area; so the twain seldom meet. I generally set four or five ducks off to one side of the crotch of the V.

• The I formation is most commonly employed in goose hunting when decoys numbering in the hundreds are used. This is often the case in snow-goose country; newspapers or diapers are set up on dowels to complement full-bodied stool, and the rig often stretches from one end of a field to the other. Snow geese seem impressed with numbers, not details.

When setting out the I, the length of the letter should follow the drift of the wind. Several sentries may set out along the I, but keep most of them around the upwind half of the letter.

Locate the blind in the middle of the letter. Although most geese will want to land up toward the head of the flock, enough decoy to the middle to cost you shots if you put your pit up front.

DECOY PROBLEMS

No matter the species of waterfowl you're hunting or the terrain where you've rigged your blocks, one of the few certainties of the sport is that ducks and geese will come to an appealing set of decoys. If they don't, you've done or are doing something wrong, and the birds will tell you what.

When there's no activity whatsoever, no birds in the air or waterfowl passing too far away to see your decoys, you're out of flight patterns. Find a different location for your blind—one that's closer to established passes, resting spots, and feeding areas.

When birds pass you at closer ranges where they surely can see your decoys (two hundred to four hundred yards out), watch their movements aloft very carefully. If they follow an arrow-straight path with purpose and dedication, again you're in the wrong place with your decoy spread. There's something about the area that simply is unattractive to ducks. Although I have no idea why, I have seen broadbill refuse to cross a sandy-colored submerged shoal to come to my decoys, and blacks flare from a telephone pole behind my blind. The puzzling thing is that this doesn't always happen; so you can't make any rules about shoals or telephone poles. But be aware that certain features of the terrain on certain days occasionally add up to places where ducks refuse to go. When you think you're in such a spot, move.

If, however, you note fly-bys tipping toward your rig, rising up for a better look, banking as if to come in, or otherwise altering their course of flight, the chances are good you're in the right spot but that there's something wrong with the way you've put your spread together.

Check your blind for good camouflage, and check those inside too. Occasionally a strong sun will find faces inside literally shining.

If the blind fits in well, look next at your decoy spread and the way you've set it, with an eye to the type of duck that's passing you by. I once changed my shooting from poor to excellent by pulling my I rig of mallards off a point and changing it to a C in a nearby cove. It was a move of less than twenty yards; we didn't even have to change the location of the blind. But where birds had flown by before, they now banked around the point and decoyed perfectly to the cove.

Another way to tempt fly-bys to come in closer is by extending the tail of a fishhook out farther. This is particularly successful on divers, but I have persuaded puddlers using a tail too. (For other persuaders, see the next chapter.)

Ducks flaring at close ranges means some detail is out of whack. The first thing to consider is your blind location: is it eyeball to eyeball with incoming birds? If so, that's your problem.

Next, check your decoys. Are any hung up with each other; is one overturned or riding awry? Perhaps they're just poor stool or poorly painted. It doesn't take much to frighten waterfowl when they're getting ready to sit in.

Note, too, where they're trying to sit down. If there's no room for them to get in—decoys packed too tightly where there should be a hole—open up a landing area.

If all these things check out, look again at your blind and the surrounding area. Shiny objects like spent casings, the jetsam of washed-up tin cans, even your gun barrel, will flare birds. Remember that those shiny or otherwise alarming objects could be under water.

As birds come in, watch and mark exactly where they flare, and try to estimate where they're looking when they do.

There was a day on the Moriches marshes when the black duck were thick and willing, but just as they got within gun range they flared wildly. I spent a half hour examining the beach and the water and, by a process of elimination as each bird flared, finally discovered they were frightened of an old sunken rubber tire that had totally escaped my notice. I pulled the tire up from the bottom, hid it under some seaweed on the shore, and the birds decoyed without blinking an eye.

Admittedly, there are no hard-and-fast rules about what draws or flares waterfowl around decoys—just an interminable bunch of variables that it's up to you to assess. But that's what's so damned intriguing and absorbing about the sport; if you're really waterfowling, you've got no time for the mundane cares of bills, work, wives, or lovers.

And when you put decoys, days, marshes, and blinds together so well that birds decoy into your lap, you know you've done something right, and all the cussing, work, waiting, and past frustration pale in the reflection of that glorious day.

9 | Hunting over Decoys

When hunting over decoys, the object of the game is to make the birds come to you. The convincing factor is the excellence of your decoy spread—the more closely it imitates a natural invitation to food, safety, and companionship, the more readily gregarious waterfowl will swing by for a look. There simply is no substitute for a carefully wrought rig and all the knowledge and planning that term implies.

But in order for your decoys to work their magnetic charm, birds must first become aware of them. It is to this attention-getting end that most waterfowling tricks are intended.

FLAGGING

One of the cardinal no-no's of waterfowling is to move when there are birds in the air. Ducks and geese are able to spot the barest flicker of activity, and it often leads their attention to a blind or boat and the hunters hiding there. This unusual degree of perception and inquisitiveness can, however, be turned into an Achilles' heel by a trick called flagging.

Flagging imitates the appearance of a resting flock. If you'll watch a raft of birds from a distance, you'll find individual members are constantly rearing out of the water to stretch and beat their wings. This act realigns feathers that have been knocked askew during the preening.

Viewed from a good distance, the flock appears a dark line on the water, with rearing birds flashing into momentary view like a block of black cardboard held up for an instant. When these flocks are several miles away, you can't see the birds on the water, but that flash of stretched wings will still reveal their position if you're looking in the right place at the right time.

Imitating this rearing and preening will attract passing birds' attention, and the way to do it is with a black flag.

The flag itself should measure around two by two feet, and be tacked to a pole 3½ feet long. When flagging passing birds you don't wave it back and forth, but shoot the flag up, snap it open, and haul it back inside the blind all in a matter of a few seconds.

The real trick to flagging, however, is not in the manipulation of the flag but in knowing when to do it.

Although all ducks and geese will respond to a flag, some species will be turned off if you flag them in close. When any bunch of birds are mere dots in the sky, you're safe to flag them to your heart's content; but once they pick up your invitation and begin to head for your spread, don't try to flag any goose but a brant, or puddle ducks in general. If one of these birds begins to veer, you might try one more snap to redirect his attention, but generally you're better off to rely on a call at this point.

Most divers and brant, on the other hand, will continue to respond to a flag until they're within gun range. This is especially true of broadbill, canvasback, and redhead. You don't have to flag when birds seem plainly bent on coming to your rig, but if they appear to lose interest a few quick flicks will usually put them back on your beam.

I'd say that of all the birds that will fall prey to a flag, broadbill amount to the ultimate suckers. I once lay in a punty and watched a broadbill pick up the tail of the rig, looking for a place to land. Each time he slowed down, seeming to have picked a spot to sit, I snapped the flag and up he came again, flapping his wings to gain altitude and get a few yards closer to that flash of black. I don't know how many times I repeated the trick—probably five. When he finally saw me in the boat and realized that something was very wrong, I doubt he was more than ten yards away, and I was laughing so hard that I never even picked up my gun. While you'll never play every bird like that particular pipe organ, just turning a flock with a flag from a half mile out will still make you feel wonderfully smug.

Don't overlook the possibility of using a flag in exactly the opposite manner too: as a means to flare birds. You'll often discover that you've set your blind in a spot you thought looked good, but where you find ducks tending to your right or left. If you'll set a flag in the marsh or on a buoy to the far side of their flight path, letting it flap in the breeze, it will flare birds in your direction.

Flagging is a surprisingly little-known technique, and I should perhaps warn you that it's lured lots more to my blind than waterfowl. Three times come to memory when other duck hunters have walked over to my hiding spot and inquired if I needed help; they'd seen my signals and thought I was trying to attract their attention.

But nothing till then, or since, has been quite so embarrassing as what my flag pulled in during a Long Island special broadbill season.

I was rigged out of Bay Shore, a mile from the beach, when I heard a helicopter approaching. I craned my neck around, and saw that it was the police.

They swung twice around my punty, rallying whole rafts of broadbill and making for some great pass shooting in the bargain; then they drifted off.

Then I heard another helicopter, this one a big Coast Guard ship. It, too, swung around the boat at a distance of a half mile, moved a few birds around, and left the scene.

I was puzzled but impressed with the unexpected cooperation I was getting. Then the picture began to come into clearer focus when my partner looked shoreward and saw some five red beacons flashing from a beach parking lot.

As it turned out, a new resident of one of the beach-front houses who'd never seen a duck hunter before, much less knew about flagging, had caught the flash of black cloth and called the Suffolk County Police and U.S. Coast Guard with the frantic news that a swimmer was in trouble—in January.

By the time the episode was over, our afternoon pastime had tied up three police cars, a special unit of the police Rescue Squad, a game warden, two helicopters, and a Coast Guard patrol boat that had been dispatched to the scene.

Given a few years' grace, I can manage to chuckle at the circumstances. But at the time, I felt awfully stupid—and still shudder at just how much that misunderstanding cost the public.

CALLING

The ability to call ducks and geese is a little like an iceberg: nine-tenths of the skill and savvy involved lies hidden from view.

To call waterfowl you must first be able to identify them, because different species have different calls. The resonant "quack" most often associated with ducks is standard only with mallards or blacks. Other types of ducks whistle, squeak, croak, chirr, and usually show little, if any, interest in a mallard call.

There's also the matter of timing and amount. You're wisest to call only when necessary, and as little as possible. Those times that qualify as "necessary" have proven to be the following:

• When distant birds are calling to your decoy spread. This occurs most often with geese, who commonly spot a rig from a mile or more away and begin making overtures. Mallards, too, occasionally call to decoy; so when you hear a distant "quack," it's a good idea to respond in kind even if you don't immediately see the bird.

• When birds show signs of veering off from your spread. It takes a little experience, but you'll come to know, almost intuitively, when an approaching bird is planning to toll to your decoys and when he's not. So long as his mind is made up, calling will only work against you since you might blow a faulty note. There comes a time, however, when a slight wobble in the wings or a minute change in direction indicates that an approaching bird is going to pass you by. When that occurs, a call will often persuade a duck or goose that he's found a happy home.

• When birds appear nervous. Especially when you're hunting mallards and blacks, you'll come across individuals or small flocks who seem to swing and circle forever. They'll skim across the outer edge of your decoy spread and gun range, very nearly tolling on each pass, then stop short, feathering the air, to gain elevation for yet another pass. If you'll blow a few low tones just as they start to set their wings, the invitation is often sufficient to get them to drop right on in. That particular success is one of the sweetest in duck hunting; you feel like you can talk to the animals!

189

Call Types   Calls are available for every species of duck and goose, but those in most common use are the mallard or black call and the Canada-goose call. Face it, you can hang just so many around your neck. I have no particular favorite when it comes to brand-name duck calls. I've found that every call maker turns out both good and bad models. Like harmonicas, the secret of a good call lies in the reed, and there doesn't seem to be any standardization in them; so keep trying out individual calls until you hear a tone that suits you.

• When sizing up a duck call, I've found that those that sound just a little high-pitched to your ears as you blow them will sound best afield. Though pitch is important, I think the most important feature of any duck call is the ease with which it can be blown. If a mere puff of breath sets the reed to vibrating, you're on the right track. It's essential that you be able to blow low, soft notes, and a call that must be blown hard to vibrate will always be loud. If that same call can be blown hard and loud without moving up to a higher pitch, or bellowing, you've found a good call—buy it before someone else does.

• Goose calls are a bit more complex than duck calls in that they produce two separate tones. I've heard awfully weird sounds come from some supposed goose calls, and they're hard to judge inside a building or shop. Get outside and have a buddy blow the call while you listen from fifty yards away. If it sounds like a Canada to your ears, it will probably sound the same way to a goose.

While it isn't necessary to be able to blow a goose call low, a responsive set of reeds is still important. By alternately cupping and uncupping your hands over the end of the call, you can produce a sound that approximates a whole flock of talking geese. A slight change in technique also will create the one-noted "honk" sound without the "ga" preceding it. Like a soft quack with mallards, the "honk" can persuade nervous geese to drop on in.

I do have a favorite in terms of goose calls: the Olt A-50 Canada Honker is, to my way of thinking, the best I've yet found on the market. But, as in all brands, there are tonal differences in the reeds of individual calls. Try several and settle on what sounds best to you.

Calling technique requires two skills: that you learn to "play" your call a little like a musical instrument, and that you know what call to issue at what time.

A combination of breath strength and the belling effect of your hands is how you play a call. Let's take a duck call first.

With the call in your mouth, ring the sounding end of the call with thumb and forefinger in the O-like "O.K." hand signal. Next, bring your fingers down and together to form a kind of sounding bell around the end of the call.

By choking that bell way down, and blowing moderately, you get a low, muffled, chirr-like sound. Increase the pressure of your breath and quickly expand your hand and the size of the bell, and you'll produce a distinct "qu-ack." That sound, blown once, and no more than twice, should redirect a bird that's considered dropping into your spread but appears to be veering off.

With your hand now in the open position, blow a series of calls beginning loud and hard, then diminishing the sounds in intensity and individual duration. The first loud quack should last about one second, with a one-second pause between it and the next sound. That next sound should not be quite so loud as the first, and of a half-second's duration. The third note should be for a quarter second, the fourth for an eighth of a second, and then you should puff out a string of low quick quacks numbering about four or five.

It's too bad words on paper don't have a sound, but the call goes roughly like this:

QUAAAAK — — — QUAAAK — QUAaaak — quaaak quack quack quack.

This call is the "highball," and it's used to attract distant ducks to your spread or to answer callers. When done right it can have an astonishing effect; I've seen birds winging along full tilt who put on the brakes and dropped into a spread like a heavy dumpling in response to that highball.

The feeding call is used to calm and encourage nervous ducks in the air. The common belief is that the feeding call is a "chucka-chucka-chucka" sound. If you've done much bird watching, you've surely heard it as birds approached a flock. But it's been my experience that the "chucka" sound amounts to an inquiry made by the birds in the air, *not* those on the ground or water.

The response the airborne birds are looking for is a low, muffled "chirr," achieved by cupping both hands over the end of the call and blowing softly. By working both hands as musicians choke a harmonica, you can get different tonal variations that simulate several birds replying. As you call, blow short rapid puffs—as if you were saying a heavy-breathed "who-who-who-who-who." Another successful technique is to allow your tongue to flutter against the roof of your mouth as you blow. This trick, incidentally, when used in conjunction with a moderately hard blow and loud tone, will often lure diving ducks with a mallard/black-type call.

Calling geese requires rather an opposite technique, in that you cup both hands and simulate several talkers when the birds are first sighted or are making inquiry. This is tricky work in that you have to alter the strength and duration of each new breath in a non-sequential string of puffs, while also belling both hands to create the desired gabbling sound. All you have to do is hear geese talking among themselves once to know what that sound is like.

Once the flock bends toward your decoys, stop gabbling and concentrate on being one bird. The call is now blown with both hands cupped over the end. Exhale softly and you'll produce the melodious "ga" part of a Canada's voice. Open your hands quickly and blow a bit harder, and you'll create the piercing "honk" of the second part.

It's very important to chop your breath short at the honk. If you don't, you'll get a three-noted call—a "ga-honk-ga"—that will put birds off.

Even though the approaching geese are making a racket equivalent to a barnyard at feeding time, be miserly in your response. About one "ga-honk" every thirty seconds is plenty.

If they seem to want to veer off, increase the frequency of the call, but don't go back to a flock gabble. If they continue toward you, decrease the frequency of the call and try to chop off the "ga" note so that you're just producing the "honk."

Geese are truly lulled by a well-blown call—far more so than ducks. But remember, calling any sort of waterfowl is an easy thing to overdo.

Practice   Surely the best practice for a beginning caller is to visit your local duck pond. Try to imitate the sounds you hear there. Try, too, to interpret to what they are a response. Note the sounds produced when incoming birds are greeted by residents, the noises that geese and ducks make when they're feeding, or the sounds from a flock at rest. If you're shy, do this early in the morning. You'll get some incredulous looks from the people who feed bread to the birds during the middle of the day. Learning to call ducks is a little like learning how to yodel. The toughest part is in finding a good time and a deserted place.

If you don't have access to a duck pond or relative wilderness, there are instructional calling records you can buy. With call in hand, you can harmonize with your stereo; but, again, you should live in a soundproof apartment or out in the woods—and have an understanding wife.

When carrying calls in the field, the best place I've found to keep them is on a string or rawhide loop around your neck. If you keep them anyplace else, you'll forget where they are or never get to them in time to respond to some 50 percent of the calling situations. Then, too, worn around your neck they can be tucked inside your jacket when it's cold. Below-freezing temperatures will lock up your reed and render the call useless unless you do this.

ANIMATION

Working lifelike movement into a decoy spread is quite important. When a breeze is blowing there's no need for artificial devices, since the yaw of the blocks on their lines produces this effect. But when it's dead calm some induced animation really helps. I've seen rigs a quarter mile apart and identical in every respect except that one had an animated decoy. The latter pulled two birds to the other hunter's one.

One way to achieve a degree of animation is simply by throwing a rock. Keep a pile of them next to you in the blind, and when a bird appears, throw one in the middle of your decoy spread. This creates a ripple that sets several decoys to bobbing and simulates some amount of life.

But I view that trick as an emergency measure—something to do when the wind drops out unexpectedly and there's no other avenue open. The dabbler decoy is a far more attractive and realistic form of animation.

To rig up a dabbler, twist a screw-eye home under the tip of a decoy's bill. You'll also need a heavy weight—heavy enough to sink that decoy—with a screw-eye set in it. I fill a coffee can with cement, and let it harden around a copper-wire ring.

The final component of a dabbler is a fishing reel with twelve-pound-test monofilament. You could use the spool the line comes on, but a reel makes it easier to wind in and take out.

After threading the line through the weight, tie it to the decoy's bill. Set the weight and block close to the middle of your decoys and take in enough line so the dabbling decoy floats normally, but is directly above the weight. Keep the reel within easy reach of your seat in the blind.

When you see birds in the air, yank on the line and the duck will dip under realistically, at the same time creating sufficient wake to move other nearby blocks around.

It is a most effective trick, and I only wish I could adapt it to field gunning. I know it would work just as well there as on water.

OTHER SURE-FIRE TRICKS THAT BRING BIRDS OVER YOUR RIG

Flagging, calling, and animated decoys do draw their share of birds and help increase your bag, but they're by no means a guarantee that every duck or goose within eyeshot will pile into your rig.

There are, however, several things you can do that will *never* fail to produce action. They are:

• Walk behind the blind to urinate.

• Decide that the way you've rigged your decoys isn't quite right and start to change them around.

• Decide the flights are over for the day and start to pick up stool.

• Pour a cup of coffee.

• Hold a sandwich in your hand with no place to lay it down but beach sand or marsh mud.

DABBLING DECOY

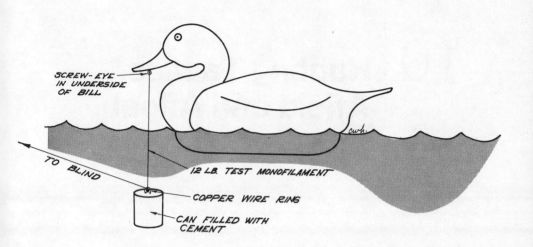

SCREW-EYE
IN UNDERSIDE
OF BILL

TO BLIND

12 LB. TEST MONOFILAMENT

COPPER WIRE RING

CAN FILLED WITH
CEMENT

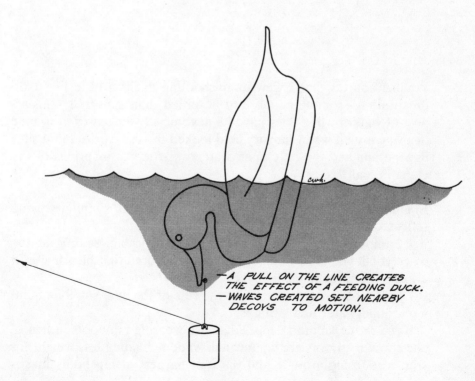

— A PULL ON THE LINE CREATES
THE EFFECT OF A FEEDING DUCK.
— WAVES CREATED SET NEARBY
DECOYS TO MOTION.

10 | Hunting Tactics Afield and Afloat

While I confess that I view jump-shooting ducks a little like I do prostitution—something more to be pitied than censored—this aspect of waterfowling does have its devotees. I've even tried it once or twice myself when January cold locked in my favorite blind sites in Montana and the only open water was the warm springs of the Gallatin Valley.

Equipment   Jump shooting is simple sport, that simplicity being reflected in the equipment required.

• Camouflage clothing of some sort is advisable, as long as the place you'll be hunting isn't so heavily pressured that blending into a background becomes a safety hazard.

• Hip boots or waders are also the rule of the day; you'll be hunting around water and swamps.

If the water isn't too deep, I'd advise wearing hip boots in lieu of chest waders. Boots are lighter than waders, holding less weight for your legs to lug around, and the foot harness in hip boots makes them a lot more comfortable for walking. Chest waders will slop around on your feet and probably raise blisters.

• Most jump shooting involves reasonably close targets; so your favorite upland gun will be a better performer in this situation than a far-reaching waterfowling piece. I'd call a 12-gauge auto with improved cylinder or modified choke on a 26-inch barrel ideal. This close-in shooting should also be reflected in your shot shells. "Express" or "high base" will provide more than enough power for 95 percent of your shots. Magnums are just too heavy. (For more information, see Chapter 11, "Waterfowl Weaponry.")

• A duck call is a valuable adjunct to jump shooting. If you carry one and blow it occasionally, you'll often elicit a response from a real bird, giving you indication of his presence and location.

Jump-shooting technique involves sneaking close to suspected waterfowl, flaring or "jumping" them so they fly, and shooting them on the wing.

Because of a waterfowl's all-seeing eyes, jump shooting over water or fields with sparse cover is well-nigh impossible. Prime spots include lakeshores, swamps, streams surrounded by plenty of cover, and twisting, deep-cut watercourses where you can use the terrain to mask your approach.

As a rule, you'll enjoy the most success if you walk against any flow of water. Signs that waterfowl are ahead will then be washed down toward you—an occasional feather plucked while preening, or aquatic vegetation torn loose by feeding birds. Using this approach, the majority of birds will also be facing upstream—into the current—providing some slight edge that way.

As you walk along, try to keep from exposing yourself unnecessarily. Use stream-side brush and natural geography to screen your body from sight of the water. When you're ready to "jump" birds, pop into view so the element of surprise produces a wild explosion of feathers and spray rather than a bird who swims to the near edge of your shot range, then takes to wing.

Whenever you see birds in the air, try to get into some sort of cover. That's where the camouflage clothing comes in. Often, a bird you've flushed and missed will have no certain idea of where you're at and, if you're hidden, will swing by, offering a good pass shot.

Hide when there are birds aloft, too. Incoming birds will occasionally pass close within gun range and, even if they don't, will often land in a spot you can mark, then walk up to.

PASS SHOOTING

Pass shooting comes closer to my idea of waterfowling, but it still misses the mark made by decoy hunting in my scale of outdoor values. Pass shooting involves first locating a duck or goose "pass"—a path birds regularly fly over going to and from feed—then building a blind or hiding there.

Equipment for pass shooting includes camouflage clothes, some sort of blind, and a far-reaching gun. In this area of waterfowling sport, full-choke shotguns and magnum loads are often the best choice, especially during pleasant weather when ducks and geese will fly high. The need for waders or boots is a matter of where you'll be hunting. Many passes are nowhere near water, in which case you'll be a lot more comfortable and warm in insulated field boots.

Blinds for the pass shooter are usually portable affairs. Often passes shift locations as new migrant birds arrive. Then, too, constant and concentrated gunning along one pass will teach birds not to fly there in the future. You've got to be able to change location when they do.

Pass-Shooting Techniques   Fifty percent of the successful pass shooter's time is spent with a pair of binoculars and an eye on the sky. You must first identify favored passes before you can hunt them.

One excellent spot to look is around the borders of preserves and refuges. Waterfowl rest in these havens by day and move out from them morning and evening to feed. If you can identify the routes they're using, you're on your way to excellent gunning.

Remember that these routes are not necessarily permanent. Waterfowl like to feed together, as well as rest together, and they will feast in one field en masse until it is picked clean, then move to another. As the destinations of flocks bent on feeding change, so will the routes they take to fly to that feed. Because a pass is hot one day doesn't mean it will be the next.

There are, however, traditional "passes": landmarks used as navigation points by migrating waterfowl year after year. If you discover one of these spots, you'll often get good shooting there every day of the season when flocks are moving through.

On any pass, traditional or temporary, I have found birds to be highly suspicious of anything new; so take great care in setting up your blind.

Several years ago I pass-shot in a hayfield on the border of the refuge near my home, during a period when the northern mallards were in. There was a haystack in the middle of the field, making for an ideal blind.

The shooting was fast, so I returned the next day and discovered the farmer had moved the haystack to his feed yard. The absence of that familiar landmark puzzled and frightened the birds; they either changed their route entirely or flew over the spot out of range.

In similar vein, a small bay on Ennis Lake used to be a major feeding pass for Canada geese leaving the safety of open water for the nearby grainfields. There was a huge muskrat lodge, long deserted by its builders, in the middle of the pass. It made for a wonderful blind. Then one day some fool burned it down by mistake or design. The geese seldom take that route anymore, and it's been four years since it was burned!

New features of the terrain will have the same effect. If you build a palace of a blind in the middle of crew-cut hay, you'll never get good gunning from the spot. In a situation like that you'd be better off to build a slit trench, or take advantage of some natural cover.

Because birds using a pass spook so readily, a flag positioned in such a way as to flare birds toward your blind can be a very effective tool.

Preserve shoots for ducks amount to a pass-shooting situation. Shooting preserves raise ducks (usually mallards) and they are encouraged to fly from pens where they feed to a source of water. Blinds are built along the route they take, and clients shoot them as they fly by.

I've been on several preserve shoots, and while the knowledge that you're dealing with pen-reared birds does take some of the excitement out of the day, this type of gunning is hardly like shooting fish in a barrel. It's difficult shooting and kind of fun. What's more, preserves often provide the only quality gunning near our larger cities and are an excellent way to introduce a youngster to the excitement, etiquette, and pleasure of hunting.

Costs for a preserve-type duck shoot usually run between five and seven dollars per bird, with a minimum kill that runs in the neighborhood of fifty to sixty dollars.

FLOATING FOR DUCKS AND GEESE

Drifting along with the current of a river and silently approaching waterfowl resting and feeding there is an effective and pleasant way to spend a hunting day.

Virtually any river-worthy craft will do, but I prefer rafts or jon boats for this job since they float low on the water and are rather easily camouflaged.

Camouflage is important in this situation; a yellow raft isn't going to work. Choose one in black or, better yet, olive. The same color is best on a jon boat and will hide you even better if you'll spray-paint light browns and marsh golds on the hull in an outline-breaking camouflage-type pattern.

I also favor the addition of boughs or marsh grass along the gunwales and hull to further mask the boat as a drifting snag or muskrat lodge.

As you're floating, take all river curves on the inside. These hold the slowest, calmest water, and the downstream side of that curve is the part of the river that will most often hold waterfowl. Pay particular attention to cuts, sloughs, and backwaters you happen upon. Because they hold slow or stagnant water, they'll be attractive to ducks and geese.

It's a wise move to scout thoroughly any river you plan to float for ducks, well in advance of the season. While you're hunting you'll be intent on spotting birds, not paying attention to the river, and you should be familiar with any and all hazards you might encounter along the way. If there's any aspect of waterfowling that eats shotguns, it's floating. Upsets—the results of ignorance, not especially dangerous water—have claimed four shotguns of friends of mine on the Madison River alone, and I'm sure countless others that I'm not aware of.

SCULLING

Because of its demands and dangers, sculling isn't a very popular form of waterfowling today. It is practiced to some extent on the Great Lakes, though sculling devotees have decreased together with the limits on redhead—one of the ducks most susceptible to this technique. Sculling still enjoys a degree of popularity on the West Coast.

There are two ways ducks are hunted by sculling. One involves locating a raft of birds, then slipping up on them with the boat; the second requires decoys.

A rig of blocks is set well offshore and the sculling boat is withdrawn to some upwind point of concealment: a tender or an onshore blind. When ducks decoy to the spread, the boat moves down on them.

In both situations the sculler works with the wind, and preferably with a partner—one man to scull, the other to shoot.

Sculling involves the dangers associated with large bodies of water and small fragile craft. The long agonizing approach required often finds a nervous flock taking to the wing before you get into range. Beset with low limits, scullers and scull boats are about as rare today as punt guns—relegated to history museums and a handful of gunners who relish reviving and reliving the past.

PART FOUR

Shotguns, Clothing, and Canine Assistance

11 | **Waterfowl Weaponry**

Ducks and geese undertake long sustained migrations, and to facilitate these movements their wings have a graceful jetlike appearance. The wings are braced by a massive bone structure and driven by lean sinewy muscles housed in a trim breast.

This body structure is in sharp contrast to the short, light, stubby wings and chunky breast common to upland birds, a class of fowl that remain in essentially the same territory throughout their lives. The flight of upland birds functions as an escape route from predators; it's a sudden burst of energy whereby they can achieve maximum speed within a few feet of takeoff—but on a flight that lasts for a few moments at the most. The ground covered by the explosion of a grouse or pheasant is measured in the hundreds of yards. The marathon of a snow goose or canvasback eats up hundreds of miles.

Other differences in adaption exist too. Anyone who's ever had marsh water slosh over the tops of his waders knows that 35-degree water next to your skin is a much colder proposition than 35-degree air. Upland birds have light, wispy feathers. Waterfowl sport a tough outer layer of closely matted feathers that gradually soften into fluffy warm down as you approach the skin. Their skin is thick and tough, too, and under it is even more insulation in the form of a layer of fat.

In comparison to other types of small game, waterfowl are rugged birds possessing a stamina and body structure that make ruffed grouse and ring-necked pheasant marshmallows by comparison. It follows, then, that weapons and ammunition used to hunt waterfowl should be chosen from the heavy end of the scatter-gunning spectrum.

Standard twelves, 3-inch magnums in 20- and 12-gauge, and 10-gauge magnums are the weapons for the serious waterfowler. And yes, I'm aware of the persistent myth that little guns—28, standard 20 and 16—"hit as hard" as heavier guns, but it isn't so.

Like most myths, this one is based on a grain of truth. If you want to talk about the individual pellet, there isn't much difference between a standard 12 and a standard 20 in terms of velocity. Measured in feet per second, with equivalent mid-power-range "express" loads, it amounts to the 12 being about 7 percent faster than the 20 (the faster a pellet is traveling, the more energy it expends on impact—the "harder it hits").

But downing a bird with a shotgun involves more than one pellet. Unless you make a lucky head or heart shot, it will usually take four pellets placed in a bird's body to bring it down. In those "equivalent" loads, the 12-gauge slings out 25 percent more shot than the 20. This creates a denser pattern in the 12, at all ranges. When the 20's pattern is too thin to place those essential four pellets into the profile of a mallard, the 12 still has a few to spare; hence it has greater "range," greater killing ability, than any standard 20.

Knockdown power is the real test of a waterfowling piece, not semantics. No matter how you juggle figures, the gun that can handle the most powder and that slings the greatest volume of shot has the potential to kill at the greatest range.

Note, however, I said "potential." There are several considerations beyond gauge and chamber length when choosing a gun for waterfowling. But for the moment let's look just at this aspect of ol' Betsy.

The 20-gauge 3-inch magnum has risen to a point of immense popularity in the last five years, and understandably so. Its 3-inch chamber will also accept 2¾-inch shells; so it easily doubles as an upland gun that's suited even for tiny quail. However, the maximum load it will handle is 1¼ oz. of shot—quite sufficient for ducks but marginal for geese. I'm a strong proponent of large shot when hunting geese, and 1¼ oz. of BB get awfully sparse at forty yards. Consider this gun if you do more upland hunting than waterfowling, if you seldom hunt geese, and if you can afford only one shotgun.

The standard 12 with a 2¾-inch chamber is slightly heavier (a pound to a pound and a half) than the 20 in a sister model. Because a light gun makes walking more pleasurable, the 12 is considered to be a bit less desirable as an upland gun. But it makes a much better waterfowling piece in that it can handle an ounce and a half of shot in front of a maximum powder charge. The standard 12 comes the closest to being an "all-around gun," especially if the brand you buy boasts interchangeable barrels. Buy two barrels, one for waterfowling and one for upland game, and, in combination with the variety of loads available, you'll have a fine companion for the smallest of upland game that's also capable of a respectable performance on big Canada geese. If you're a one-gun man who likes to hunt everything, this is the choice for you.

If you can afford a shotgun that will be used exclusively on waterfowl, I strongly recommend the 12-gauge chambered for 3-inch magnum shells. This weapon will also take 2¾-inch shells; so on those rare days when the blacks are decoying to your hat brim you can use the lighter loads. But when they're swinging by way out there, or you've set your sights on a Christmas goose, this is the gun that will bring down the table meat. The newest 3-inch mags can toss out 1⅞ oz. of shot, affording a tight pattern at long ranges, even with big goose-sized loads. Because they're heavy guns, however, they do poor double duty in the uplands—unless you're interested in building up your muscles.

If you're an idiot savant like me who believes that goose hunting is to waterfowling what Ferrari is to sports cars, you might want to invest in a 10-gauge 3½-inch magnum. These brutes sling a full 2 oz. of lead around, and are capable of phenomenal ranges. The best shot I've made to date on a goose is an unscientific seventy-five yards, arrived at by guess, by gosh, and by triangulation. But the estimates were made by hunting buddies, not me, and the guy who paced the ground distance from blind to bird (the goose was swinging right to left, not going away) was 6'3"; so if anything the estimates were probably conservative.

Remember, though, the 10-banger is not a panacea but a highly specialized tool. They're tricky to learn how to shoot because their pattern is fist-tight at forty yards; they're heavy as a steamer trunk and difficult to swing (though once you get them going you'll have no follow-through problems). They're also expensive little devils to feed, with shells currently going for ten bucks a box—when you can find them.

Choke and Barrel Length   Once you've settled on the gauge and chamber that best suit your tastes, choke and barrel length are the next considerations. Choke is the degree of constriction machined into the end of your barrel that, combined with that barrel's length, determines the rate at which your shot pattern will expand. Since a major factor in bringing down a bird is pellet concentration, choke and barrel length play a major part in the range of your shotgun.

The standard barrel lengths are 30 inches, 28 inches, and 26 inches, and most factory models also have a standard choke for each length: full on the 30-inch barrel, modified on the 28, and improved cylinder on the 26.

Since the manufacture of modern arms began, a 30-inch full-choke barrel has been standard equipment on any "duck gun" worthy of the name, but it's a cliché worth debating.

True, the 30-inch full-choke barrel will give you the tightest pattern, therefore the greatest potential reach; but when you get down to brass casings, just how many birds per day offer a shot in the forty-five- to fifty-five-yard range?

For some unfathomable reason, duck hunters tend to remember, they scheme to outsmart, and they consistently lay all their plans around those birds that will hang just within the pale of killing range: birds who are missed more often than they're hit. "But oh, if I could just stretch that pattern out another five yards!" they say.

So let's say they do, and that they occasionally take those ducks at sixty yards. There will still be ducks passing within a "pale," but that range is now five yards farther out. Barrel-stretching can go on ad absurdum. Then, too, the farther out you're reaching, the more difficult the birds are to hit in the first place, *and* the more cripples you're bound to be responsible for.

In the meanwhile, look at what's happening with close-decoying birds—those within thirty-five to forty yards. With a tight-shooting barrel you're slinging a pie-plate-sized pattern at this range. This increases the chance you'll miss your target entirely; and if you connect right on the button your dinner is reduced to a puff of feathers and lead-laced mincemeat.

I can conjure up something of a personal testimonial in this matter of range too. I used to use a 10-gauge mag with 30-inch full and full barrels on ducks. The gun got me my birds, and I must admit I still have a childish fascination with pulling down mallards from nose-bleed altitudes. But one day the safety on Big Bertha went on the fritz and I had to use my modified-choke twelve. I immediately discovered both a jump in my daily bag and fewer cripples to chase around. I was foregoing the far-out shots and doing a lot better on clean close-in kills.

Since that time the latter gun has seen a lot of duty in my blind and I've come to believe its 28-inch barrel and modified choke are the best combination for most waterfowling situations. (though I do wish it were chambered for 3-inch mags).

With the knowledge that you don't have the farthest reaching barrel on the marsh, you'll pass up ducks at debatable ranges and concentrate on those within reasonable distances. The increased size of your pattern at these ranges will then decrease the margin of misses. (See also Choke Chart.)

CHOKE CHART: 12-Gauge, 2¾-inch Chamber

20 yards	Full	16-inch spread
	Modified	20
	Improved Cylinder	26
30 yards	Full	26
	Modified	32
	Improved Cylinder	38
40 yards	Full	40
	Modified	45
	Improved Cylinder	60

NOTE: the modified spread creates an ideal middle ground, opening up to cover a wide area long before full choke, yet holding together to create good pellet density long after improved cylinder has spread to the point of disintegration.

Variable Chokes   If settling on one choke for all time unsettles you, another possible route to take is to install a variable choke on your scattergun. These devices, typified by the Cutts Compensator and Poly-choke, allow you to set your choke for whatever the situation seems to demand. If you want to go the variable-choke route, you'll find it best to mount these chokes on a short (26-inch) barrel, since it helps keep the gun in balance.

Weight   The weight of the weapon comes next in my personal order of importance. "For every action there is an opposite and equal reaction" is a basic tenet of Newtonian physics; translated to waterfowling that means "the heavier the gun, the less the kick." By virtue of the fact that you'll be shooting the most powerful of modern shells, you'll be wise to steer clear of so-called lightweight models and stick to the standard weights in whatever type of gun you choose.

Lightweights are popular because they're easy to carry afield, and if you do a lot of jump shooting you might overlook this heavyweight rule of thumb. But pass shooting and hunting over decoys is sedentary sport; gun-toting doesn't enter the picture. Choose a heavy shotgun that is nevertheless comfortable and swings easily, and you'll develop neither sore shoulder nor an anticipatory flinch. By way of specifics, I'd say the lightest weights for waterfowling pieces should run: standard 12-gauge—7 pounds; 12-gauge, 3-inch magnum—8½ pounds; 10-gauge—10½ pounds.

Stock length   A matter of no small importance that rates high as a cause of poor shooting. The problem arises as a result of the weather cycle of a typical waterfowling season; it usually begins in warm October and ends in frigid December or January. During the warmer months you wear light clothing, and gradually add layers of garments as the thermometer drops. By season's end you've got an extra inch or two of padding between your shoulder and the gun butt, increasing the distance of trigger pull and consequently decreasing your accuracy if your gun was fitted in the warm comfort of a sporting goods store.

To compensate for this condition, I either cut down the stocks on my waterfowling pieces or buy them two inches too short in the first place. By adding a $3.00 pull-on rubber "butt boot" and an extra butt insert, I get a good fit in warm weather as well as plenty of cushioning against a near-bare shoulder. When I find myself piling on clothing, I simply peel off the butt boot, lean on the cushioning effect of cloth, and again have a well-fitted stock.

Action   I've purposely left the question of action to last—not because it's unimportant, but because it's personal. Autos, pumps,

and doubles all have their fans. When you cut through all the supposedly logical reasons why Harry recommends his pump—because
it will outshoot any other make or style—you come to realize that
Harry really likes the gun because he's shot it a lot. He knows the
weapon and how to use it, and, I suspect, more important, every
time he sees it in his gun rack or hefts it afield, it brings back warm
memories: that double he dropped during a snowstorm, and that
straight-on shot at a great old gander that somehow he bobbled.
You can't divorce a gun from personality or its past; so there's valid-
ity to the advice that you should get the action and model that appeals to you in feel and looks. It will be the easiest to learn to love—
and use.

Browning

Browning's A-5 automatic,
chambered for 3-inch mags,
is one of the most popular
waterfowling guns in America
today, with an impressive record of reliability.

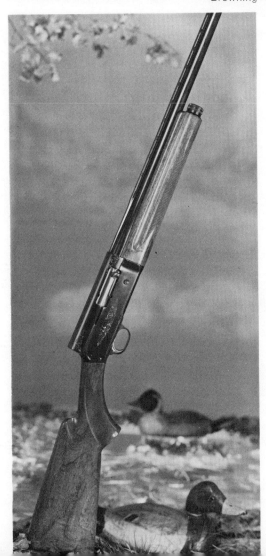

• AUTOS. In terms of cold hard facts, however, the semiautomatic is hard to beat in terms of efficiency. Three pulls of the trigger deliver three shots with no manual activity on your part beyond crooking your finger. Autos fall into two classes (gas-operated and recoil-operated), and it's generally true that the gas-operated mechanisms kick less. If you plan to reload shells, however—and this might well be in order if you buy a 3-inch mag—autos will not feed correctly unless your casings are letter-perfect, a condition that often can't be judged by eye. Autos also require the most babying in terms of maintenance. They'll jam if they're dirty or overly oiled, especially in frigid weather.

Savage Arms

The Savage model 30-D comes very close to the ultimate all-around shotgun. With its pump action, 3-inch mag chambering, and the availability of a 28-inch modified barrel, you can shoot any load in this weapon from the lightest field weight to the heaviest magnums, for any bird from dove to geese.

• Pump-action fans point out that the manual activity required to shuck a shell is actually a good thing, requiring of the shooter a split-second's pause and resighting before touching off another shell. With autos there is a tendency to keep banging away without correcting for a miss, until all shells are gone. Pumps also stand up well under typical waterfowling conditions—miserable weather and a surfeit of dirt. They'll also accept malformed reloads more easily than an auto, and they hold the auto's three shells.

Remington

Remington's entry into the waterfowling field includes the pump action 870 "wingmaster" and the model 1100 auto. Both weapons are available in 3-inch magnum chambering.

• Doubles fall into two categories: those with barrels arranged side by side and those with barrels arranged one on top of the other. Logically enough, the former is called a side-by-side, the latter an over/under. Which type is best for you is strictly a matter of personal preference. Some people prefer the sighting plane of a single tube, and this accounts for most of the over/under's popularity. Generally, the over/under will cost more than a sister side-by-side.

Doubles offer several advantages over pumps and autos. For one thing, by virtue of the fact that you have two barrels, you can have two chokes: a modified for close-swinging birds and a full for those far out. Although doubles only have two shots, they're far faster than either pumps or autos to reload. With automatic ejectors, it's quite easy to learn how to get off four shots during each toll, though automatic ejectors usually push the price of a factory-produced double well beyond that of a pump or auto.

Doubles are also the safest of the three types in that they can be carried or racked in the blind broken—in a position to see if the weapon is loaded or unloaded, yet ready to shoot at the snap of the breech. They'll also accept and shoot the vilest-looking reloads you'd care to put together, a fact that warms the heart of many a 10-gauge fan. Most 10-gauge guns are doubles, and it's just as well; if I couldn't reload my 10-gauge shells, saving about six bucks a box, I'm afraid my wife would have to go barefoot.

Savage Arms

Savage's model 333 over/under comes in 3-inch magnum chambering, with auto ejectors and a tang safety, at a very reasonable price. Other manufacturers of duck- and goose-worthy over/unders include Browning, Remington, Winchester, and Beretta.

SHOT AND SHELLS

There are three types of shotgun shells available today, and at one time or another, all three loads are of use to the waterfowler.

• Low base, low brass, and field loads are all names for the shells holding the smallest charge of powder and pushing the lightest amount of lead. While these loads are far too light for birds on the wing, they are handy to dispatch cripples.

• High base, high brass, express, or "duck and pheasant" loads are the next category up the power scale. These cartridges boost your power and pattern by about 20 percent over the field load. They're useful during those times when birds are offering a shot at from thirty to forty yards, a situation that sometimes arises jump shooting, decoy hunting over a small pothole, or pass shooting during a high wind.

• For most duck and goose hunting, however, it's the magnum load that's the wisest choice. This powder/shot combination increases power and range 40 to 50 percent over field loads, affording a standard 12 a reach up to an honest fifty-five yards (I've heard waterfowlers claim of clean kills beyond that range with this shell, but doubt the wisdom of such a shot).

Beyond the characteristics of the loads themselves, there are a few other features to look for in a good shell for ducks and geese. Waterproofing is a virtual necessity; I've yet to see a duck-hunting trip where at least a few shells didn't end up in the drink. This points in the direction of plastic upper casings, a wise choice in another way because they hold their shape (no swelling or ovaling out at the crimp) and always feed well. Plastic also comes clean with a wipe on your pants; if your shell doesn't end up in the water, it's bound to drop into some mud.

One word of caution about plastic, however: in recent years an all-plastic casing with no brass at the base has appeared on the market. It is a good idea in theory, but not in practice as of the writing of this book. The primer tends to pop out of some of them after being exploded, and it will foul any gun mechanism short of a double-barreled weapon.

Plastic collars that line the interior of a shell casing receive my stamp of approval. These prevent direct contact of lead shot with the steel walls of a gun barrel, and prevent deformation of the pellet (which in turn causes the pellet to assume an erratic flight and results in a poor pattern). Perhaps the best device of all is the plastic "piston" insert, which both protects the shot and holds it together, preventing so-called stringing out—a situation that finds the last pellet in a charge following far behind the first. Your pattern will be far more effective if all pellets travel on the same plane, reaching the target essentially the same instant.

Shot sizes to use for waterfowl are a subject of argument equal to the "best" gauge and the "best" barrel-length/choke combination.

And like these other two areas of debate, they are subjects upon which I have my opinions.

First let's look at relative sizes of shot and how they're measured.

"The smaller the identifying number, the larger the shot" is the rule here; #7½ , the smallest shot within reason to use on a duck, is about the size of a pinhead; 00 buck, the largest shot-shell load short of a solid slug (which is illegal), is about half the size of a marble. A sampling of some of the sizes in between, the smallest first, would include #6, which is roughly the diameter of a pencil lead; #4, about the thickness of a coat-hanger wire; #2, the diameter of a lighter flint; BB, the same size as the ammunition used in BB guns; #4 buck, about the size of a .22 bullet; and "buck," roughly the size of a pencil.

When assessing the most effective shot under a given circumstance, there are several factors to be considered; among them are pattern, energy, and range.

If you were to take a handful of sand and throw it as hard as you could, you'd be splattering a myriad of tiny particles over everything within a relatively short distance. Take a handful of marbles and throw them hard, and you'd get much greater range but poor coverage—a thin pattern along the entire flight path of the projectiles. Allowing some latitude for poetic license, this is essentially the difference between #7½ shot and 00 buck, both of which I've seen used on waterfowl at one time or another.

The justifications for each are rather interesting. In terms of #7½ shot, proponents rightfully claim a denser pattern. But more ingenious and quite common is the notion that these tiny pellets will 1) penetrate more deeply because they're small (like a needle versus a blunt arrowhead), and 2) pass through the armor of feathers more easily than larger shot, which tends to "ball up."

The matter of penetration would be true *if* both large and small pellets possessed the same amount of energy in flight. But it's physically impossible for this to happen when both pellets are traveling at the same rate of speed. For example, #8 "trap shot" at sixty yards has a piddling .69 foot-pounds of energy per pellet; #2 shot, propelled by an equivalent charge, has a whopping 5.23 foot-pounds of energy. Sure, some penetration will be lost in the #2 shot because its greater bulk creates greater resistance, but that resistance also translates into shocking power, another factor that helps bring down a bird.

That smaller shot will find its way through feathers is also doubtful. Because the shot is smaller, individual pellets won't carry the volume of "balled" feather fiber into the meat that fours or sixes will. However, proportionately, when I've cleaned birds I've found 7½'s buried the feather fibers just as readily as larger shot. There's just less of it torn loose by each pellet.

At the other end of the scale, 00 buck (I've seen many hunters use this on geese) has a pretty fantastic range; indeed, if a pellet connects with a vital spot it will kill at 100 yards and beyond. But with only nine pellets to each 2¾-inch 12-gauge cartridge, you hardly have what you would call a pattern at that kind of a range.

The wisest choice in shot sizes, then, lies somewhere between these two extremes and, to my way of thinking, involves the following:

• Early in the season I use #6's or #5's on ducks and #2 shot backed up by BB for geese.

• Late in the season I switch to #4's for ducks and BB's backed up by #4 buckshot on geese. This heavier shot is dictated by thickening feathers and fat layers.

A few words might be in order on that goose choice, too. First, if there's any bird that subjects the hunter to sky-busting and poor range judgment, it's the goose. After shooting at three-pound ducks, when a twelve-pound goose comes gliding in he looks like a blimp as sixty-five yards. I'm as guilty of this poor judgment as anybody; so, to prevent crippling a bird through my own stupidity, I opt for big shot that packs a lot of energy at long ranges.

Realize, too, that I'm using a 10-gauge 3½ -inch magnum on these birds, with a cartridge that contains about as many BB's as a standard 12 has #2's, and fifty-six #4 buck pellets—roughly the same number of BB's that a 12 packs. With this number of pellets I still get a decent pattern at long ranges.

SIGHTS AND SCOPES

Purists might snort at the thought of a sight or scope on a shotgun, but I think they have a place in waterfowling, especially for tyros.

With the exception of jump shooting, you'll have a long time to line up on your target, and a sight forces you to slow down and think before triggering a shot. This will, in turn, result in more and cleaner kills.

One of the most consistent faults I've observed among clients

I've guided and friends with whom I've hunted is the assumption that 150-odd pellets affords them the latitude to point their barrel in the general direction of the target in order to bring it down. This attitude usually results in a shot that's made too quickly, too casually, and that misses its target. The "slow down and think" nature of a sight helps counter this tendency. Flock shooting is another sin avoided by the use of a sight—it forces you to pick out a single bird.

Waterfowling is also a long-range shotgun sport, and in any kind of distance shooting, from big-game rifles down to slingshots, the farther you are from your target, the greater the need for precise aiming. Sights afford that kind of precision.

• The front bead is the most common form of shotgun sight on the market, and it comes attached to most factory models. Of the bead types, I strongly favor the red glass that picks up light and stands out as you swing. It's much easier to find than an ivory or steel bead, especially in low-light conditions. Using this type of bead, you can train yourself to use the shallow notch found in most shotgun receivers as a rear sight.

Another route to go is the Slug-Site, a commercial device that can be stuck to the receiver of your shotgun and removed at will. Essentially this gadget is both a rear and front sight, housed on a seven-inch-long piece of flat iron that's held in place by a sticky substance. Slug-Sites are available as a mail-order item from Slug-Site Co., 3835 University, Des Moines, Iowa 50311.

• One variety of shotgun sights I can't personally recommend is constructed of two O-rings that rest along either side of the shotgun muzzle. The idea, when using these, is to encircle a passing bird with the ring before triggering your shot. It works, but only at relatively close ranges. And the sight's construction and location make hell out of casing and uncasing a gun.

• Special shotgun scopes are relatively new to the market, and I've been impressed with those I've tried. They don't magnify an image like rifle scopes, but rather project a red dot out to the point of impact. Surely most ingenious, and a bit baffling, are those that show a dot in the middle of a clear see-through ring mounted on the receiver. The dot seems to hang in midair; you find your bird, determine the correct lead, and put the dot there; if your calculations are correct the bird comes down.

The problem with all these sights, however, is that they encourage one-eyed shooting: the monocular squint of the rifleman. Shotguns should be aimed with *both* eyes open. For that reason my favorite sight is Normark's Single-point. This device resembles a rifle scope in shape and mounting, but differs from all other scopes on the market in that you can't see through it.

To understand its operation, focus your eyes on a distant point and hold a finger in front of one eye. Both eyes will appear to be seeing the finger, and seeing through it at the same time. One eye will project your finger's image on whatever you're looking at.

This is exactly the way the Single-point works. If you close one eye and try to look through the scope, all you'll see is a red dot in the middle of a black field. Open both eyes, and your viewing eye projects that dot on the target. You *must* shoot this device with both eyes open, and combined with the red-dot assurance of where your shot will hit, you learn the nuances of lining up and leading quickly. Once that skill is developed, you can remove the scope entirely and become a purist yourself, shooting by "instinct," which, incidentally, I don't believe exists.

PATTERNING AND PRACTICE

Learning to estimate range, and having some idea of what your gun is capable of doing, is far more critical to waterfowling than to other shotgun sports. The upland gunner usually has a flash of a shot offered at close ranges that is immediately swallowed up by trees or a hedgerow. The duck or goose hunter frequently sees his quarry a minute or more prior to its decoying or passing within range. Because of the anxiety and anticipation associated with watching a bird loom larger and larger while you're forced to wait, powerless to do a damn thing about it, shooting too soon, or long after birds have passed from range, are common mistakes.

You'll enjoy a sobering and instructive experience that will help eliminate these tendencies if you pattern your shotgun before the season.

Set up a target against some hay or straw bales, and mark off thirty, forty, fifty, and sixty yards. You'll learn even more if you bring plenty of box cardboard and shoot into it. If your pellets pass through the cardboard, you're relatively safe to assume they're carrying enough killing power to penetrate feather and skin. Shoot whatever assortment of powder and shot loads you plan to use the coming season.

It would also pay to have two cutout facsimiles of an average-sized duck, viewed from profile and straight on. After each shot, lay those facsimiles against the pattern that's revealed in the cardboard, counting as a clean kill the placement of four pellets in the body or head—four pellets that *pass through* the cardboard, that is.

I promise you'll come to understand how utterly easy it is to miss the proverbial "sitting duck," and you'll learn the futility of barrel stretching in the bargain.

Other things that might well be revealed are the patterning quirks of your shotgun. Many guns will pattern a particular load combination better than it will others. My 12 auto, for example, blows holes using #2's, but patterns fours, fives, and sixes perfectly. It isn't a matter of make, either—just individual barrels and their characteristics.

This is important information to have when choosing your loads, for patterning is usually the secret of a top-notch duck shot who claims #4, or #6, or whatever, is the ultimate shot size to use because it's downed him so many birds. Actually, it just patterns best in his barrel.

12 | Clothing for the Waterfowler

The pursuit of waterfowl on this continent has found me in blinds all the way from The Pas in northern Manitoba to a town called Teacapan, sixty miles south of Mazatlan, Mexico, and eight hundred miles below the United States border.

If those relatively wide travels have taught me anything about outerwear, it's that a serious duck hunter could well amass a wardrobe that would rival the combined holdings of the nation's ten best-dressed men. For starters, there's the matter of color.

You should have a suit to match every shade you encounter during the season. If opening day dawns on the rich greens of growing things, olive drab blends the best. If you hunt the northern marshes, where the green of early season turns a rich brown with the frosts of fall, you'll need clothing to blend into this background as well. In both cases, a camouflage pattern in the proper hue will best break up your outline.

Other colors you might need include solid white for hunting around snow cover, black for gunning off the rock jetties along the Northeast Coast, and gray for shooting from punties over open water.

In terms of material and design, a loose-fitting outer jacket-and-pants set of tight-weave windbreaker cloth is the most versatile garment. This outer covering allows you to dress for virtually any climate, from warm to cool to cold, by adding to or subtracting from the clothes you wear underneath. I also like a jacket that has a hood; it breaks up the outline of your neck and head, as well as providing protection from the elements.

The one exception I make to this basic outfit is when I'm hunting in very hot weather. High temperatures occasionally come with the duck season down south, and are the rule in Mexico. In these conditions a suit of see-through camouflage netting is the best way to remain hidden and cool.

One feature I strongly recommend be incorporated into any outer hunting jacket is elastic shell pockets. Although a box of shells will probably be within easy reach most of the time, when you have to chase a cripple, you either forget to grab extras entirely or don't bring enough. With a dozen or so shells tucked firmly in your two pockets, you'll always have the firepower to dispatch a wounded bird.

Careful attention to color and hue is all that's required for outerwear, but when you're hunting in extremely cold temperatures the clothing you wear under your suit becomes of primary importance. When you're dressing for bitterly cold weather, remember that several articles of light clothing will keep you warmer than one heavy jacket of equivalent weight.

• A sampling of the kind of clothing that keeps you warm includes cotton underwear as the basic undergarment. Although this light underwear might not do much to keep you warm, it plays an important part in the overall function of your clothes in that it absorbs perspiration. The physical effort required in walking to a blind across a muddy marsh, setting out decoys, or digging a pit usually has you sweating before you settle down to wait. It's that moisture that eventually chills you unless you make some provision for it to be absorbed by your clothing. Cotton does this job best.

• Insulated underwear goes over the cotton. Although some brands of the insulated stuff come with a cotton liner sewn to the inside, if you buy this variety you'll have to wash it a lot, and washing will cause undue wear. Rather, buy the unlined underwear, and put it over your cotton garments. Waffle-knit underwear holds the least heat, Dacron or other synthetic-fiber-filled garments fall in the middle of the road, and down is the most efficient insulator of all.

221

It would be misleading to say any one of them is preferable for all seasons. Down underwear at 40 above would be intolerably hot, and waffle-knit at zero would be ineffective. Choose the garment that best suits you at the temperatures you plan to encounter.

Underwear bottoms deserve some thought too. In pits and punties I've found a matched suit of insulated underwear to be impractical. My lower extremities hold warmth better than my upper extremities; so when I wear a complete set of Dacron underwear my legs often get too warm and begin to perspire. I usually wear heavy tops and light bottoms. One exception I make is when I'll be doing a lot of wading in cold water. There's nothing that will leech warmth from the body faster than contact with cold water through rubber waders; so I always wear heavy bottoms for winter wading.

• Shirts are next, and I'd recommend either wool shirts or thick flannellike "moleskin." I lean a bit toward moleskin material since it both affords warmth and will break the wind. Pants can be either wool or brushed denim. I prefer the brushed denim since it, too, cuts wind better than wool and just feels more comfortable.

• A sweater and then a jacket are the final components of cold-weather clothing. The bulkier the sweater, the warmer it will be. It is tiny compartments of trapped dead air that keep you warm, not the weight of cloth; so the more air you can keep close to your body the more efficiently your clothes will hold in warmth. Jackets can range all the way from your windbreaker ducksuit to a separate Alaska-type parka, depending on the temperature. Down filling will keep you the warmest.

• The best all-around headgear for the waterfowler is the narrow-brimmed "Jones" cap. The brim is turned up on the sides and down in front so rainwater or spray won't run down your neck. In addition, most of these caps come with ear flaps; so they will keep you warm in very cold weather. In truly bitter weather, when either the thermometer or wind-chill factor approaches 0 degrees, I prefer to wear a wool "watchcap." These caps can be pulled well over your ears and down your neck, and there's something about wool that seems to generate heat. You must wear a hood with a watchcap, though. Wool is warm, but unless you cover it with some sort of a windbreak the lightest breeze will eat through it.

While we're on the subject of winds, if you commonly encounter cold weather when you're waterfowling, always buy an outer ducksuit with drawstrings: drawstrings around the hood, around the bottom of the parka, and around the cuffs (elastic banding is actually best here). These drawstrings discourage easy entry of cold air, another critical factor when the thermometer plummets toward zero.

• Keeping hands and feet warm is similarly a matter of layers of covering. The most effective arrangement for your hands is a pair of common wool gloves, covered by shooting mittens. No glove with individual fingers will keep your hands warm when it's really cold because there's so much surface area exposed to the air.

Mittens suitable for shooting fall into two categories: those with palm slits through which you work your fingers when you're ready to shoot, and those that expose only your trigger finger. The full mitten with the shooting slits is the warmest, though it takes a little time to work your fingers into position. That should create no great hardships in a blind, but it will be a problem for the jump-shooter. If you like to walk for your ducks, choose the mitten with the exposed index finger. Shooting gloves are available in right- and left-hand models.

Your feet—if anything like mine—will be the most difficult part of your body to keep warm. When your hands get cold, you can always tuck them under your armpits, but that's a tough trick to match with your feet unless you're into yoga.

The only way I've found to keep my feet reasonably warm is to buy large boots expressly for my duck-hunting trips. I get them one and a half sizes too big.

All that room has a reason: I cram a lot into it. First, and this I've found most important, I wear a pair of "wick-dry" socks. These are special socks engineered to transfer moisture away from your skin, and, indeed, they do just that. Next I wear a pair of heavy wool socks—thick-knitted things that seem to weigh a pound apiece. Finally, and nearly as important as the wick-dry socks, I wear a pair of "slipper socks." These are wool socks with flexible leather soles. There is something about having an extra sole inside a boot that really makes a difference in warmth. An old duck-hunting partner who recently migrated to the great beyond gave me the clue—when the weather was cold he always put several layers of newspaper in the bottom of his boots. I tried the trick and it worked. Then I tried leather and foam-rubber boot inserts and they worked better. Then I tried slipper socks. To date I've found nothing quite so warm as they.

• Footgear has a lot to do with warmth. Rubber is the least desirable material because of the moisture problem—perspiration can't escape rubber as it will through the pores of leather. So if you won't be wading or standing on damp ground, an insulated leather boot will prove the best. Both Sears and Browning make superior models according to tests performed by my feet.

If you will be standing in water or on marshy ground, rubber is the only material that will keep water out. No matter how "waterproofed" boot manufacturers claim their leather product to be, moisture will eventually work its way through the leather. If, however, the water won't be deep where you'll be walking or standing, you might consider L. L. Bean's rubber-and-leather boot. The lower half of the foot is rubber and the upper half leather. Since warm air rises, this allows for plenty of moisture transfer through the top of the boot, and none through the bottom.

• If you'll be doing any wading you'll have to wear rubber footwear, and I'd recommend you get the best on the market. Light inexpensive waders might be welcome if you're hunting in warmer climates, but unless you'd be willing to swim in the water you're wading, get heavy, cloth-backed, real rubber boots.

Any brand of water-oriented duck hunting is bound to bring you in contact with some form of sharp edge: barbed wire, thorny bushes, sharp snags, splinters or nails in driftwood, broken glass, sharp tin cans—a whole nightmare of materials just waiting to puncture a pair of boots. And there is nothing, absolutely nothing, so dispiriting as tearing a big hole in your knee or pants seat with three dozen decoys out in four-foot-deep, 35-degree water.

The best boots I've found are the "commercial quality" chest waders manufactured by Red Ball. They're the favored brand of clam diggers and commercial fishermen on the East Coast, which says something about their endurance. They're not cheap—about sixty bucks at current prices—but I can count on at least six years' use from each pair I buy. That use includes breaking ice, digging clams, climbing barbed-wire fences, walking through thick woods, and, of course, duck hunting. I use them all year round and I know they actually save me money, having gone through my share of "bargain" waders before settling on these.

I feel as strongly about boot style too. As far as I'm concerned, hip boots are a useless death trap around any water that will be over your head. In all but isolated instances, when you're decoy hunting hip boots won't be high enough to provide real freedom of movement either. Water will lap dangerously close to their tops as you stretch to retrieve a cripple or to place your outermost stool.

They fill quickly with water, and the way they snap firmly around your calves they're impossible to get off in a hurry. Chest waders, on the other hand, will hold air and act as a life preserver if you wear them with a quick-release belt around their top. If water starts to trickle in, bend at the waist, your feet thrust upward, and the air trapped in your legs will keep you afloat forever. They slide off easily, too, and once off, again make a perfect life preserver if you cradle your body in the V of the crotch and use the air trapped in the legs for flotation.

KEEPING DRY

Any serious waterfowling is bound to involve its share of rain. That's another plus for chest waders: with a rubber-hooded parka worn outside the boots, it's impossible for rain to get in.

When you know you'll be faced with rain, tote along a long-brimmed baseball-type cap to keep rain off your face. What little water drips from your parka hood will then be directed to the tip of the cap's peak and away from you.

Rubber gloves are a blessing even when its not raining. They'll keep your hands dry, and consequently at least tolerably warm, when you're picking up stool from cold water.

Make it a rule *never* to step into water for any purpose wearing any glove but rubber. If you wear your shooting mittens, they're sure to get wet and will be rendered useless. If you forget rubber gloves, go bare-handed even in the coldest weather. Warm dry gloves back in the boat or blind are more important than brief comfort at the risk of wetting them.

13 | **Waterfowling Dogs**

There are many breeds that qualify as waterfowling dogs. The spaniels were bred with an eye toward retrieving over water, and, indeed, the Irish water spaniel and springer spaniel are specialists at this. Lou Peck, a good friend of mine who is a Brittany breeder and trainer, claims that about half the dogs he trains enjoy retrieving ducks as much as working upland game. It surprises many people, but the kinky, curly coat of a standard poodle makes that breed a good water dog. In fact they were developed in France with just that function in mind. And I've got to give some due to downright mutts; I've seen a few dogs of dubious parentage that made passable, though hardly polished, retrievers.

But I'd classify all of the aforementioned breeds off-beat if work as a waterfowler will be your dog's primary function. Some of them are essentially upland dogs; others have been bred for bench, for show, and as pets for so long that the pure hunting strain isn't there.

To approach this matter from a different angle: the qualities that make a poodle popular among prospective owners are intelligence, appearance, and, because they don't lose their hair, cleanliness.

The dogs that are in demand, and the pups of those dogs, possess those qualities first, and the old hunting ability comes as less than an afterthought. Even though they might once have been bred to hunt, purchasing these now-popular house pets means that you could end up with a strain that doesn't have the spirit that makes him quiver at the sound of a shot, or show the bad manners but admirable exuberance of occasionally breaking at the sight of a falling bird.

My feelings and advice are to stick with those breeds that are still primarily gun dogs rather than pets or the pampered possessions of the social elite. In terms of waterfowling, that boils down to two choices: the Chesapeake retriever or the Labrador retriever.

The Chesapeake Bay retriever is truly an American product, bred to take the cold salt waters of the northeast. They have the reputation of being hard-headed, single-minded, one-man dogs that are difficult to train, but they also are incredibly tough. Chessies have been known to break two hundred yards of ice to get to a downed bird. They've retrieved cripples from a wild surf and bucked surging currents that would have swept other dogs under.

I've been sorely tempted to get a Chessie and try him out every time round when I had to buy a new duck dog. But I haven't—for several reasons.

First, in all my hours spent in a blind, I have yet to see a working Chesapeake. Gunners have extolled their virtues and told me about friends who had friends whose Chessies performed miracles, but I still haven't *seen* a working dog. I can't help but wonder why.

Second, upon inquiry to Chesapeake breeders (who are few), I never found one who would sell me a dog that was finished, or even started. They had pups aplenty, but the adults they had on hand were all "show" dogs or field-trial specialists. The absence of available working dogs, "meat dogs" if you will, struck me as strange and triggered another red light.

Finally, an old gunner's explanation of the Chesapeake mystique really made sense. "A Chessie," he said, "is the finest dog God ever created for the waterfowler. They'll retrieve a thousand birds a day, break inch-thick slush ice to get to each one, and give nary a shiver. They'll order their lives around you; they don't want nobody else. They're tough, they're loyal, they're strong, and they're willing, but they're hard-headed. They can't change.

"When I was shooting seventy-five birds a day, I had a Chesapeake that I'd put up against any other dog on this earth. But that same animal could never exist on three or four birds a day like the limits are now. Chessies aren't gentlemen; they're made to do an honest job, like a workhorse. And if you don't give them their job, a tough, hard, nearly impossible job to do, it breaks their spirit or something. A Chessie that's a house pet is worse than worthless, but Lord what a dog they were for gunning when there were birds to shoot."

Labrador retrievers have been my waterfowling dogs. They're a friendly breed, good around kids and quite affectionate; yet they possess real drive, instinct, and desire to hunt.

I've owned several, and in terms of drawbacks about the only one I can cite is that I wish they were a little hardier. I do a lot of hunting in cold climates: in late fall in Montana, and the even colder water temperatures of the upper northeast coast in January. After two or three retrieves in that kind of frigid waters a Lab starts to shiver. Some gunners claim the dogs are "nervous," but I know mine and he's just damnably cold. I have found, however, that I can keep the dog reasonably comfortable if I keep a terrycloth towel in the blind with which to rub him down quickly when he leaves the water. Some dry bedding to lie or sit on inside the blind helps too.

It might be worth pointing out that Labs also do excellent double duty as upland dogs. They flush rather than point, a slight disadvantage to my way of thinking, but they're naturals at ferreting out pheasant and grouse and will bring them back, assuming you can hit them.

Buying a Dog   Before you buy a dog, you'd do well to ask yourself if you really want one. Owning any sort of working hunter has its pains as well as pleasures.

In purely pragmatic terms, I'd say that the number of times you go waterfowling is a good yardstick of your need for a dog. If you're a casual hunter who ventures afield two or three times a season, a dog will probably amount to little more than another source of frustration—unless you enjoy dog training as a pastime unto itself.

If you've worked with your dog all year long on some sort of regular basis, he'll know your commands and desires well enough to perform on spotty field trips. But you simply can't take a dog who's been a pet for nine months and expect him to do anything right on opening day—even if he was a finished and polished dog when you first got him.

My dogs have always fouled up the first few days I had them out—breaking as birds tolled, and refusing to sit still in the blind—but they've been good lusty hunters, and the excitement of doing the thing for which they were made is just too much to bear at first. They behaved like kids at the Christmas tree, tearing into every present at once; utterly undisciplined. Yet I can't help but term their intense interest admirable, and I have trouble fighting back a grin when I reproach them. They know that they did wrong, but their whole demeanor says to me, "But dammit boss—this is such *great* fun!"

Then, on about the third trip out, they begin to settle down and behave. The initial excitement is over and they can look at what's happening more objectively. They come to realize that incoming birds won't go down unless you shoot them, and that if they leave the blind before your command you'll be displeased.

A good working dog does take time, patience, and exposure; so if you don't hunt a lot and have neither the time nor desire to maintain a regular training program, I'd advise strongly against buying one. You'll spend the few days you do get out on the marsh beating your dog and apologizing to your partners in the blind instead of hunting.

On the other hand, if you're afield every weekend and spend stormy evenings thinking up excuses that will keep you away from the office the next morning, you'll find a retriever adds yet another dimension to waterfowling.

Part of the pleasure is in watching that dog work for you: hitting the water with a mighty splash, and churning his way to a downed duck. But there's the ritual too.

In this age of superscience and myth debunking, man is pitifully short of rituals. Training and using a dog is as much a part of the waterfowling ritual as painting your stool, setting a rig, and building a blind. It's doing things the right way—creating the whole picture. Away from the blind, you'll enjoy a bond between man and dog that was forged in the field into a relationship that never exists between a mere "pet" and his "owner."

Selecting a Gunning Dog   There are two ways to buy a dog: as a puppy or as a trained adult.

In both cases it's important to know something about the animal's background and parentage. The dog should have papers issued by the American Kennel Club (AKC) attesting to the fact that he is pedigreed. This is the only way you can be sure that you're getting a pure strain, without possible undesirable crossbred traits.

The dog should have been vaccinated for distemper and rabies, and have been x-rayed for signs of hip displasia. This disease has become tragically common among many breeds, and virtually always means the animal must be destroyed in its second or third year.

I also feel it's important that the animal come from either top working dogs or field-trial champions no more than three generations back in its lineage. My advice is based on that matter of breeding "pets" rather than hunters, mentioned earlier.

Buying a puppy is surely the most common route most people take. If you buy from a kennel, a well-bred pup will cost from 75 to 150 dollars, depending on bloodlines. Occasionally you can buy a puppy privately, with perfectly acceptable lineage, for 35 dollars up.

Trained dogs are understandably more expensive. "Started" dogs are usually a year to a year and a half old, and have been taught the basics of hunting by a professional trainer. Started dogs will cost from 150 dollars to 400, depending on the amount of training that's gone into them and the promise they show as hunters. "Finished" dogs are just what the name implies: mature animals, fully trained, that are ready for work right now. These dogs are admittedly costly — usually 500 to 1,000 dollars for a young animal with a long working life ahead.

There are many pros and cons involving the way to go about acquiring a hunting partner. When raised from puppyhood, the dog gets a chance to know you and grow with your family. *But* amateur trainers seldom turn out good working dogs.

Laziness is generally the reason. You start with noble intent, then, in reality, never spend enough time training the dog, nor do you do it at the right time. Even when you expend lots of energy on training, the chances are that you'll put up with bad habits without realizing it, that in ignorance you'll teach your dog bad habits, or that you'll let your dog outfox you. The World's Greatest Authority on how to train a dog badly has spoken; I've tried it twice and neither time ended up with a really first-line dog. Both were excellent hunters, but they were also spoiled brats who could play on my affections like an only child.

The finished dog is at the other extreme. They're just too expensive for me, and I can't help but feel that when one man, the dog's trainer, has been the only authority and human the animal has known, that man will always be that dog's master. You will only be the dog's owner; there will be something very important missing from your relationship.

230

Speaking for myself, I prefer to buy the year-old started dog, and that's the satisfactory route I've taken with my last two Labs. The dog is still young enough to develop an attachment to you, yet is well schooled in basic discipline, form, and etiquette. You also have the advantage of seeing and knowing what kind of a hunter you're buying.

Another route that seems acceptable is to buy a puppy, raise him in your home to a trainable age, and then turn him over to a professional handler for schooling. As is obvious, I have severe doubts that anyone who's dandled a puppy on his lap is capable of doling out proper discipline to that dog. And I also have a hunch that puppy, and later the mature dog, might not be capable of taking discipline from such a master seriously, without the intervention of a stern and able third party.

In both the started dog and trained puppy you'll find the ultimate investment will be about the same. That's yet another reason for not buying a retriever unless you truly plan to use it.

USING THE RETRIEVER

I've purposely skipped dog training. The ins and outs of teaching a dog new tricks deserve a book, and, indeed, there are many such excellent books on the market. *Charles Morgan on Retrievers, Training Your Retriever* by James Lamb Tree, and *Water Dog* by Wolters are some works I'd recommend.

Instead, let me say a few words about hunter training.

When dogs are trained by a pro, the acts they are expected to perform, the commands you give, and the motions you go through to elicit a response from the dog are rather standard. It's important that *you* learn exactly how to work with a dog, for each word and each gesture has its proper response. If you don't execute them correctly the dog will become confused and not perform; this is a fault of your training, not the dog's.

Sending a Dog on a Retrieve   Command the dog to heel. "Heel-up" is the usual term. He should sit at your side with his head at about your thigh. Sweep your hand in an arc that begins at the dog's head and ends pointing in the direction of the bird or dummy. Arc your hand twice, saying, "Dead bird, dead bird."

This gives the dog a "line"—a direction. He might well know

exactly where the bird fell, but if he didn't see the fall this shows him approximately where to look.

The fetching command is usually "Back." At the sound of that word the dog should take off like a bolt of lightning.

The dog should travel on a straight line to the bird and return over the same route. He should deliver the bird to your hand, sitting at heel. If he looks for direction bringing the bird in, say "Fetch it here," or blow several short blasts on a whistle. Once you have the bird, you can send the dog out again for a double, using the same hand-arc/"Dead bird" sequence.

If the dog hasn't marked the fall, he must make what is known as a blind retrieve. Give the dog a line with your hand and send him, "Back." If he makes an approach that will miss the bird, one long whistle blast means the dog should stop and look at you. A broad obvious sweep of your hand to left or right, coupled with the command "Over," will send the dog in that direction. If he stops short of the felled bird, the command "Back" will send him out farther. Some dogs also are trained to get direction from various whistle blasts.

Finding a Lost Bird   Occasionally, neither you nor the dog will know exactly where a bird fell. In this case, walk the dog over to the probable area and say "Dead." The dog will glue his head to the ground and search for the downed bird with real dedication. The command "Dead" will get the same response at a distance. If the dog is having trouble locating a scent and you know where the bird hit, "Dead" will tell him he's in the immediate area of the fall and he'll search more carefully.

PART FIVE

Table Fare

14 | Preparing Waterfowl for the Table

There's a tradition in the Strung house that on Thanksgiving we serve both turkey and wild goose. It started many years ago when we invited our regular complement of eighteen to twenty-two dinner guests, and discovered the eighteen-pound turkey we had in the freezer just might not have enough meat on its bones to fill our famished diners. So Sil defrosted a ten-pound wild goose I'd shot a few weeks before, stoked up the old wood-burning stove I use to heat my workshop, and cooked it too.

We were right about the turkey. By the time it passed full around the table, it had been reduced to a pile of white, bare bones. But except for the slices of goose that Sil and I had taken, the Canada was untouched.

Then someone who hadn't gotten a full share of turkey took the first plunge, hesitantly carving a slice of breast meat from the goose. "Hey—this isn't bad at all!" he said, and persuaded his companion to try a bite. She agreed, and passed the word along; and soon the goose, too, was nothing but bone.

But there's more to the story. The guests assembled around the table enjoyed the goose so much that those who returned the following year begged for more. And since that second year, it's the goose, not the turkey, that's reduced to a pile of rubble within five minutes of its being set on the table.

Fishy—greasy—gamey—they're all adjectives used to describe waterfowl as table fare by those who have never tried it. Once they do, those descriptive terms change to "Delicious," "Outa sight," "Something else!"

There is some savvy connected with properly preparing waterfowl, just as there is for different types of domestic meats. Unlike domestic fowl you buy in the supermarket, however, care of waterfowl is a beginning-to-end procedure that begins soon after the bird is brought to hand.

Plucking is the first order of business when you wish to serve the bird as a roast.

• Dry-plucking means that you pull the feathers free from the carcass with your hands. This can be done at home (outside, or you'll have feathers all over the kitchen), or as a means to pass slack time right in the blind. It's generally accepted that dry-plucking results in the finest tasting meat.

Begin by cradling the bird back-down on your knees, and tease the breast feathers free. The stout outer feathers will pull out first, leaving soft, fluffy down. Down usually comes loose if you rub it hard with you thumb in slow, deliberate sweeps.

Work out from the breast, stripping feathers clean of the sides, then around to the back. Tail and wing feathers are removed last. They're well anchored and often must be pulled loose one at a time. It's not necessary to pluck the wings beyond the first joint; the scant meat that lies beyond doesn't justify the work involved.

When the carcass is relatively free of feathers, sever the legs and wings by cutting through the first joint with a sharp knife. Cutting through the neck requires a bit more effort. Use a heavy knife or cleaver and cutting board.

It's an Augean task to pluck a carcass perfectly clean of feathers, and rather than spend the time, I prefer to burn residual pin feathers and hair off with a propane torch. Just a quick once-over with this hot flame cleans the carcass perfectly. Any open flame will produce the same results, but not quite as efficiently as the easy-to-direct flame of a torch.

• Wet-plucking is easier than dry-plucking, but it requires extensive preparation and creates something of a mess. As a rule I reserve this technique for times when I have many birds to clean—ten or more.

You'll need a five-gallon bucket or pot half filled with water, a stove, and a few drops of detergent. Heat the water to within 10 degrees of boiling (212 degrees at sea level), and stir in a teaspoonful of detergent. Immerse the unplucked carcasses of two to four ducks in the slightly soapy water and stir them gently for about fifteen seconds.

The detergent action allows the water to penetrate the duck's oily feathers, then the heat loosens the feather-butts once the water reaches the skin. Keep a close watch on the birds; they're ready to be plucked as soon as breast and wing feathers pull loose easily. If you leave the carcass in the water too long the heat will work in reverse, holding the feather-butts more secure than they were in the first place.

Water temperature is quite critical to this operation. If it's too hot or too cold the feathers won't come loose; so it's a good idea to check the temperature of the water with a thermometer before dunking each batch of ducks.

When done correctly, removing feathers from the carcass requires no more than a rubbing motion with your hand. Birds will strip as easily as willow leaves from a slender branch.

• Paraffin plucking is a little expensive, but it's the easiest of the three methods. After a cursory dry-plucking, immerse the partially defeathered carcass in melted paraffin wax. Withdraw the bird; after the wax hardens, feathers and wax coating can be peeled from the carcass like a banana peel.

Cleaning a plucked bird begins with an incision from the anus to the rear of the bottom breastbone. Note that I discuss cleaning *after* plucking; if you clean before plucking, feathers will get in the way and you'll end up with a messier and more difficult job than is necessary.

Remove all stomach contents by sliding the back of your fingers along the inside of the breast and scooping the entrails out. There will probably be a strong, somewhat sour odor. Don't interpret this as the meat having gone "bad." All fowl smell terrible when you clean them—even farm-fresh chickens.

From the removed entrails you might want to rescue the liver, heart, and gizzard. The gizzard is ball-round, dark in color, and hard, and must be cut in half to remove the tough lining and gravel or sand that will be contained therein. The gizzard serves to initially grind up and partially digest a bird's food. The gizzard, heart, and liver are all delicious to eat and make an excellent stock for stuffing and gravy. Goose liver pâté needs no more recommendation than to mention it.

Give the body cavity a quick rinsing with cold water, and run your index finger on either side of the backbone up toward the breast. You'll be able to feel a soft, jellylike substance. These are the lungs, one on each side of the backbone, and they should be removed. Farther inside the cavity you'll feel hard cartilaginous organs. These are the digestive tract and larynx, and they too should be removed.

The crop is the final organ to clean. It's located just where the neck joins the breast on the outside, and if it's full, it will be swollen with grain, rice, or whatever foods the birds were feeding on. Make a large enough incision to free the contents, and rinse out the empty crop. The bird is now cleaned.

Other methods of cleaning waterfowl exist and, at times, are in order.

• Skinning rather than plucking the bird is one method I don't recommend. When you remove the skin, the resulting meat cooks dry. So dry, in fact, that any meat other than the breast gets frizzled. If the breast is all that you are interested in, there are faster, simpler methods to get at it.

• Breast fillets are obtained by plucking a clean line down the middle of the breastbone; you'll be able to feel the bone in the center of the breast. With a sharp knife, cut cleanly down on either side of the bone. Pull the meat away from the bone with one hand, and slice away bone-to-meat attachments with the knife. When you reach the side of the carcass, you'll begin to run out of meat and into skin. Now reverse your fillet, separating skin and flesh until you return to the original cut. Each carcass will provide you with two chunks of boneless, skinless meat. With a little practice, you can fillet a duck in less than two minutes' time.

• Breast removal is even faster, but a little trickier to learn. It works especially well on small birds: doves, teal, coot, and the like.

Lay the cleaned bird on the ground on its back, wings spread outward. Stand with one foot on each wing, and grab one leg in each hand. Pull up sharply and cleanly, and the breast should pop free of the body and entrails.

I must confess that when I do this I end up with a bit more cleanup than is indicated here, but even with that extra work, it's still a quick way to dress a bird. I have seen others, more adept at this technique than I, breast coot out as easily as shucking corn.

Curing and aging is important to both the flavor and the texture of game birds. "Curing" the meat amounts to nothing more than over-night immersion in a strong brine solution.

This draws any remaining blood from the meat tissue, resulting in a milder flavor to the meat. It isn't a prerequisite to cooking; some people, myself included, prefer a strong flavor in wildfowl.

On the other hand, I am a firm and constant believer in aging meat. Allowing the carcass to remain for several days in cool temperatures before freezing it or eating it results in a breakdown of muscle tissue and more tender meat.

The simplest way to age a carcass is in the refrigerator. Cover a cleaned bird with aluminum foil or wax paper, to prevent drying, and leave it there for at least three days.

I prefer to "hang" birds in the traditional British manner: to age them in a cool backshed/meathouse on my property before cleaning and plucking them. But to do this correctly you must have ideal temperatures and be able to judge accurately when the birds are ready for cleaning. Both factors are so variable, depending on weather and the condition of the bird itself, that any description of the yard-sticks I use would be misleading 90 percent of the time. One sign that should give a clue, however, is feather resistance. When the feathers just above the tail can be plucked free of the skin with ease, the bird is usually ready for dressing.

Butchering   When should you leave a bird whole for roasting and when should you simply breast it out?

• When a duck or goose gets caught squarely in your pattern and is overly shot-up, breasting the bird out is usually best. It's also a wise move to do this soon after the kill, without any hanging, since blood-shot meat spoils quickly.

• The larger species of waterfowl, in good condition—geese, mallards, canvasback, and pintail—virtually demand a roast. It's almost sinful to use just their breasts and miss the meat you end up discarding, as well as to miss the heady flavors that can be imparted to the birds through different types of stuffing.

• Smaller birds like teal and bufflehead have so little meat on their backs and thighs that the time you'd spend plucking them isn't really justified. Breast these birds out. This is also recommended for ducks that eat fish: mergansers, and any diving species that have been feeding on mussels and crustacea for several weeks. The chunks of breast are more responsive to flavor-altering marinades than whole carcasses because there's more surface area exposed to the sauce.

DUCKFEATHERS!

Another reason why I usually prefer to dry-pluck waterfowl is that their feathers and down are useful.

Many of the outer feathers of geese and ducks are used in the manufacture of artificial fishing flies. I'm a fly-tier myself, but even if you're not it's a good bet one of your friends is. If so, you can probably engineer a feathers-for-flies trade that will keep you in fishing tackle all year long.

Down is one of the best insulators known to man and waterfowl is its source. The best down comes from geese but duck down is quite close in quality. I save all the down from the ducks and geese I shoot and my wife uses it to make sleeping bags for us. It's a unique pleasure to spend a warm night under cold stars, kept cozy by down from the birds you shot. It's also something of a financial pleasure; down is worth twenty to thirty dollars per pound.

15 | Cooking Waterfowl

Before discussing how to cook waterfowl properly, it might be worth pointing out how *not* to cook them.

To parboil waterfowl is a persistent myth that seems to hang on and on and on, the justification for the boiling being that it removes all the grease in ducks and geese.

In fact, waterfowl have very little fat. The practice probably comes from the domestic duck and goose, for these birds are fatty indeed. But waterfowl live a hard life, one that doesn't afford unlimited food and the buildup of fat reserves. The amount of fat they do carry is just about right to keep the meat rich and moist. If you parboil the birds, you'll end up with dry, coarse meat.

Improper cooking time is also commonly responsible for mistakes and second-rate eating. As a rule, those times cited for domestic fowl are utterly wrong for waterfowl. Again, it's a matter of the kind of existence waterfowl endure; they're neither pampered nor over-fed, and they develop extensive muscle structure. When you cook them using the same guidelines you would for chicken or turkey, you only toughen muscle fiber and make for overly chewy meat.

That is the reason why wildfowl are traditionally cooked "rare," with plenty of pink meat evident. It's a little like steak; a rare steak will always be more tender than a well-done steak.

Following that analogy (if you can't get used to the idea of rare duck), the same steak can be cooked to a point where it will be even more tender than when rare—swiss steak is one example of this. If you cook and cook and cook wildfowl at low temperatures (250 to 300 degrees), you'll end up with tender meat that literally falls off the bone. Cooking wildfowl in this manner also results in a milder flavor than when you cook it rare.

Altering the flavor of the meat, when you deem it to have an objectionable odor (fishy, strong, etc.) can be accomplished in several ways.

• Marinades are solutions of liquids and spices that both tenderize and flavor meat. The basic stocks for waterfowl marinades come from a variety of sources (milk, orange juice, and wine, for example). Several marinades are included in the recipes that follow.

• Cooking the bird in sauerkraut.

• Stuffing it. There are many varieties of stuffing that are delicacies in their own right, but the principal reason for stuffing is to lend pleasant flavors to the meat. Birds may also be simply "stuffed" with an onion, carrot, parsley, or celery stalks. These vegetables both attract unwanted flavors and impart flavors of their own to whatever meat they're cooked with.

RECIPES

Virtually any recipe for domestic fowl will work as well with duck or goose, so if you have a favorite chicken or turkey dish, by all means try it out on your next batch of waterfowl.

Don't forget your trusty cookbook either; the suggestions there for poultry dishes provide a rich source for experimentation and remarkable dining.

There are, however, a few ways of preparing waterfowl that Sil and I consider outstanding. They are dishes, stuffings, and marinades that are the first to pop into my head when asked, "How do you want your duck tonight?", and they're reproduced here in the hopes you'll find the proof of the pudding as delightful as we do.

MARINADES FOR WATERFOWL

When marinating, place fowl in a stainless steel pan or glass bowl, as most marinades contain an acid that will cause a chemical breakdown of metals.

1 chopped onion	1/2 teaspoon salt
1 minced clove garlic	1/2 teaspoon pepper
1/2 cup white wine or vermouth	1/2 teaspoon celery seed
1/2 cup salad oil	1/2 teaspoon poultry seasoning

Mix all ingredients and let stand for a couple of hours. Place duck pieces in mixture and marinate for three to five hours. Then broil duck till done, or barbecue over open coals.

SOY MARINADE

1/2 cup soy sauce	1 clove garlic
1/2 cup red wine	1/2 teaspoon curry powder
1/4 teaspoon powdered ginger	

Combine all ingredients and mix well. Place duck breasts in marinade and refrigerate for three to five hours.

SAUERKRAUT DRESSING FOR DUCKS

This recipe can be used as a conventional stuffing or when using duck breasts in a casserole.

Drain and chop one 27-ounce can of sauerkraut. Mix with 1 chopped tart apple, 1/4 cup minced onion, 3 to 4 tablespoons of brown sugar, 1/2 cup raisins, and 1/4 teaspoon thyme. Salt and pepper to taste.

GIBLET STUFFING

1/4 pound margarine	1/4 teaspoon paprika
1 medium-sized onion minced	1/4 teaspoon poultry seasoning
2 stalks celery diced	2 cups bread crumbs
giblets of bird diced	1 egg
1/4 cup diced mushrooms	salt and pepper to taste
1/2 teaspoon parsley	

Melt margarine in skillet and sauté the onion, celery, giblets, and mushrooms. Add bread crumbs, egg, and seasonings. Mix well. Cook until lightly browned and not sticky.

APPLE-SAUSAGE DRESSING FOR GOOSE OR DUCK

1/4 cup minced onion	1 egg
1/4 cup diced celery	salt and pepper to taste
1/2 cup breakfast sausage	1/4 teaspoon paprika
1 diced tart apple	1/8 teaspoon thyme
2 cups bread crumbs	1 teaspoon parsley

Sauté onions, celery, sausage, and apple in skillet. Add bread crumbs, egg, and seasonings and mix well. Cook until lightly browned and not sticky.

ROAST WILD DUCK

1 duck for each two people	1/2 cup orange juice
salt and pepper to taste	1/2 cup Madeira wine

Rub cavity of bird with salt and pepper. Place duck in tin foil in roasting pan. Cook covered at 450 degrees for 15 minutes. Reduce heat to 300 and continue cooking, basting frequently with mixture of juice and wine, till tender — about 2 hours.

BROILED DUCK

Split the ducks in half by cutting down the breast. Butter halves well, and sprinkle with salt, pepper, poultry seasoning, and paprika. Broil them, basting with melted butter until desired doneness. Approximately 8 to 12 minutes a side.

SAUTEED DUCK BREASTS

1/4 pound margarine	3 lbs duck breasts
1/2 cup milk	1 cup Italian Flavored bread crumbs
1 egg	

Melt margarine in skillet. Combine milk and egg; dip duck breasts into liquid and then into bread crumbs. Cook until golden brown, then turn. Reduce heat and simmer until desired doneness, about 30 to 40 minutes.

Epilogue

It is winter in Montana. Not by the calendar perhaps, but looking from my study window I see the tangled branches of cottonwood and quaking aspen etched against a pink winter sunset: the classic Currier and Ives winter scene. The frost is in the ground, too, rock-hard under a skiff of snow.

Perhaps most significant, the ducks and geese have left. Except for a few hardy mallards that will ply the local warm springs for the duration of the cold weather, gunning is done for the year, and I, too, am ready to leave.

In another week I will fly to New York, then in a month to Florida and after that Mexico. To do a little fishing, perhaps, but, more important, some duck shooting. I suddenly realize that writing this book cost me dearly. I've done very little waterfowling this season; ironic perhaps, but in keeping with the advice of an old friend who once warned me about making work out of the thing you love the most: "You'll never find the time to enjoy yourself," he said.

It's been a year in the doing, and I suppose I haven't really found the time to enjoy waterfowling—to immerse myself in a gray morning, to languish in the sounds and smells of a marsh. But I have dates with a black duck on Long Island, some broadbill in northern Florida, and a bunch of pintail in Altata, Sinaloa, that will, in part, make up for those missed opportunities.

And those missed opportunities have provided a reward all their own. *Misty Mornings and Moonless Nights* is its name. It has been fun to write, and there's always a pleasure in learning, and telling, and remembering glorious moments afield. In short, I've enjoyed this book. I hope you'll do likewise.

Norman Strung
December 3, 1973

Recommended Reading

Chapelle, Howard I., *American Small Sailing Craft,* (W. W. Norton and Co., 1951).

Connett, Eugene V., *Duck Decoys, How to Make, Paint and Rig Them,* (Greene Pub. Co.).

Coykendall, Ralf, *Duck Decoys and How to Rig Them,* (Henry Holt, 1955).

Earnest, Adele, *Art of the Decoy: American Bird Carvings,* (Bramhall House).

Hines, Bob, *Ducks at a Distance,* (U.S. Dept. of Interior, Fish and Wildlife Service, Boston, Mass.).

Hochbaum, H. Albert, *Travels and Traditions of Waterfowl,* (Branford Co., 1955).

Kortright, F. H., *Ducks, Geese and Swans of North America,* (Stackpole, 1942).

Linduska, Joseph P., *Waterfowl Tomorrow,* (U.S. Government Printing Office, 1964).

Mackey, William F., Jr., *American Bird Decoys,* (Dutton Co., 1965).

Walsh, Harry M., *The Outlaw Gunner,* (Tidewater Publishers, 1971).

Status of Waterfowl Yearly Fall Flight Forecast, (U.S. Dept. of Interior, Fish and Wildlife Service, Boston, Mass. 02109).

Duck Identification Guide for the Hunter, (U.S. Dept. of Interior, Fish and Wildlife Service, Boston, Mass. 02109).

Index

Index

Index